WALDEN TWO

WALDEN TWO

BY

B. F. SKINNER

WITH A NEW INTRODUCTION
BY THE AUTHOR

PRENTICE HALL
Englewood Cliffs, NJ 07632

Library of Congress Cataloging in Publication Data
Skinner, Burrhus Frederic,
   Walden Two.

I. Title.
$PZ_3.S6_28_{25}W_{a5}$ $[PS_{3537}.K_{527}]$ $8_{13}'._5'_4$ 41339
ISBN 0-02-411521-5
ISBN 0-02-411511-8 pkb.

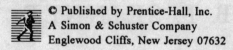 © Published by Prentice-Hall, Inc.
A Simon & Schuster Company
Englewood Cliffs, New Jersey 07632

Printed in the United States of America

35

ISBN   0-02-411510-X

Prentice-Hall International (UK) Limited, *London*
Prentice-Hall of Australia Pty. Limited, *Sydney*
Prentice-Hall Canada Inc., *Toronto*
Prentice-Hall Hispanoamericana, S.A., *Mexico*
Prentice-Hall of India Private Limited, *New Delhi*
Prentice-Hall of Japan, Inc., *Tokyo*
Simon & Schuster Asia Pte. Ltd., *Singapore*
Editora Prentice-Hall do Brasil, Ltda., *Rio de Janeiro*

WALDEN TWO REVISITED

THE EARLY summer of 1945, when I wrote *Walden Two*, was not a bad time for Western Civilization. Hitler was dead, and one of the most barbaric regimes in history was coming to an end. The Depression of the thirties had been forgotten. Communism was no longer a threat, for Russia was a trusted ally. It would be another month or two before Hiroshima would be the testing ground for a horrible new weapon. A few cities had a touch of smog but no one worried about the environment as a whole. There were wartime shortages, but industry would soon turn again to devoting unlimited resources to the fulfillment of unlimited desires. The industrial revolution was said to have stilled the voice of Thomas Robert Malthus.

The dissatisfactions which led me to write *Walden Two* were personal. I had seen my wife and her friends struggling to save themselves from domesticity, wincing as they printed "housewife" in those blanks asking for occupation. Our older daughter had just finished first grade, and there is nothing like a first child's first year in school to turn one's thoughts to education. We were soon to leave Minnesota and move to Indiana and I had been in search of housing. I would be leaving a group of talented young string players who had put up with my inadequacies at the piano and I was not sure I could ever replace them. I had just finished a productive year on a Guggenheim Fellowship, but I had accepted the chairmanship of a department at Indiana and was not sure when I would again have time for science or scholarship. Was there not something to be done about problems of that sort? Was there not by any chance something a science of behavior could do?

It was probably a good thing that these were small provincial problems, because I might not have had the courage to tackle bigger ones. In *Behavior of Organisms*, published seven years earlier, I had refused to apply my results outside the laboratory. "Let him extrapolate who will," I had said. But, of course, I had speculated about the technology that a science of behavior implied and about the differences it could make. I had recently been taking the implications seriously because I had been meeting once a month with a group of philosophers and critics (among them Herbert Feigl, Alburey Castell, and Robert Penn Warren) where the control of human behavior had emerged as a central topic.

That all this should come together in a novel about a utopian community was probably due to the fact that a colleague, Alice F. Tyler, had sent me a copy of her new book, *Freedom's Ferment*, a study of perfectionist movements in America in the nineteenth century.* With two months to spare before moving to Indiana, I decided to write an account of how I thought a group of, say, a thousand people might have solved the problems of their daily lives with the help of behavioral engineering.

Two publishers turned *Walden Two* down, and Macmillan published it only on condition that I write an introductory text for them. These editorial judgments were, at the time, quite correct. One or two distinguished critics took the book seriously, but the public left it alone for a dozen years. Then it began to sell, and the annual sales rose steadily on a compound interest curve.

There were, I think, two reasons for the awakened interest. The "behavioral engineering" I had so frequently mentioned in the book was, at the time, little more than science fiction. I had thought that an experimental analysis of behavior could be applied to practical problems, but I had not proved it. The 1950's, however, saw the beginnings of what the public has come to know as behavior modification. There were early experiments on psychotic and retarded persons, and then on teaching machines and programmed instruction, and some of the settings in which these experiments were

* Tyler, A. F. *Freedom's Ferment*. Minneapolis, Univ. of Minnesota Press, 1944.

conducted were in essence communities. And in the sixties applications to other fields, such as counseling and the design of incentive systems, came even closer to what I had described in *Walden Two*. A technology of behavior was no longer a figment of the imagination. Indeed, to many people it was altogether too real.

But there was, I think, a better reason why more and more people began to read the book. The world was beginning to face problems of an entirely new order of magnitude—the exhaustion of resources, the pollution of the environment, overpopulation, and the possibility of a nuclear holocaust, to mention only four. Physical and biological technologies could, of course, help. We could find new sources of energy and make better use of those we had. The world could feed itself by growing more nutritious grains and eating grain rather than meat. More reliable methods of contraception could keep the population within bounds. Impregnable defenses could make a nuclear war impossible. But that would happen only if human behavior changed, and how it could be changed was still an unanswered question. How were people to be induced to use new forms of energy, to eat grain rather than meat, and to limit the size of their families; and how were atomic stockpiles to be kept out of the hands of desperate leaders?

From time to time policy makers in high places have been urged to pay more attention to the behavioral sciences. The National Research Council, the operative arm of the National Academy of Sciences, made one such proposal a number of years ago, pointing out that useful "insights in policy formulation" had been developed. But it implied that the chief role of the behavioral sciences was to collect facts and insisted, possibly to reassure policy makers who might be alarmed by the ambitions of scientists, that "knowledge is no substitute for wisdom or common sense in making decisions." Science would get the facts but Congress or the President would make the decisions—with wisdom and common sense.

It is true that when the behavioral sciences have gone beyond the collection of facts to recommend courses of action and have done so by predicting consequences, they have not been too helpful. Not all economists agree, for example, on how an increase or reduction in taxes or a change in interest rates will affect business, prices, or unemployment, and political scientists are no more likely to agree on the consequences of domestic or international policies. In anthropology, sociology, and psychology the preferred formulations are those that do not dictate action. A thoroughgoing developmentalism, for example, almost denies the possibility of effective action. Applied psychology is usually a mixture of science and common sense, and Freud regarded therapy as a minor contribution of psychoanalysis.

From the very beginning the application of an experimental analysis of behavior was different. It was doubly concerned with consequences. Behavior could be changed by changing its consequences—that was operant conditioning—but it could be changed because other kinds of consequences would then follow. Psychotic and retarded persons would lead better lives, time and energy of teachers and students would be saved, homes would be pleasanter social environments, people would work more effectively while enjoying what they were doing, and so on.

These are the kinds of achievements traditionally expected from wisdom and common sense, but Frazier, the protagonist of *Walden Two,* insists that they are within reach of a special behavioral science which can take the place of wisdom and common sense and with happier results. And what has happened in the past twenty-five years has increased the plausibility of his achievement—a community in which the most important problems of daily life, as well as certain aspects of economics and government, are solved.

Frazier's critics will protest. What can we conclude from a successful community of a thousand people? Try those principles on New York City, say, or on the State

Department and see what happens. The world is a vast and complex space. What works for a small group will be far short of what is needed for a nation or the world as a whole.

Frazier might answer by calling Walden Two a pilot experiment. Industries do not invest in large plants until they have tried a new process on a smaller scale. If we want to find out how people can live together without quarreling, can produce the goods they need without working too hard, or can raise and educate their children more efficiently, let us start with units of manageable size before moving on to larger problems.

But a more cogent answer is this: what is so wonderful about being big? It is often said that the world is suffering from the ills of bigness, and we now have some clinical examples in our large cities. Many cities are probably past the point of good government because too many things are wrong. Should we not rather ask whether we need cities? With modern systems of communication and transportation, businesses do not need to be within walking or taxicab distances of each other, and how many people must one be near in order to live a happy life? People who flock to cities looking for jobs and more interesting lives will flock back again if jobs and more interesting lives are to be found where they came from. It has been suggested that, with modern systems of communication, the America of the future may be simply a network of small towns. But should we not say Walden Twos? A few skeletons of cities may survive, like the bones of dinosaurs in museums, as the remains of a passing phase in the evolution of a way of life.

The British economist E. F. Schumacher, in his remarkable book *Small Is Beautiful*,* has discussed the problems that come from bigness and has outlined a technology appropriate to systems of intermediate size. Many current projects dealing with new sources of en-

* Schumacher, E. F. *Small Is Beautiful*. New York, Harper Torchbooks, 1973.

ergy and new forms of agriculture seem ideally suited to development by small communities. A network of small towns or Walden Twos would have its own problems, but the astonishing fact is that it could much more easily solve many of the crucial problems facing the world today. Although a small community does not bring out "human nature in all its essential goodness" (small towns have never supported that romantic dream), it makes it possible to arrange more effective "contingencies of reinforcement" according to the principles of an applied behavior analysis. We need not look too closely at practices derived from such principles to survey some of those which could solve basic problems in a small community.

To induce people to adapt to new ways of living which are less consuming and hence less polluting, we do not need to speak of frugality or austerity as if we meant sacrifice. There are contingencies of reinforcement in which people continue to pursue (and even overtake) happiness while consuming far less than they now consume. The experimental analysis of behavior has clearly shown that it is not the quantity of goods that counts (as the law of supply and demand suggests) but the contingent relation between goods and behavior. That is why, to the amazement of the American tourist, there are people in the world who are happier than we are, while possessing far less. Inflation is said to be the most serious problem in the world today. It has been defined, not ineptly, as spending more than one has. In an experimental community contingencies of reinforcement which encourage unnecessary spending can be corrected. As for pollution, small communities are optimal for recycling materials and avoiding wasteful methods of distribution.

The basic research has also shown how important it is for everyone, young and old, women and men, not only to receive goods but to engage in their production. That does not mean that we should all work like eager beavers according to the Protestant work-ethic. There are many ways of saving labor, but they should not, as

Frazier points out, be used to save laborers and hence to increase unemployment. Simply by dividing the total amount of wages Americans receive each year by the number of people who want jobs, we arrive at a perfectly reasonable annual wage for everyone. But that means a reduction in the standard of living for many people, which, as things now stand, is probably impossible. In a series of small communities, however, everyone would have a job because work, as well as wages, could be divided among workers. And good incentive conditions—for example, those in which people make not money, but the things that money buys—do not require what we call hard work.

If the world is to save any part of its resources for the future, it must reduce not only consumption but the number of consumers. It should be easy to change the birth rate in an experimental community. Parents would not need children for economic security, the childless could spend as much time with children as they liked, and the community would function as a large and affectionate family in which everyone would play parental and filial roles. Blood ties would then be a minor issue.

People are more likely to treat each other with friendship and affection if they are not in competition for personal or professional status. But good personal relations also depend upon immediate signs of commendation or censure, supported perhaps by simple rules or codes. The bigness of a large city is troublesome precisely because we meet so many people whom we shall never see again and whose commendation or censure is therefore meaningless. The problem cannot really be solved by delegating censure to a police force and the law courts. Those who have used behavior modification in family counseling or in institutions know how to arrange the face-to-face conditions which promote interpersonal respect and love.

We could solve many of the problems of delinquency and crime if we could change the early environment of offenders. One need not be a bleeding heart to argue that many young people today have simply not been prepared by their homes or school to lead successful lives within the law or, if prepared, do not have the chance to do so by getting jobs. Offenders are seldom improved by being sent to prison, and judges therefore tend to reduce or suspend sentences, but crime, unpunished, then increases. We all know how early environments can be improved, and a much neglected experiment reported by Cohen and Filipczak* has demonstrated that occasional offenders can be rehabilitated.

Children are our most valuable resources and they are now shamefully wasted. Wonderful things can be done in the first years of life, but we leave them to people whose mistakes range all the way from child abuse to overprotection and the lavishing of affection on the wrong behavior. We give small children little chance to develop good relationships with their peers or with adults, especially in the single-parent home, which is on the increase. That is all changed when children are, from the very first, part of a larger community.

City schools show how much harm bigness can do to education, and education is important because it is concerned with the transmission and hence the survival of a culture. We know how to solve many educational problems with programmed instruction and good contingency management, saving resources and the time and effort of teachers and students. Small communities are ideal settings for new kinds of instruction, free from interference by administrators, politicians, and organizations of teachers.

In spite of our lip service to freedom, we do very little to further the development of the individual. How many Americans can say that they are doing the kinds of things they are best qualified to do and most enjoy doing? What opportunities have they had to choose fields related to their talents or to the interests and skills they acquired in early life? Women, only just beginning

* Cohen, H. L., and Filipczak, J. *A New Learning Environment.* San Francisco, Jossey-Bass, 1971.

to be able to choose not to be housewives, can now discover how hard it is to choose the right profession when they are young or to change to a different one later on.

And once one is lucky enough to be doing what one likes, what are the chances of being successful? How easily can artists, composers, and writers bring their work to the attention of those who will enjoy it and whose reactions will shape behavior in creative ways? Those who know the importance of contingencies of reinforcement know how people can be led to discover the things they do best and the things from which they will get the greatest satisfaction.

Although sometimes questioned, the survival value of art, music, literature, games, and other activities not tied to the serious business of life is clear enough. A culture must positively reinforce the behavior of those who support it and must avoid creating negative reinforcers from which its members will escape through defection. A world which has been made beautiful and exciting by artists, composers, writers, and performers is as important for survival as one which satisfies biological needs.

The effective use of leisure is almost completely neglected in modern life. We boast of our short workday and week, but what we do with the free time we have to spend is nothing of which we can be very proud. The leisure classes have almost always turned to alcohol and other drugs, to gambling, and to watching other people lead exhausting or dangerous lives, and we are no exception. Thanks to television millions of Americans now lead the exciting and dangerous lives of other people. Many states are legalizing gambling and have set up lotteries of their own. Alcohol and drugs are consumed in ever-increasing quantities. One may spend one's life in these ways and be essentially unchanged at the end of it. These uses of leisure are due to some basic behavioral processes, but the same processes, in a different environment, lead people to develop their skills and capacities to the fullest possible extent.

Are we quite sure of all this? Perhaps not, but Walden

Two can help us make sure. Even as part of a larger design, a community serves as a pilot experiment. The question is simply whether it works, and one way or the other, the answer is usually clear. When that is the case, we can increase our understanding of human behavior with the greatest possible speed. Here is possibly our best chance to answer the really important questions facing the world today—questions not about economics or government but about the daily lives of human beings.

Yes, but what about economics and government? Must we not answer those questions too? I am not sure we must. Consider the following economic propositions. The first is from Henry David Thoreau's *Walden*: by reducing the amount of goods we consume, we can reduce the amount of time we spend in unpleasant labor. The second appears to assert just the opposite: we must all consume as much as possible so that everyone can have a job. I submit that the first is more reasonable, even though the second is defended by many people today. Indeed, it might be argued that if America were to convert to a network of small communities, our economy would be wrecked. But something is wrong when it is the system that must be saved rather than the way of life that the system is supposed to serve.

But what about government? Surely I am not suggesting that we can get along without a federal government? But how much of it is needed? One great share of our national budget goes to the Department of Health, Education, and Welfare. Health? Education? Welfare? But an experimental community like Walden Two *is* health, education, and welfare! The only reason we have a vast federal department is that millions of people find themselves trapped in overgrown, unworkable living spaces.

Another large share of the budget goes to the Department of Defense. Am I suggesting that we can get along without that? How can we preserve the peace of the world if we do not possess the most powerful weapons, together with an industry that continues to develop even more powerful ones? But we have weapons only because other countries have them, and although we feel threatened by countries with comparable military power, particularly the Bomb, the real threat may be the countries that have next to nothing. A few highly industrialized nations cannot long continue to face the rest of the world while consuming and polluting the environment as they do. A way of life in which each person used only a fair share of the resources of the world and yet somehow enjoyed life would be a real step toward world peace. It is a pattern that could easily be copied, and I was heartened recently when someone from the State Department called to tell me that he thought America ought to stop trying to export the "American way of life" and export Walden Twos instead. A state defined by repressive, formal, legal, social controls based on physical force is not necessary in the development of civilization,* and although such a state has certainly figured in our own development, we may be ready to move on to another stage.

Suppose we do know what is needed for the good life; how are we to bring it about? In America we almost instinctively move to change things by political action: we pass laws, we vote for new leaders. But a good many people are beginning to wonder. They have lost faith in a democratic process in which the so-called will of the people is obviously controlled in undemocratic ways. And there is always the question whether a government based on punitive sanctions is inappropriate if we are to solve problems nonpunitively.

It has been argued that the solution might be socialism, but it has often been pointed out that socialism, like capitalism, is committed to growth, and hence to overconsumption and pollution. Certainly Russia after fifty years is not a model we wish to emulate. China may be closer to the solutions I have been talking about, but a Communist revolution in America is hard to imagine. It would be a bloody affair, and there is always

* See Service, Elman. *Origins of the State and Civilization.* New York, Norton, 1975.

Lenin's question to be answered: How much suffering can one impose upon those now living for the sake of those who will follow? And can we be sure that those who follow will be any better off?

Fortunately, there is another possibility. An important theme in *Walden Two* is that political action is to be avoided. Historians have stopped writing about wars and conquering heroes and empires, and what they have turned to instead, though far less dramatic, is far more important. The great cultural revolutions have not started with politics. The great men who are said to have made a difference in human affairs—Confucius, Buddha, Jesus, the scholars and scientists of the Revival of Learning, the leaders of the Enlightenment, Marx—were not political leaders. They did not change history by running for office. We need not aspire to their eminence in order to profit from their example. What is needed is not a new political leader or a new kind of government but further knowledge about human behavior and new ways of applying that knowledge to the design of cultural practices.

It is now widely recognized that great changes must be made in the American way of life. Not only can we not face the rest of the world while consuming and polluting as we do, we cannot for long face ourselves while acknowledging the violence and chaos in which we live. The choice is clear: either we do nothing and allow a miserable and probably catastrophic future to overtake us, or we use our knowledge about human behavior to create a social environment in which we shall live productive and creative lives and do so without jeopardizing the chances that those who follow us will be able to do the same. Something like a Walden Two would not be a bad start.

B. F. SKINNER

January, 1976

WALDEN TWO

HE TURNED up one day in the doorway of my office. He was already out of uniform, but he had not yet lost the leathery tan which testified to his military service. He was tall and fair and he had the pleasant, easy smile of the successful college graduate. He might have been any one of half a dozen former students whom I vaguely remembered.

He stood hesitantly for a moment, as if at attention, then stretched out his hand and came forward.

"Hello, sir," he said brightly. I fumbled for the name and he added, "Rogers, sir. 'Forty-one."

"Oh, Rogers, Rogers, by all means," I said. "Glad to see you. Come in and sit down."

He turned to the door, and I saw that he had brought with him another young man showing the same history of wind and sun.

"Professor Burris, this is Lieutenant Jamnik. We were together in the Philippines, sir."

Jamnik shook hands shyly. He was shorter than Rogers by three or four inches, and heavily built. His thin lips failed him as he tried to smile, and he was apparently quite unaware of the force of his grip. Not a college man, I judged, and a bit frightened at meeting a professor. Perhaps Rogers had made it harder by calling me "sir." This had nothing to do with any former military rank of mine, and must have been a carry-over from preparatory school days.

I offered them cigarettes and asked the usual questions. Had they seen the new emergency housing arrangements—the trailer camps and the reconstructed barracks? What did they think of the Quonset classrooms? And so on. Rogers replied appropriately enough, but he seemed impatient with small talk. At the first opportunity, with a quick glance at Jamnik, he pressed his hands together and entered huskily upon what seemed to be a prepared speech.

"Jamnik and I have done a good deal of talking during the past two years, sir," he said, "about things in general. We were doing patrol work and it was pretty dull. So we talked a lot, and one day I got to telling him your idea about a sort of Utopian community."

I am not sure that I can explain why this innocent remark staggered me. For several years the conviction had been forcing itself upon me that I was unable to contemplate my former students without emotion. The plain fact was that they frightened me. I avoided them upon every occasion and tried to forget them. So far as I could see, their pitiful display of erudition was all I had to show for my life as a teacher, and I looked upon that handiwork not only without satisfaction, but with actual dismay.

What distressed me was the clear evidence that my teaching had missed the mark. I could understand why young and irresponsible spirits might forget much of what I had taught them, but I could never reconcile myself to the uncanny precision with which they recalled unimportant details. My visitors, returning at commencement time, would gape with ignorance when I alluded to a field that we had once explored together—or so I thought—but they would gleefully remind me, word for word, of my smart reply to some question from the class or the impromptu digression with which I had once filled out a miscalculated hour. I would have been glad to agree to let them all proceed henceforth in complete ignorance of the science of psychology, if they would forget my opinion of chocolate sodas or the story of the amusing episode on a Spanish streetcar.

I came to wait for these irrelevancies as a guilty man must wait for references to his crime. And now, here was another! My idea about a sort of Utopian community! I made a wild stab at recollection. It was true, I had once read up on nineteenth-century American communities. There had been a queer duck in graduate school named Frazier, who was interested in them. I did not know him well, but I used to hear him talk. Perhaps it was because of him that I had once thought about making one more try at something like a community, with the benefit of modern techniques. But that was years ago. Had I ever told a class about it? And, good God, just what had I told them?

"You see, sir," Rogers went on, "Jamnik and I are like a lot of other young people right now. We can't make up our minds. We don't know what we want to do. I was going into law, you remember." I nodded, dishonestly. "But that's out now. I've talked it over with my father, and I don't want to do that. And I guess Jamnik never had any plans at all, did you, Steve?"

Jamnik moved nervously.

"I had a job in a shipping department before the war," he said, with a shrug. "You wouldn't call it 'plans.'"

"What we don't see, sir, is why we have to take up where we left off. Why isn't this a good time to get a fresh start? From the very beginning. Why not get some people together and set up a social system somewhere that will really work? There are a lot of things about the way we're all living now that are completely insane—as you used to say." I winced, but Rogers was too preoccupied to notice. "Why can't we do something about it? Why can't we *go on* doing something about it?"

There was an embarrassing silence.

"You fellows have done a pretty good job up to now," I said hurriedly. I regretted the remark, for I was sure Rogers would be fed up with civilian humility, but as it happened, I gave him a cue.

"It's a funny thing, sir, but in a way, fighting a war is easy. At least you know what you want and how to get it. But we don't even know how to begin to fight the mess we're in now. *Whom* are we fighting? What kind of war is it? Do you see what I mean, sir?"

"I know what you mean," I said, and I meant it. As the war had come to an end, I looked forward to a quick return to my old life, but a year of questionable peace had seen no great change. During the war I had assumed an appropriate sense of social responsibility, in spite of a contrary inclination of long standing; I now found my-

3

self unable to discard it. My new interest in social problems and my good will appeared to have exactly no effect whatsoever upon society. I could not see that they were of the slightest value to anyone. Yet I continued to pay for them day after day with a sustained feeling of frustration and depression.

"A lot of people who feel that way go into politics," I said.

"Yes, I know. But I remember what you said about that, too." I drew another quick breath. This must have been one of my hotter days. "I didn't understand you at the time," Rogers continued. "In fact, if you don't mind my saying it, I used to think you were sort of immoral—in a civic sense, I mean. But I can see your point now, and so does Steve. Politics really wouldn't give us the chance we want. You see, we want to *do* something—we want to find out what's the matter with people, why they can't live together without fighting all the time. We want to find out what people really want, what they need in order to be happy, and how they can get it without stealing it from somebody else. You can't do that in politics. You can't try something, first one way and then another, like an experiment. The politicians guess at all the answers and spend their time persuading people they're right—but they must know they're only guessing, that they haven't really *proved* anything."

This was Frazier's line, without any doubt. There was little in Rogers' youthful enthusiasm to remind me of Frazier himself, but the argument was clearly the same. In some benighted moment I must have made the transplant.

"Why don't we just start all over again the right way?" Rogers continued with great difficulty, almost in anguish, as if he were being forced to accuse me of some egregious shortcoming.

"Some of us feel that we can eventually find the answer in teaching and research," I said defensively.

"In research, maybe," said Rogers quickly. "In teaching, no. It's all right to stir people up, get them interested.

4

That's better than nothing. But in the long run you're only passing the buck—if you see what I mean, sir." He stopped in embarrassment.

"For heaven's sake, don't apologize," I said. "You can't hurt me there. That's not my Achilles' heel."

"What I mean is, you've got to do the job yourself if it's ever going to be done. Not just whip somebody else up to it. Maybe in your research you are getting close to the answer. I wouldn't know."

I demurred. "I'm afraid the answer is still a long way off."

"Well, that's what I mean, sir. It's a job for research, but not the kind you can do in a university, or in a laboratory anywhere. I mean you've got to experiment, and *experiment with your own life!* Not just sit back—not just sit back in an ivory tower somewhere—as if your own life weren't all mixed up in it." He stopped again. Perhaps this *was* my Achilles' heel.

I missed my chance to give him a reassuring word. I was thinking of Frazier and of how remarkably well his ideas had survived transplantation. A professional thought occurred to me: perhaps this was the test of the goodness of an idea, of its internal consistency. But Rogers' voice broke through.

"Have you ever heard of a man named Frazier, sir?"

The swivel chair in which I had been leaning back against my desk skidded forward and I kept from falling with a quick, awkward movement. It must have been amusing, for I heard muffled laughter mingled with expressions of alarm. I placed the chair squarely on the floor and sat down again. I groped for a phrase to regain my composure, but I found none. I readjusted my coat.

"Did you say *Frazier?*" I said.

"Yes, sir, Frazier. T. E. Frazier. He wrote an article for an old magazine that Steve—Jamnik, here—ran across in the PX. He was starting a community something like the one you used to talk about."

"So he really started it," I said distantly, still somewhat shaken.

5

"Do you know him, sir?"

"At one time I knew him. At least, it must be the same man. We were at graduate school together. I haven't seen or heard from him in ten years—or it must be longer than that. He was the man that—well, some of the ideas I gave you about Utopias—he and I used to toss them about a bit, you see. As a matter of fact, they were mostly his ideas."

"You don't know what he has done since?" said Rogers, and I sensed a note of disillusionment in his manner.

"No, but I'd like to."

"Oh, we don't know either, sir. You see, this article was more like a program. It was written a long time ago. It gave you the impression he was ready to get under way, but we don't know whether he ever did. We thought it would be worth while to find out what happened. It might give us some ideas."

I reached for the yearbook of my professional society. Frazier was not listed as a member. In a minute or two I had located an issue eight years old. He was there— *T. E. Frazier*—with his degrees and the universities which had granted them. No current university affiliation was recorded; evidently he had given up teaching, or perhaps had never begun. From what I remembered of him I was not surprised. In graduate school he had once taken a red pencil to a magazine article written by the president of the university, treating it like a theme in English composition. He had corrected the punctuation, improved the word order, and by reducing several passages to logical symbols, he had disclosed a lot of bad thinking. Then he had signed and mailed it to the president, with a grade of C minus.

The mailing address in the yearbook was a surprise. At that time Frazier had been living in a neighboring state not more than a hundred miles away. The address read: *Walden Two, R. D. 1, Canton.*

"Walden Two," I repeated slowly, after reporting these facts to my visitors. We were silent for a moment.

"Do you suppose—?" said Rogers.

6

"Sure!" said Jamnik, suddenly free of embarrassment, though he spoke only to Rogers. "His community! There was a lot in this article about What's-his-name's Walden. Don't you remember, Rodge?"

I began to see light.

"Walden Two. Walden the Second. Of course. And quite like Frazier—fancying himself a sort of second Thoreau."

We fell silent again. I glanced at the clock above my desk. I had a lecture in ten minutes and had not been through my notes.

"I'll tell you what I'll do," I said, standing up. "I'll drop Frazier a line. I never knew him well, you understand, but he'll remember me. I'll ask him what's going on—if anything *is* going on."

"Will you, sir? That will be great!"

"At least we'll find out whether Walden Two is still in existence. The chances are it was all a pipe dream and has long ago vanished into thin air. But I'll put a return address on the envelope, and we'll soon know."

"I think you'll find him there, sir," said Rogers. "This article didn't sound like a pipe dream exactly, would you say, Steve?"

Jamnik thought a moment, like a navigator making a swift calculation.

"He'll be there," he said quietly.

2

JAMNIK was right. Frazier was there.

And so was Walden Two—"quite according to plan," Frazier wrote with a self-assurance which sounded familiar.

"As for your questions," his letter continued, "wait six months, and I promise a full report. We are preparing a series of articles which should be just what you want. But if you can't wait—and I hope you can't—come and see Walden Two now. Bring your young friends with you—we are always looking for converts—and anyone else you like. We can accommodate a party of ten."

Bus schedules on the nearest highway and other information were added.

I threw the letter across my desk impatiently. Its reality was strangely disturbing. It had been amusing enough to recall Frazier as an interesting figure in my graduate school days; it was quite another thing to make contact with him again now. I found that he was pleasanter as a memory. But here was his letter, and what was to be done about it? I was annoyed at having got myself in for something, and I regretted my offer to help Rogers and Jamnik.

To make matters worse, the whole venture began to build itself up at an alarming rate. I had scarcely finished Frazier's letter when the phone rang. It was Rogers. He had wanted to avoid bothering me, he said, and had waited in silence. I glanced at my calendar and noticed that he had waited for exactly the three days needed for the promptest of replies. I told him about Frazier's letter and agreed to meet him and Jamnik in my office early that afternoon.

At lunch I ran into a colleague from the Philosophy Department named Augustine Castle. As fellow bachelors living at the Club, we saw a great deal of each other, but I could hardly call him a friend. It was an impersonal acquaintanceship. I conversed with him as I might publish "A Reply to Professor Castle" in a professional journal. We usually talked about the one subject common to our respective fields—the nature and limitations of human knowledge—and it was a source of gratification to both of us that we disagreed violently and exhaustively. His position precessed slightly with the years and could variously be called intuitionism, rationalism, or—I suspected—Thomism. I could sum him up, to my satisfaction and perhaps with condescension, as "a Philosopher."

In his preoccupation with Mind, Castle had let himself put on too much weight. His florid face was undistinguished except for a pair of sharp eyes and a badly trimmed black mustache. He conversed extremely well, if rather legalistically. I had fallen into his carefully laid traps so often that I had devised a standard method of getting out of them. It was not profound; I would simply ask him to define his terms. That annoyed him and set me free.

As soon as we had ordered, Castle began to report on the progress he had been making in something called "justification." It was, he insisted, the real answer to the logical positivists. But Walden Two was on my mind and I could marshal very little enthusiasm for justification. Although I scarcely expected Castle to be interested, I broke in to tell him something about Frazier and my curious discovery of his present whereabouts. To my surprise he was fascinated. It turned out that he had once given a course in the Utopias, from Plato and More and Bacon's *New Atlantis* down to *Looking Backward* and even Shangri-La! In case Rogers and Jamnik were interested and we made the trip, could he by any chance go along? I recalled Frazier's "party of ten" and invited him to join us.

Rogers and Jamnik were outside my office when I returned from lunch, and they were not alone. Rogers had brought his fiancée, Barbara Macklin. She was à tall, pretty girl with shoulder-length blond hair. She had an easy confidence which might almost have been called boldness. I seemed to remember that they had been engaged before Rogers joined the Navy—that would have been at least three years ago, poor man. Another girl of about the same age, shorter than Barbara and by no means so well groomed, was introduced somewhat more informally by Jamnik as "my girl," and by Rogers as Mary Grove.

We sat down in my office, the girls in the chairs and the rest of us as comfortably as possible on my desk and a table. I read Frazier's letter aloud and passed it around for inspection. "Walden Two" and the address were printed in faint block letters across the top of the paper. Frazier's hand was large and almost childish, and he had used a stub pen and jet-black ink.

Rogers had searched the library for a copy of Frazier's old article, and he read it to us. It set forth the argument Rogers had outlined three days before. Political action was of no use in building a better world, and men of good will had better turn to other measures as soon as possible. Any group of people could secure economic self-sufficiency with the help of modern technology, and the psychological problems of group living could be solved with available principles of "behavioral engineering."

I cannot recall that anyone raised the question whether we were to visit Walden Two. We simply proceeded to set a date. I phoned Castle. So far as he and I were concerned, the only free time in the near future was almost upon us. It was now Monday, and we could leave on Wednesday for the rest of the week, which was given over to a sort of pre-examination reading period. This was received by the others as a great stroke of luck, and so it was settled. The girls, I realized with something of a shock, had been accepted as members of the party from the very first.

I wired Frazier when we would arrive, telling him not to bother to reply, but he sent an acknowledgment anyway:

On Tuesday I worked up the examination material to which I had intended to devote the whole week, and on Wednesday morning, rather breathless from my new tempo, I found myself on a train, with Rogers beside me discussing the problems of returning servicemen. In the seat ahead, Castle was talking with somewhat greater animation to Barbara, who was listening with studied attention. Across the aisle sat Steve Jamnik, with his girl's head on his shoulder.

Walden Two was about thirty miles from the largest city in the state, which we reached in time for an early lunch. We checked bus schedules and had coffee and sandwiches in the station. Before one o'clock we were already in the suburbs, heading east. The highway followed a river which has cut deeply into its northern bank, and the road wound precariously between a steep bluff on the left and the river on the right, sharing a narrow embankment with a railroad.

An hour later our bus passed over a small bridge and hissed to a stop. We were left standing at the side of the road as the bus drew away in a popping roar.

Across the road a station wagon was drawn off the highway. It was deserted. I looked up and down the road, but could see no one. I walked over to the bridge and looked into the creek bed beneath. As I returned, a few pebbles rolled down the bank near the station wagon, and I looked up in time to see Frazier scrambling to his feet. He had been lying on a wide ledge of stone. He waved an arm gracefully in the air.

"Hello!" he shouted. "Be right down."

We crossed the road as he jogged down the bank on his heels. He looked very much as I remembered him. He was not tall, but a suit of some white washable material gave an impression of height. He had grown a small, scarcely visible beard. The cheap straw hat far back on his head might have been purchased at any general store. He shook my hand warmly, and as I introduced my companions, he greeted each of them with a smile which succeeded in being friendly in spite of an intensely searching glance.

He led the way toward the station wagon.

"Just having a little nap," he said, waving his hand toward the stone ledge. "I thought you might make the earlier bus. You've had a dirty trip. Sorry I couldn't meet you in the city, but we can't spare our cars and trucks for long at this time of year."

I protested that the bus had been quite comfortable. We were taking our places on the rather stiff seats in the station wagon, and it was not difficult to be convincing.

We left the main highway immediately and drove north along the creek, at the bottom of a small ravine. We then slowly climbed the east bank and emerged in the midst of some prosperous farm land, which could not have been seen from the river level. There were a few farmhouses and barns dotted about, and ahead and far up the sloping field to the right, a series of buildings of another sort. They were earth-colored and seemed to be built of stone or concrete, in a simple functional design. There were several wings and extensions which gave the impression of not having been built at the same time or according to a single plan. They were arranged in several levels or tiers, following the rise of the land. Frazier allowed us to survey them in silence.

After perhaps half a mile we left the ravine behind and crossed the creek on a small wooden bridge. We turned off the main road and followed the stream to the right along a private driveway. On our left were other buildings of the same functional style. Frazier still ventured no information.

"What are those buildings?" I said.

"Part of Walden Two," said Frazier. But that was all.

We passed through a grove of young pines and emerged to find a small pond on our right. Ahead, at the upper edge of a gentle slope of closely cropped land and at the foot of a wooded hill, were the main buildings. They now seemed surprisingly extensive. We followed a looping drive which brought us to the lowest level. We unloaded our baggage, and Frazier turned the station wagon over to a young man who had apparently been waiting for it. We carried our bags into a hallway, and Frazier showed us to our rooms. They were all alike—rather small, but with large windows looking out over the very pleasant countryside across which we had just driven. We were assigned to the rooms in pairs, the two girls in one, Rogers and Jamnik in another, and Castle and I in a third.

"You will want to clean up and rest a bit," said Frazier, "so I will leave you here until three o'clock." He departed abruptly.

Castle and I inspected our room. There was a double-decker bunk built against the left wall. Half of the right wall was recessed for shelves and cupboards which served as a bookcase and dresser. A hinged table could be dropped from the remaining wall space. A small clothes closet was fitted into the corner at the foot of the bunk. There were two comfortable chairs, made of heavy plywood, which appeared to be a local product.

The total effect was pleasant. The beds were covered with printed spreads, which were quite handsome against the natural finish of the woodwork and the earth-colored walls. A piece of the same material hung at one side of the broad window.

We unpacked quickly, washed up in a bathroom across the hall, and found ourselves with nothing to do. I did not feel like wandering about the building or grounds until we were invited to do so. But Frazier had not said so much as "make yourselves at home." On the contrary, he had said "rest a bit." But we were in no mood for resting, and I resented the way he had arranged our time without consulting us. We were not children to be sent off for naps. I was also annoyed by his dramatic silence. It seemed to be a trick designed to stimulate our curiosity.

But it was quite unnecessary, and it suggested that Frazier had been insensitive to our evident interest. I felt like apologizing to my companions.

For lack of something better to do, Castle and I stretched out on our bunks. I took the upper deck and was glad to find that the mattress was quite comfortable. I had feared that some sort of Spartan asceticism would be demanded of us. We began a desultory conversation, but I soon found myself thinking of Frazier asleep on his sunny ledge along the road. It was a relaxing thought, and my irritability subsided. The bed grew more and more comfortable, and my remarks to Castle became brief and vague.

Half an hour later Castle woke me and reported that the others were outside. I had slept soundly and found it difficult to clear my head. I had neatly confirmed Frazier's prediction that I would want to rest, but as I thought of it, my irritation returned.

There was a knock at the door, and I scrambled down from my bunk as Castle answered it. It was Frazier. He was smiling and very cordial, but I knew that I looked sleepy, and I fancied that his smile was not without a trace of self-satisfaction.

W E HAVE much to see and much to talk about," said
Frazier when we had assembled out of doors, "and
I suggest that we start slowly. We shall have fifty or
sixty hours together. What do you say to a leisurely
start? Shall we walk down to the pond and then back for
a cup of tea?"

We thought this an excellent idea, especially the tea,
which would make up for our hurried lunch in the bus
station. We set out across the field to the south, skirting
a fairly large flock of sheep. The sheep were kept together by a single length of string, carrying occasional
bits of cloth like a kite-tail, and supported on poles stuck
into the ground to form a square fold. Rogers commented
on this insubstantial arrangement.

"We wanted an expanse of cropped grass in our front
yard," Frazier explained, "but it's too close to the buildings for a regular sheep pasture. It's used a great deal by
the children. In fact, we all use it as a sort of lawn. By
the way"—he turned particularly to Castle and me—"do
you remember Veblen's analysis of the lawn in the
Theory of the Leisure Class?"

"I do, indeed," said Castle. "It was supposed to rep-
resent a bit of choice but conspicuously unconsumed pasture." Castle's diction was always precise, but occasionally, as in this instance, he burlesqued himself with
added delicacy.

"That's right," said Frazier, with a slight smile. "Well,
this is our lawn. But we consume it. Indirectly, of course
—through our sheep. And the advantage is that it doesn't
consume us. Have you ever pushed a lawn mower? The
stupidest machine ever invented—for one of the stupidest of purposes. But I digress. We solved our problem
with a portable electric fence which could be used to
move our flock of sheep about the lawn like a gigantic
mowing machine, but leaving most of it free at any time.
At night the sheep are taken across the brook to the main

fold. But we soon found that the sheep kept to the enclosure and quite clear of the fence, which didn't need to be electrified. So we substituted a piece of string, which is easier to move around."

"What about the new lambs?" Barbara asked, turning her head at a slight angle and looking at Frazier from the corners of her eyes.

"They stray," Frazier conceded, "but they cause no trouble and soon learn to keep with the flock. The curious thing is—you will be interested in this, Burris—the curious thing is that most of these sheep have never been shocked by the fence. Most of them were born after we took the wire away. It has become a tradition among our sheep never to approach string. The lambs acquire it from their elders, whose judgment they never question."

"It's fortunate that sheep don't talk," said Castle. "One of them would be sure to ask 'Why?' The Philosophical Lambkin."

"And some day a Skeptical Lambkin would put his nose on the string and nothing would happen and the whole sheepfold would be shaken to its very foundations," I added.

"And after him, the stampede!" said Castle.

"I should have told you," said Frazier soberly, "that no small part of the force of tradition is due to the quiet creature you see yonder." He pointed to a beautiful sheep dog, which was watching us from a respectful distance. "We call him the Bishop."

We walked on in silence, but Castle pretended to be troubled.

"Leaving us," he said hesitantly, "with the question of the relative merits of electricity and the wrath of God."

Frazier was amused, but only briefly.

"Except for the hills on the other side of the river," he said, "all the land you see from here belongs to Walden Two. We aren't quite so affluent as that may sound, for we are bounded on three sides by wooded hills which cut off any distant view. We bought it all for taxes. There were seven or eight farms here—badly run-down—three of them abandoned. The road through the ravine goes on over the hill to a few surviving farms on the other side. It's a county road, but we keep it in repair by way of working out our county taxes. We built the other roads ourselves."

We had begun by clustering about Frazier, listening as well as our walking formation would permit. Steve and the two girls soon dropped a little behind, apparently preferring the countryside at first hand to Frazier's rather labored phrases. As we drew close to the pond, Frazier paused to close ranks.

"The pond is our own work," he said after a moment. "It covers some swamp land and stores a bit of water against a dry spell. As you see, we have a few ducks—more for the children than anything else, though we get an occasional dinner from them." We moved on toward a small boat landing at the edge of the water.

"One of our medical people took quite an interest in the pond. He has it nicely balanced, he tells me. At the first the water was brown and slimy. You can see how clear it is now." Frazier picked up an oar from a small flat-bottomed boat moored at the landing and, with some effort, plunged it straight down. The full length was visible and shining white.

We soon had a pleasanter demonstration, for a group of six or eight young people who had been following us at a distance arrived at the pond. They changed into bathing suits in a thicket which seemed to have been especially trimmed for the purpose, and then ran abreast to the landing and plunged in with a single splash, their brightly colored suits gleaming beneath the surface as they glided outward.

We stood watching them as they swam about near a small float, while Frazier talked on. He pointed out the truck gardens beyond the dam, a pine grove which had been set out five years ago to screen the workshops from the living quarters, and a strip of birches which separated the truck gardens from the sheep pasture and supplied some choice firewood. He was talking about trivia, but he seemed to know it. Indeed, he made a point of it. Each reference was tossed off in the most casual way. Yet there was a note of quiet enthusiasm, or even passion, in his voice. He loved these simple facts. He was fascinated by these trade treaties with nature.

We inspected the dam and the sluiceway, and Frazier then turned us about. We walked back along the shore of the pond and followed what was called the Upper Brook in the direction of the building farthest to the east. Presently we passed a large and fragrant bed of mint growing in the moist soil near the brook. A rustic fence of woven branches separated it from the sheepfold.

"No mint for the lambs?" said Castle.

"They are brought together under more favorable circumstances in the dining room," said Frazier dryly.

All the main buildings were now in plain sight.

"What's that building material?" I asked. "Concrete?"

Frazier had his own plan of exposition.

"We used the old farm buildings as living quarters until we could put up the original unit you see on our left," he began, as if I had not spoken. "Some of them were too valuable to tear down. There's a nice old stone house near the river, which we converted into a sort of granary. The original barns are all still in use, except one which stood on the site of our modern dairy barn.

"The main buildings, of course, we put up ourselves. The material, Burris, is rammed earth, although a few walls are made of stone from that old quarry you see above the buildings on Stone Hill. The cost was fantastically low when you consider either the cubic footage, as our architects do, or, what seems to me more important, the amount of living that goes on inside. Our community now has nearly a thousand members. If we were not living in the buildings you see before you, we should be occupying some two hundred and fifty dwelling houses and working in a hundred offices, shops, stores and warehouses. It's an enormous simplification and a great saving of time and money."

We had reached several child-size tables with attached benches. They appeared to be designed for picnics, but we later discovered them in use in a sort of out-of-doors school. Frazier sat down on a bench with his back to the table, upon which he rested his elbows. The girls took places on either side of him, and the rest of us dropped upon the ground.

"One advantage of cooperative housing," Frazier said, "is that we can deal with the weather. Edward Bellamy tried it, you remember. The streets of his Boston of the future were to be covered when it rained."

"Wasn't it H. G. Wells who supposed that cities would eventually be built in enormous caves, where weather could be manufactured to taste?" said Castle.

"I had forgotten that," said Frazier, slightly annoyed. "Of course, the technical problem is difficult if you think of a community unit as large as a city. But as I was going to say—Bellamy was admittedly ahead of his time in the invention of covered streets, though the idea is anticipated in the marquees and canopies of the rich. But he doesn't seem to have realized quite how much the control of weather contributes. Except in some very favorable climates, which won't solve the problem for all of us, it's still necessary to provide oneself with a raincoat, one or more overcoats, an umbrella, rubbers, overshoes, gloves, hats, a scarf, perhaps ear muffs, not to mention special undergarments of various sorts. And in spite of all that, we frequently get wet and chilled and, in due course, influenza."

"What a horrible picture!" said Barbara.

"But a true one. And that's only the beginning. It's only when we conquer the weather, or move into a favorable climate, that we understand its tyranny. No wonder the *nouveau* Californian is ecstatic! He has a new birth of freedom. He realizes how often he used to surrender to the inconvenience of a bad night—how many times he was kept from seeing his friends, or from going to the theater or a concert or party."

I thought Frazier was building up his point beyond reason.

"Well, what do you do here when it rains, except let it rain?" I said.

"In a community unit of this size," Frazier continued undisturbed, "it was feasible to connect all the personal rooms with the common rooms, dining rooms, theater, and library. You can see how we did it from the arrangement of the buildings. All our entertainments, social functions, dinners, and other personal engagements take place as planned. We never have to go out of doors at all."

"How about going to work?" asked Rodge.

"That's an exception only when we work out of doors. In bad weather our trucks ferry us back and forth between our living quarters and the workshops beyond the pines."

"But I like to be out of doors in bad weather," said Barbara. "I love to walk in the rain."

"Of course you do," said Frazier, sitting up. "In the right kind of rain at the right time! A good rain is something to be savored and enjoyed. But I'll wager you don't feel that way about all kinds of weather." He dropped back as if to resume his argument.

"A clear, cold day?" said Barbara. It was obvious that she was merely trying to hold Frazier's attention, and he was annoyed.

"I'm talking about inclement weather—the inconvenient or plain nasty kind," he said gruffly.

Barbara missed the overtones, or at least was not disturbed by them.

"That long passageway with all the windows—is that what you mean?" she said. She took a cigarette from a case and Frazier began to slap his pockets in a vain search for a match. He accepted a folder from Barbara, struck a match, and held it awkwardly.

"That's what we call the 'Ladder,'" he said, brightening. "It connects the children's quarters with the main rooms. It used to be called 'Jacob's Ladder'—all the little angels going up and down, you know. Our architects caught themselves in time to make something more than a mere passageway out of it. They weren't satisfied to devote so much space to a single function and broke it up into a series of stages or alcoves furnished with benches, chairs, and tables. There's a magnificent view. At this time of day you'll find groups there taking tea. In the morning there's a sort of prolonged coffee hour. Many devotees carry their breakfast there. It's always full of life. But since it's our next stop," he added, rising from his bench and looking at Barbara and Mary, "why do I bother to tell you all this?"

I thought I knew the answer but held my tongue.

"Who were your architects?" asked Rodge, as we headed across the field toward the foot of the ladder. "Were they members of the community?"

"They were among the very first, though seniority is never discussed among us. They were a young couple interested in modern housing and willing to work within the limits of our initial poverty. It would be hard to exaggerate what they have contributed to Walden Two."

"What do they find to do now?" said Castle. "They must have abandoned their profession."

"By no means," said Frazier. "They were also interested in interior design, especially in inexpensive modern furniture which could be mass-produced. Our most flourishing industry is the manufacture of some unusual pieces which they designed."

"But they have ceased to be architects in the strict sense of the word," insisted Castle. He seemed anxious to press what appeared to be a case of personal sacrifice for the sake of the community.

"You wouldn't say that," said Frazier, "if you could see them now. They had a few lean years, professionally speaking, but they've really got their reward. You must remember that we were forced to build Walden Two by easy stages. Our quarters have some obvious disadvantages. But imagine what it would mean to an architect to design an entire community as a whole!"

"Is that what they are doing?" said Barbara.

"I promise you that story all in good time," said Frazier with a cryptic smile. "I'm arranging for you to meet the architects themselves, and I think it's only fair to give them the pleasure of astonishing you."

"Astonish the bourgeoisie!" I muttered to Castle. But Castle did not seem to share my annoyance at Frazier's tactics. In fact, he seemed to be taken in.

"Do you suppose they *are* building another one?" he whispered.

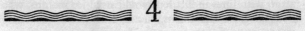

4

FROM the bottom of the passageway called the Ladder, a solid bank of flowers seemed to stretch above us until a slight turn in the passageway cut off the view. Actually, the flowers filled large boxes which separated the stages and could just be seen one above the other from where we stood. Short flights of stairs ran along the windowless north wall, which was covered with paintings.

The passageway made a very acceptable gallery. It was not always possible to get a view sufficiently distant for my taste, but the lighting was excellent. The artists were all unfamiliar, but the work was extraordinarily good. Frazier saw that I was interested and seemed to be alarmed at a possible disarrangement of plans.

"Tomorrow," he said pointedly, "we shall find time to survey the artistic activities of Walden Two. As you may imagine, art flourishes here." And he pressed forward.

I felt that this called for some show of resistance and therefore followed at a leisurely pace, stopping to examine several paintings at length. They were surprisingly vigorous and fresh, in many styles, and almost without exception competently handled. I had seen many professional shows less interesting from a technical point of view and certainly much less exciting.

Suddenly I found myself surrounded by a group of men and women who were joining a party on two of the stages. Someone, mistaking me for one of them, took my arm and passed me along to a charming young woman who made a place beside her on a bench against a flower box. I began to stammer a protest but she smiled reassuringly and I sat down in silence. She made some remark —I remember only that it was friendly and rather clever —and I could respond only by staring at her. All at once the archetypal theme of an old nightmare possessed me. I saw myself on the podium of a world-famous orchestra, tapping the stand and raising my baton in the air, trying wildly to remember what was to be played. Or I was an actor, with lines industriously rehearsed for months, who now, as the curtain rose, found himself on the wrong stage.

I sat for what must have been several minutes in paralyzed silence. I could not move but I was thinking fast. Desperately I tried to understand myself. The scene before me was simple enough. These were delightful people. Their conversation had a measure and cadence more often found in well-wrought fiction than in fact. They were pleasant and well-mannered, yet perfectly candid; they were lively, but not boisterous; affectionate, but not effusive. But they were of another world, and I could not even be sure they were speaking a language I knew. A cold fear seized me. I roused myself with great effort and pulled myself to my feet. I muttered something which to my astonishment sounded like "Good friend—must see 'im," and made a dash for it.

I found Frazier and the others somewhat more than halfway up the Ladder. They had stopped at an alcove in which an attractive woman of perhaps thirty-five had apparently been waiting for us. She was remarkably well-dressed, but in great simplicity of style. Her dark hair was drawn tightly against her head. As my panic subsided, and in turn my shame at the thought of my bad manners, I came under the spell of the pictures again, and she began to remind me of a piece of modern sculpture done in a shining dark wood.

"Strange as it may seem," said Frazier, with a suggestion that he had been waiting for me, "there are many things about Walden Two of which I am not competent to speak, especially things of interest to the ladies." He bowed slightly to Barbara and Mary. "So I have asked Mrs. Meyerson to help me. She is in charge of Clothing for Women, but she can answer most of your questions in other fields. Besides, she's very good company." He glanced warmly at Mrs. Meyerson, who gave him a condescending pat on the shoulder.

"You are so heavy-handed, Fraze," she said. She turned to the girls and added brightly, "Shall we get some tea?"

When they had left, Frazier broke into a quiet laugh.

"Our tea service will amuse you," he said. "We used to have the usual cups, saucers, and bread-and-butter plates. But one of our teachers, at what I suppose you would call the 'college level,' developed a class in domestic practices. They got out of hand and began to study *our* practices—here at Walden Two! One project was to analyze our tea service, which is a sort of coffee service, too, in the morning. Their recommendations were so sensible that we immediately adopted them. I think you will agree that it's a nice little job in domestic engineering."

"That's all very interesting," said Castle, "but I hope you aren't going to attribute the success of your community to trivial technical achievements of that sort. After all, a slight improvement in a tea service won't shake the world."

"We shake the world in other ways," said Frazier, without a smile. "The actual achievement is beside the point. The main thing is, we encourage our people to view every habit and custom with an eye to possible improvement. A constantly experimental attitude toward everything— that's all we need. Solutions to problems of every sort follow almost miraculously."

" '*Almost* miraculously?' " said Castle. "You lay no claim to miracles, Mr. Frazier?"

Frazier was puzzled.

"As to your remark about the triviality of what you have seen so far," he said with some warmth, "I must remind you that we have agreed upon an easy start. I promise you heavier fare tomorrow and still heavier thereafter. You will see real achievements, never fear. But our friends are returning. It's time to go for tea. We might have lost the alcove if we had all gone together."

I made a hasty attempt to evaluate this bit of antisocial scheming, but gave it up. Frazier urged us along to discover the tea service for ourselves, but I saw that the girls were carrying tall glasses, set in braided grass jackets, to which loops of string were attached so that the glasses could be carried like pails. They also carried squarish dishes containing bread and butter.

From the top of the Ladder we entered a small room in which chairs and tables, many in use, were arranged somewhat in the manner of a small hotel lobby. Near the door stood a large tea cart, containing urns of tea, hot water, and coffee. On another cart stood several large pitchers of iced drinks. I spotted a supply of the tall glasses and square dishes on shelves underneath.

I think Frazier had intended to make light of the engineered tea service, but Castle had challenged him and he accordingly entered upon a zealous defense. He demonstrated the "technique" by filling a glass with tea to the level of two cups marked on a scale fixed beside the tap. He dropped in a slice of lemon and then slipped the glass into a jacket which he took from a small bin.

"Cups and saucers were immediately discarded by our young domestic engineers," he said soberly. "It's practically impossible to carry a full cup of tea without spilling, especially down the stairs of the Ladder. We always serve ourselves, and we needed a container from which tea could be drunk with pleasure and which would also serve as a convenient carrier. These young people knew nothing of the Russian practice of using glasses for tea but they naturally hit on it as a solution. They improved on the Russians by using very large glasses. Three cupfuls will leave ample margin against spilling. Only the most voracious make more than one trip to the tea cart. A large glass emphasizes the odor and flavor of the tea, just as it does for brandy. The glass, you see, is extraordinarily thin. It's pleasant to drink from and very light."

"I've never seen a Russian swinging his tea like a lantern," I said.

"So much the worse for the Russians," said Frazier. "I can't give you the actual figures, but some experiments proved that the jackets were worth while. They were omitted on alternate days for a month or so and members of the class stood about and counted spillings."

Castle had been trying to meet Frazier's aggressive

demonstration by pretending to be amused. He may have felt that Frazier was baiting him and that a sense of humor was his only defense. But his occasional chuckling failed to disturb Frazier and eventually seemed rather silly. Finally his amusement passed out of control and into open contempt. As Frazier described this trivial application of scientific method, Castle turned his back with a snort of disgust and walked straight away from us. After half a dozen steps, he turned squarely around and came back, shaking his head and shrugging his shoulders with evident embarrassment. Frazier saw his advantage but was apparently not satisfied that the victory was secure. Instead of dropping the subject, he pressed on as if it were an issue in world politics.

"You can see for yourselves how much more smoothly the tea rides when the glass is carried like a pail," he said, swinging his glass in graceful arcs and pointing to the tea, which was scarcely disturbed. "Moreover, our young engineers had other problems, which they solved at the same time. Tea must be kept warm, especially if you pour yourself two or three cups at a time. Now, a teacup is the worst possible conserver of heat . . ."

He continued in this way for some time. Then he stopped and stared at Castle as if waiting for comment. Castle said nothing. Instead, he awkwardly poured himself tea and arranged his glass in its jacket. I followed his example, and Frazier, smiling broadly, strode off down the Ladder. Rodge and Steve took glasses of the iced drinks, and we all spread butter and jam on large slices of bread.

The square dishes proved to be of the same thin glass. One edge was rolled under to permit a firm grip, and the dish was so deep that our bread was quite safe on the journey back to the alcove. Although I felt a little strange swinging my tea beside me like a censer, I had to admit that it was the first time I had ever felt secure on such a voyage.

5

I CAN understand why a builder of Utopias would choose to have only beautiful women about him," I said to Frazier when we had settled ourselves with our tea, "but I'm amazed at your success."

Frazier looked at me very seriously.

"I assure you there was no deliberate choice," he said earnestly. "We tried to get a representative sample—a true cross section. We failed in some respects, but I can't see how a selection could have been made, even unconsciously, on the basis of personal appearance. Do you think so, Rachel?"

"I'm sure you're right, Fraze," said Mrs. Meyerson, though I am not sure she understood the point.

"But most women are not so attractive as this," I said, with a wave of my hand to indicate the length of the passageway.

"So that's why you were dawdling!" said Frazier dryly. "I thought you were looking at the pictures."

"A great many women can be quite attractive," said Mrs. Meyerson quickly. "Each in her own way. Here we are not so much at the mercy of commercial designers, and many of our women manage to appear quite beautiful simply because they are not required to dress within strict limits."

"For the moment," said Frazier, "that very fact will prevent Mr. Burris from fully enjoying this hobby of his." He turned to me. "Going out of style isn't a natural process, but a manipulated change which destroys the beauty of last year's dress in order to make it worthless. We opposed this by broadening our tastes. But the required change has not yet taken place in you. In a day or so you will know what I mean. Little touches which now seem out of style and which, in spite of what you say, must mar your appreciation, will then appear natural and pleasing. You will discover that a line or feature is never in itself dated, just as you eventually come to regard the dress of another country as beautiful, even though you first judge it comical or ugly."

This seemed unforgivably patronizing.

"Nothing is interfering with my appreciation of beauty at this very moment," I said. I happened to be looking directly at Mrs. Meyerson as I spoke.

"Come, come," said Frazier. " 'Politics and flattery are strangers here.' "

"I think Miss Macklin will understand what Mr. Frazier is trying to say," said Mrs. Meyerson, coming to my aid. "Would you care to tell us what you think of our dress?"

Barbara was caught unprepared.

"It's a little hard to say," she began. "I don't think I'd notice anything unusual about any one of you. Together, though—I don't know. Something about the hair, for one thing. It's very attractive, but not always—in style."

"Please don't be embarrassed. You are quite right."

"Yet there *is* a style about it," Barbara hastened to add. "You are like women from different countries. And many of you are beautiful."

"Thank you, my dear. I wasn't fishing. We do have, I think, a rather cosmopolitan air—because we encourage variety. Nevertheless, we're not exactly out of fashion, as you have very generously said."

"A curious case of eating your cake and having it too," said Castle. "You seem to be in and out at the same time. Pray, how do you manage to do it?"

"You are puzzled," said Mrs. Meyerson, as she might have said "You are hurt" to a child. "Well, I suppose the answer is we compromise. But it's not quite that. At least it's not just taking the easy way out—we spent a lot of time on it. We solved the problem by—experimenting, would you say?" She turned to Frazier.

"No," he said flatly, without looking at her. "Intuition."

"By intuition, then," Mrs. Meyerson cheerfully agreed. "We want to avoid the waste which is imposed by changing styles, but we don't want to be wholly out of fashion.

So we simply change styles more slowly, just slowly enough so we needn't throw away clothing which is still in good condition."

"You understand, of course," said Frazier, "that we can't give castoffs to anyone else because there's no one in Walden Two who has any use for them."

"But don't you get farther and farther out of style?" asked Castle.

"No," said Mrs. Meyerson. "We simply chose the kind of clothes which suffer the slowest change—suits, sweaters and skirts, or blouses and skirts, and so on. You won't find half a dozen 'party dresses' among us—and those aren't from the community supply. Yet each of us has something that would be in good taste except at very formal functions."

"Full dress," said Frazier by way of parenthesis, "is a form of conspicuous consumption which doesn't amuse us—except when we see it in others."

"I'm surprised that a Utopia has anything but lounging pajamas," said Castle glumly.

Mrs. Meyerson laughed gaily.

"Many people are surprised that we dress up," she said. "But we have our reasons. Fraze could tell you more about them than I. It isn't that we mind being thought queer, I'm sure. Perhaps we don't want to think ourselves queer."

"That's putting it very well, Rachel," said Frazier. He turned to the rest of us. "You must remember that we aren't really cut off from the world and don't want to be. Our art and literature, our movies, our radio, and our occasional excursions outside the community keep us in constant touch with American life. A complete break would be more trouble than it's worth. Also, it would be unfair to our children to make them feel out of place or ill at ease among outsiders. It might suggest that life at Walden Two was somehow odd or even inferior."

"But isn't dressing up precisely the sort of unnecessary trouble that a Utopia should dispense with?" said Castle.

"I'm sure there was no dressing for the occasion at Walden One."

"It really isn't so much trouble," said Mrs. Meyerson. "Our dress isn't severe; it's just enough to meet current standards."

"And we have time for trouble," said Frazier. "You're thinking of dressing in the usual rush, after driving home from a late appointment at the office through rush-hour traffic to reach a dinner party in time for cocktails. None of that here, you see. We have plenty of time for everything. We like a break between the active part of the day and the quieter social hours at dinner and in the evening. A bath and a change are an important point in the day's schedule. They are psychologically refreshing.

"As for your reference to Thoreau," Frazier added after a moment, "remember that his experiment was concerned with subsistence and solitude. Dressing is a social mechanism which he could neglect."

I had noticed a distant rustling. Presently several children passed the alcove, and others soon followed. A similar migration was in progress out of doors, threading its way among a series of flower beds.

"It's suppertime for the angels," Frazier explained.

The children were of various ages—some as young as seven or eight, others at least thirteen or fourteen. They were all shining clean, in gay and well-fitted but utilitarian clothes. There seemed to be no adults with them, but they were well-behaved. They spoke quietly and moved quickly along. Many of them greeted Mrs. Meyerson and Frazier and smiled pleasantly at all of us.

One of them, a boy of about ten, stepped into the alcove and, going quickly to Mrs. Meyerson, gave her an affectionate hug.

"Hello, Rachel," he said. "Are you coming?"

"I haven't forgotten," she said. She stood up and turned to Frazier. "It's Deborah's debut in the dining room. I must run along."

She arranged to join us after lunch the next day, ex-

31

plaining quite frankly that she wanted to give Barbara and Mary a more accurate view of Walden Two than they could expect from Frazier, and then she and the boy left.

"Mrs. Meyerson's children," Frazier explained, nodding after them. "Delightful! Like all our children! Deborah is seven today and is 'coming out' in the main dining room. The younger children take their meals in their own building until their seventh birthday. It's quite an event when they move up. Perhaps we can catch a glimpse of Deborah later in her big moment."

The children had all passed and we returned to our discussion.

"If you don't mind my saying it," I said, "your men seem to be dressed a shade below your women in point of excellence as well as formality."

"Quite right," said Frazier. "It's not really a sex difference—I insist. We haven't quite freed ourselves from the culture from which we came. Men are less dependent upon clothes, even here. For this time of day a jacket or sweater or perhaps a leather coat in cooler weather will suffice. And no tie. Definitely no tie."

"My throat gets cold," said Castle.

"What if someone liked to be really shabby?" I said. "Would you permit him to follow his whim?"

"I can't imagine it," said Frazier, "but I know you can. You are thinking of a world in which a fine suit is a mark of wealth, as well as a means to wealth. A shabby suit is a sign of poverty or a protest against the whole confounded system. Either is unthinkable here."

"Not quite unthinkable, I should say," said Castle. "It might be a sign of indolence or simple carelessness."

"Both of which are born of weariness," said Frazier distantly. He seemed to be listening for something. Suddenly he rose and looked toward the top of the Ladder. "But more of that later on," he said. "It has been a most interesting discussion. We must continue it soon. Now I think we must go." He spoke in a mechanical way and immediately picked up his glass and plate and started up the Ladder. We followed, but his speed increased, and he soon outstripped us and went into the main building.

As we neared the top of the Ladder we heard children singing:

"Happy birthday to you. Happy birthday to you."

We left our dishes in a large basket near the door, and I led the way toward the music. Frazier was standing in the doorway of a dining room. He seemed to sense our approach and moved impatiently inside. I did not like to follow.

Through the door we could see that the room had been slightly darkened for the occasion. As the song was sung again and again, two silent figures moved from table to table. One of them, an older child, carried a birthday cake upon which seven candles sparkled in the dusk. She stopped at each table and allowed the children to read the inscription. The other figure was a child of seven, in her best dress, solemn as a nun, glowing with pride.

In a moment the procession came to an end, and the smaller child returned quickly to her table, where Mrs. Meyerson was sitting. The candles were blown out and the business of cutting the cake began. As the lights came up, I stepped far enough inside the door to catch a glimpse of Frazier, but I withdrew quickly and urged the others away. Frazier was standing alone and unnoticed against a wall, his face twisted by an exaggerated expression of affection. I thought I saw a tear on his cheek.

6

OUR GUEST quarters were at the end of the main building farthest from the Ladder and on the lowest level. Frazier met us there at seven o'clock. We filed up a narrow staircase and found ourselves at one end of a broad corridor called the "Walk." This ran the full length of the building, curving slightly as the building followed the contour of the hill. The sun had not yet set and the evening promised to be fine, but there was a good deal going on indoors. The Walk was dotted with strollers, who seemed to be there for the sake of greeting others like themselves or to settle their dinners. I was reminded of the deck of a large liner.

As we joined in this procession Frazier called our attention to various common rooms, arranged on either side of the corridor. On our right were reading rooms, libraries, and small lounges with chairs and tables grouped for conversation or games. These rooms looked out upon the Walden Two landscape from which we had seen the building during the afternoon. They were all occupied.

"Why are so many people indoors on such a beautiful evening?" I asked.

"Probably just because they don't need to be," said Frazier. "The inhabitants of Walden Two can get out any time of day. They have no reason to wait for the day's work to be over, or the children put to bed. Nor have they any interest in getting away from the same four walls."

On our left were rather more businesslike rooms, with large skylights but no windows. Some were furnished for music, with pianos, phonographs, and shelves of music and records. Others appeared to be group studios. Various works of art in progress stood about, but the rooms were serving now for informal meetings. The dining rooms were on this side of the corridor, near the Ladder.

I was struck by the absence of large crowds. For some reason the word "community" had suggested barn-sized halls full of noisy people, like a church social or bazaar or county fair. I confessed my surprise and Frazier laughed heartily.

"What good are crowds?" he said.

"Well, I don't know," I said. "But how can you avoid them?"

"Are they useful? Are they interesting?"

"Some people get a certain thrill from being part of a crowd," said Castle.

"A symptom of loneliness," said Frazier flatly. "Consider the average housewife." He turned and slowed his pace to make sure that the girls could hear him. "How does the average housewife spend most of her day? Alone! Whom does she see? Tradespeople, or her younger children, or two or three neighbors—not two or three friends, just two or three people who happen to be within reach. Is it surprising that she finds the noise and bustle of a large crowd like food to a starving man? Of course she gets a thrill from a crowd! And the bigger the crowd the better—the surer she is that for a time at least she will not be lonely. But why should anyone who isn't starved for friendship or affection enjoy a crowd?"

"You can meet interesting people," said Barbara hesitantly. She was naturally opposed to this line of argument.

"Not efficiently," said Frazier gently. "We have much better arrangements for bringing together compatible people with common interests."

"What about a spectacle—a show?" I said. "Doesn't that naturally mean a crowd?"

"Not at all. Our theater holds about two hundred. That's our largest crowd. When a play or movie happens to interest all of us—and that's rare—it's simply repeated until we have all seen it. The actors are glad of the chance to repeat their performance, and the film doesn't care. The same is true of concerts. I grant you that some events—a championship tennis match, say—can't be repeated. But matches aren't important here. We are not hero-worshipers."

"But you can't very well solve the problem of a lecturer that way," said Castle. "Speaking as one who makes a living at it, I can say that I don't welcome the chance to play more than one performance."

"We solve the problem of the lecturer by dispensing with him. The lecture is a most inefficient method of diffusing culture. It became obsolete with the invention of printing. It survives only in our universities and their lay imitators, and a few other backward institutions." He glared at Castle. "Why don't you just hand printed lectures to your students? Yes, I know. Because they won't read them. A fine institution it is that must solve that problem with platform chicanery!" He made an effort to control his growing contempt, and went on more quietly. "Perhaps something can be said for an exhibition, for the antics of the speaker, and I know about 'audience participation.' But granting, Mr. Castle, that you are justified in wishing to make a personal appearance, let me ask this: On what conceivable subject could you possibly address all of us?"

Castle was puzzled, and said nothing.

"You mean," I said, "that Mr. Castle could speak on no topic which would interest more than two hundred of you?"

"That's just what I mean, and two hundred is putting it high. We aren't a selected group, and our tastes vary. We have no fads. No one tells us we 'ought to take an interest' in this or that. You couldn't count on snob-appeal, either, for we have no reason to pretend to be interested in high-brow or timely topics. What would you speak on to get a large audience?"

"But a really clever lecturer ought to be able to find a subject that would entertain more than a small theaterful, even so," I said.

"*Entertain* is another matter," said Frazier. "It's a theatrical performance. And such a lecturer is glad to repeat his performance, as our actors do."

"I accept the distinction," said Castle, "and I'll stick to serious informative discussions. But I submit that there are subjects of—well, I see that I can't say economic importance, but let me say, political importance, which must be interesting to everyone because they are crucial for everyone."

Frazier laughed triumphantly.

"You can no more say 'political' than you can say 'economic,' " he said. "You will find a few of us interested in politics, because we are charged with that interest on behalf of the community. But you can address the lot of us quite comfortably in one of the smaller common rooms."

"You mean to say," said Castle slowly and with a challenging stare, "that all of your members interested in, say, a discussion of world peace could be put in one of these small rooms?"

"In one corner!" said Frazier, fairly crowing at his success in disconcerting us.

"What about an interest in the affairs of the community?" I said.

"In the other corner," said Frazier, laughing heartily. "But we must talk about that later on. No, the simple fact is, there's no good reason for bringing people together in large numbers. Crowds are unpleasant and unhealthful. They are unnecessary to the more valuable forms of personal and social relations, and they are dangerous. The mob rushes in where individuals fear to tread, and Führers deceive themselves as to their support."

"I hope you won't deny that you are all interested in *eating*," said Castle. "What about a crowd in your dining room?"

"An excellent point," said Frazier, "and one which illustrates my final complaint against crowds: they are expensive. They demand elaborate space and equipment which stand idle most of the time. Look at your stadiums and theaters—or restaurants, for that matter. Here things are different. We simply stagger the daily schedules of our members. As a result our equipment is, in many cases, almost constantly in use. We can do this because we aren't bound by the timetables of stores, businesses, and schools. 'From nine till five' means nothing to us. You will find us breakfasting anytime between five and ten in the morning. Luncheon begins immediately thereafter and lasts until midafternoon. The children have definite hours, on the early side. Adults dine as early as five-thirty or as late as nine. Our dining rooms, Mr. Castle, seat about two hundred. As you will see in a moment, there are no large rooms and no crowding."

"I suppose members are assigned to particular eating shifts?" I said, and I must confess that I hoped to uncover a bit of regimentation.

Frazier snorted in disgust.

"Absolutely not!" he said. "The most we ever need is a notice on the bulletin board pointing out that less crowded rooms will be found at certain hours."

"But if I ask someone to meet me for dinner, how do I know his schedule isn't three or four hours ahead of mine?" I said.

"It is often hard to make a date for a meal. But meetings are easily arranged at Walden Two, so it doesn't matter. And there's a compensating gain: by changing schedule, we can get a change of faces from time to time." Frazier stopped and laughed uneasily, as if he had been betrayed into confessing some slight dissatisfaction. He rallied quickly and struck out with increasing energy.

"An amazing piece of cultural engineering—the staggered schedule! The effect is almost unbelievable. We need less equipment of all sorts. Bathrooms, for example. If you have ever stayed at a summer hotel which didn't have private baths, you remember the shaving-hour and dinner-hour rushes. With a staggered schedule we get along with limited installations quite conveniently. The tea- and coffee-hour facilities do triple duty. And we can avoid strong preferences for certain performances at the theater or for the use of the tennis courts or for working hours. Our equipment is used fifteen or eighteen hours a day without undue hardship for those on the early or late shifts.

"But perhaps the most valuable result"—Frazier paused for a moment, to see if we could anticipate him—"is psychological. We're utterly free of that institutional atmosphere which is inevitable when everyone is doing the same thing at the same time. Our days have a roundness, a flexibility, a diversity, a flow. It's all quite pleasing and healthful."

We had stopped for most of this harangue in one of the lounges. Without another word Frazier moved on toward the dining rooms, like a guide who has finished a little speech in one corner of a cathedral and shepherds his flock to the next point of interest.

7

T HE DINING rooms proved to be even smaller than
Frazier's remarks had suggested. Each contained perhaps half a dozen tables of different sizes. The rooms
were decorated in various styles. It was possible to dine
briskly in a white-walled room bustling with speed and
efficiency, or at leisure in a pine-paneled Early American
dining room in beeswax candlelight, or in an English inn
whose walls carried racing pictures, or in a colorful Swedish room. Two carefully designed modern rooms, one
with booths along one wall, came off well by comparison.

I was rather offended by this architectural hodge-
podge. The purpose, Frazier explained, had been to
make the children feel at home in some of the interiors
they would encounter outside the community. Through
some principle of behavior which I did not fully understand, it appeared that the ingestion of food had something to do with the development of aesthetic preferences or tolerances. The same effect could not have been
so easily obtained by decorating the lounges in different
styles.

The period rooms were grouped about a serving room
which was operated like a cafeteria, although there was
no calculated display of foods or production-line delivery.
I was reminded, rather, of a buffet supper. As we entered, we followed Frazier's example and took trays.
They were of the same thin glass we had seen in the tea
service. Frazier took a napkin from a compartment bearing his name, which also contained some mail which he
ignored. The rest of us took fresh napkins from a drawer.

"We have made out very well in our linen manufac-
tory," Frazier said, waving his napkin at us. "No wonder
it has always been a luxury. A very durable cloth, and
pleasant to use. I suppose you expected paper," he added
suddenly, looking at me.

There were three main dishes on the menu—a sort of

goulash, a soufflé, and lamb chops. A small poster described the goulash, gave something of its history, and showed its country of origin on a small map. Frazier called our attention to the poster and explained that new dishes from all parts of the world were constantly being tried out and included in the Walden Two menus according to demand. We all took the goulash and added salad and fruit tarts to our trays. Frazier urged us to take bread and butter also. It was the same bread that we had had at tea, and it had been delicious, but by force of habit we all started to pass it by. Bread was apparently a favorite topic of Frazier's and served as text for another guidebook harangue.

"The commercial baker," he said as he made sure that we all got thick slices, "tries to produce a satisfactory loaf with the fewest and cheapest materials. Here the goal is in the other direction. Our cooks have to prepare the food we produce so that it will be eaten. They want to get as much *into* a loaf of bread as possible. It would be no achievement whatsoever to make an equally delicious loaf with less butter or cheaper starches. They would only have to prepare what they had saved in some other form."

He looked at us with raised eyebrows, like a magician who has just performed an astonishing feat, and then led the way toward one of the modern rooms, where we found a brightly colored table against which our glass trays glistened. The trays were elliptical, with a large depression at each end. Smaller compartments and a recess for a cup filled the middle section. We all put the trays down parallel to the edge of the table, but Frazier showed us how to arrange them spokewise around the table, so that we could have the main dish conveniently in front of us, with the cup and smaller compartments within easy reach. When we were ready for dessert, the tray could be reversed. A small cabinet built into the table contained silverware and condiments.

In spite of Castle's obvious impatience with the details of a domestic technology, Frazier talked at length about the trays. One of their innumerable advantages was the transparency, which saved two operations in the kitchen because the tray could be seen to be clean on both sides at once. As Frazier made this point, Castle snorted.

"Mr. Castle is amused," said Frazier, bearing down hard. "Or perhaps it isn't amusement. It might be interesting to ask him to perform an experiment. Mr. Castle, would you mind turning one of these trays over from side to side one thousand times? Perhaps you will concede the result. Either you would work quickly and finish with painfully cramped muscles, or else slowly and be bored. Either would be objectionable. Yet some one of us would be compelled to do just that three times a day if our trays were opaque. And it would be *some one of us*, remember, not an 'inferior' person, hired at low wages. Our consciences are clearer than that! Do you see, now, why—but you see the point." Frazier fluttered both hands in the air in token of an easy victory.

"The main advantage of the tray," he went on, "is the enormous saving in labor. You will see what I mean when we visit the dishwashery. Commercial restaurants would give anything to follow our lead, but it requires a bit of cultural engineering that's out of their reach."

He apparently expected someone to ask for further details about "cultural engineering," but we were all busy with our dinners and we finished them in silence. We carried our empty trays to a window which opened into a utility room, and Frazier then turned and led the way toward the Walk. Mary whispered something to Barbara, who said to Frazier, "Aren't we going to see the dishwashing?"

"So soon after dinner?" said Frazier, with heavy surprise. He seemed proud of having achieved a degree of delicacy, but he turned immediately toward the utility room.

On the other side of the window through which we

had pushèd our trays, a very pretty girl, who seemed to be on excellent terms with Frazier, received each tray, removed inedible objects, and flipped it upside down on a chain carrier. It immediately passed out of sight under a hood, where we were told it was sprayed with skim milk, which together with all the edible waste would go to the pigs.

A distinguished man with a full beard, who stopped Frazier to ask if he thought the library should acquire a more up-to-date musical encyclopedia, received the tray from the milk bath and placed it upside down on a set of revolving brushes which fitted the dishlike depressions. At the same time the tray was flooded with hot soapy water. The man then examined it briefly—saving, I suppose, one of the operations which were supposed to exhaust Castle—and placed it in a rack. When a rack was full, it was lowered into a rinsing vat and carried to a sterilizer.

Meanwhile the cups and silverware received similar treatment in separate production lines under the control of the same operators.

"All your dishwashing seems to be done by two people," I said.

Frazier nodded violently. "And with four or five shifts a day you can say eight or ten people at most," he said. "Compare that with two hundred and fifty housewives washing two hundred and fifty sets of miscellaneous dishes three times a day and you will see what we gain by industrializing housewifery." He pronounced it "huz-zifry" and I missed the reference.

"But don't give us too much credit," he went on. "We're less mechanized in our dishwashing than many large hotels and restaurants. We simply make mass production available to everyone as a consequence of co-operative living. We can beat the hotels by introducing labor-saving practices which require a bit of cultural engineering." He paused a moment, but again no one asked the question he was waiting for. "The glass tray, for example," he said almost petulantly. "A very important advance, but impossible for the restaurant which must cater to people of established tastes, you see."

We made a brief inspection of the kitchen and bakery, which were apparently not distinguished by any contribution from cultural engineering, and then returned to the Walk.

8

WE FOUND space near the windows of a small lounge and drew up chairs so that we could look out over the slowly darkening landscape. Frazier seemed to have no particular discussion prepared and he had begun to look a little tired. Castle must have been full of things to say, but he apparently felt that I should open the conversation.

"We are grateful for your kindness," I said to Frazier, "not only in asking us to visit Walden Two but in giving us so much of your time. I'm afraid it's something of an imposition."

"On the contrary," said Frazier. "I'm fully paid for talking with you. Two labor-credits are allowed each day for taking charge of guests of Walden Two. I can use only one of them, but it's a bargain even so, because I'm more than fairly paid by your company."

"Labor-credits?" I said.

"I'm sorry. I had forgotten. Labor-credits are a sort of money. But they're not coins or bills—just entries in a ledger. All goods and services are free, as you saw in the dining room this evening. Each of us pays for what he uses with twelve hundred labor-credits each year—say, four credits for each workday. We change the value according to the needs of the community. At two hours of work per credit—an eight-hour day—we could operate at a handsome profit. We're satisfied to keep just a shade beyond breaking even. The profit system is bad even when the worker gets the profits, because the strain of overwork isn't relieved by even a large reward. All we ask is to make expenses, with a slight margin of safety; we adjust the value of the labor-credit accordingly. At present it's about one hour of work per credit."

"Your members work only four hours a day?" I said. There was an overtone of outraged virtue in my voice, as if I had asked if they were all adulterous.

"On the average," Frazier replied casually. In spite of

45

our obvious interest he went on at once to another point. "A credit system also makes it possible to evaluate a job in terms of the willingness of the members to undertake it. After all, a man isn't doing more or less than his share because of the time he puts in; it's what he's doing that counts. So we simply assign different credit values to different kinds of work, and adjust them from time to time on the basis of demand. Bellamy suggested the principle in *Looking Backward*."

"An unpleasant job like cleaning sewers has a high value, I suppose," I said.

"Exactly. Somewhere around one and a half credits per hour. The sewer man works a little over two hours a day. Pleasanter jobs have lower values—say point seven or point eight. That means five hours a day, or even more. Working in the flower gardens has a very low value—point one. No one makes a living at it, but many people like to spend a little time that way, and we give them credit. In the long run, when the values have been adjusted, all kinds of work are equally desirable. If they weren't, there would be a demand for the more desirable, and the credit value would be changed. Once in a while we manipulate a preference, if some job seems to be avoided without cause."

"I suppose you put phonographs in your dormitories which repeat 'I like to work in sewers. Sewers are lots of fun,'" said Castle.

"No, Walden Two isn't that kind of brave new world," said Frazier. "We don't *propagandize*. That's a basic principle. I don't deny that it would be possible. We could make the heaviest work appear most honorable and desirable. Something of the sort has always been done by well-organized governments—to facilitate the recruiting of armies, for example. But not here. You may say that we propagandize *all* labor, if you like, but I see no objection to that. If we can make work pleasanter by proper training, why shouldn't we? But I digress."

"What about the knowledge and skill required in many jobs?" said Castle. "Doesn't that interfere with free bidding? Certainly you can't allow just anyone to work as a doctor."

"No, of course not. The principle has to be modified where long training is needed. Still, the preferences of the community as a whole determine the final value. If our doctors were conspicuously overworked *according to our standards,* it would be hard to get young people to choose that profession. We must see to it that there are enough doctors to bring the average schedule within range of the Walden Two standard."

"What if nobody wanted to be a doctor?" I said.

"Our trouble is the other way round."

"I thought as much," said Castle. "Too many of your young members will want to go into interesting lines in spite of the work load. What do you do, then?"

"Let them know how many places will be available, and let them decide. We're glad to have more than enough doctors, of course, and could always find some sort of work for them, but we can't offer more of a strictly medical practice than our disgustingly good health affords."

"Then you don't offer complete personal freedom, do you?" said Castle, with ill-concealed excitement. "You haven't really resolved the conflict between a *laissez-faire* and a planned society."

"I think we have. Yes. But you must know more about our educational system before I can show you how. The fact is, it's very unlikely that anyone at Walden Two will set his heart on a course of action so firmly that he'll be unhappy if it isn't open to him. That's as true of the choice of a girl as of a profession. Personal jealousy is almost unknown among us, and for a simple reason: we provide a broad experience and many attractive alternatives. The tender sentiment of the 'one and only' has less to do with constancy of heart than with singleness of opportunity. The chances are that our superfluous young premedic will find other courses open to him which will very soon prove equally attractive."

"There's another case, too," I said. "You must have

some sort of government. I don't see how you can permit a free choice of jobs there."

"Our only government is a Board of Planners," said Frazier, with a change of tone which suggested that I had set off another standard harangue. "The name goes back to the days when Walden Two existed only on paper. There are six Planners, usually three men and three women. The sexes are on such equal terms here that no one guards equality very jealously. They may serve for ten years, but no longer. Three of us who've been on the Board since the beginning retire this year.

"The Planners are charged with the success of the community. They make policies, review the work of the Managers, keep an eye on the state of the nation in general. They also have certain judicial functions. They're allowed six hundred credits a year for their services, which leaves two credits still due each day. At least one must be worked out in straight physical labor. That's why I can claim only one credit for acting as your Virgil through *il paradiso.*"

"It was Beatrice," I corrected.

"How do you choose your Planners?" said Rodge.

"The Board selects a replacement from a pair of names supplied by the Managers."

"The members don't vote for them?" said Castle.

"*No,*" said Frazier emphatically.

"What are Managers?" I said hastily.

"What the name implies: specialists in charge of the divisions and services of Walden Two. There are Managers of Food, Health, Play, Arts, Dentistry, Dairy, various industries, Supply, Labor, Nursery School, Advanced Education, and dozens of others. They requisition labor according to their needs, and their job is the managerial function which survives after they've assigned as much as possible to others. They're the hardest workers among us. It's an exceptional person who seeks and finds a place as Manager. He must have ability and a real concern for the welfare of the community."

"*They* are elected by the members, I suppose?" said Castle, but it was obvious that he hoped for nothing of the sort.

"The Managers aren't honorific personages, but carefully trained and tested specialists. How could the members gauge their ability? No, these are very much like Civil Service jobs. You work up to be a Manager—through intermediate positions which carry a good deal of responsibility and provide the necessary apprenticeship."

"Then the members have no voice whatsoever," said Castle in a carefully controlled voice, as if he were filing the point away for future use.

"Nor do they wish to have," said Frazier flatly.

"Do you count your professional people as Managers?" I said, again hastily.

"Some of them. The Manager of Health is one of our doctors—Mr. Meyerson. But the word 'profession' has little meaning here. All professional training is paid for by the community and is looked upon as part of our common capital, exactly like any other tool."

"*Mr.* Meyerson?" I said. "Your doctor is not an M.D.? Not a real physician?"

"As real as they come, with a degree from a top-ranking medical school. But we don't use honorific titles. Why call him *Doctor* Meyerson? We don't call our Dairy Manager *Dairyman* Larson. The medical profession has been slow to give up the chicanery of prescientific medicine. It's abandoning the hocus-pocus of the ciphered prescription, but the honorific title is still too dear. In Walden Two—"

"Then you distinguish only Planners, Managers, and Workers," I said to prevent what threatened to be a major distraction.

"And Scientists. The community supports a certain amount of research. Experiments are in progress in plant and animal breeding, the control of infant behavior, educational processes of several sorts, and the use of some of our raw materials. Scientists receive the same labor-credits as Managers—two or three per day depending upon the work."

"No pure science?" exclaimed Castle with mock surprise.

"Only in our spare time," said Frazier. "And I shan't be much disturbed by your elevated eyebrows until you show me where any other condition prevails. Our policy is better than that of your educational institutions, where the would-be scientist pays his way by teaching."

"Have you forgotten our centers of pure research?" I said.

"Pure? If you mean completely unshackled with respect to means and ends, I challenge you to name five. It's otherwise pay-as-you-go. Do you know of any 'pure' scientist in our universities who wouldn't settle for two hours of physical labor each day instead of the soul-searching work he's now compelled to do in the name of education?"

I had no ready answer, for I had to consider the cultural engineering needed to equate the two possibilities. My silence began to seem significant, and I cast about for a question along a different line.

"Why should everyone engage in menial work?" I asked. "Isn't that really a misuse of manpower if a man has special talents or abilities?"

"There's no misuse. Some of us would be smart enough to get along without doing physical work, but we're also smart enough to know that in the long run it would mean trouble. A leisure class would grow like a cancer until the strain upon the rest of the community became intolerable. We might escape the consequences in our own lifetime, but we couldn't visualize a permanent society on such a plan. The really intelligent man doesn't want to feel that his work is being done by anyone else. He's sensitive enough to be disturbed by slight resentments which, multiplied a millionfold, mean his downfall. Perhaps he remembers his own reactions when others have imposed on him; perhaps he has had a more

severe ethical training. Call it conscience, if you like."
He threw his head back and studied the ceiling. When
he resumed, his tone was dramatically far-away.

"That's the virtue of Walden Two which pleases me
most. I was never happy in being waited on. I could
never enjoy the fleshpots for thinking of what might be
going on below stairs." It was obviously a borrowed expression, for Frazier's early life had not been affluent.
But he suddenly continued in a loud, clear voice which
could leave no doubt of his sincerity, "Here a man can
hold up his head and say, 'I've done my share!'"

He seemed ashamed of his excitement, of his show of
sentiment, and I felt a strange affection for him. Castle
missed the overtones and broke in abruptly.

"But can't superior ability be held in check so it won't
lead to tyranny? And isn't it possible to convince the
menial laborer that he's only doing the kind of work for
which he's best suited and that the smart fellow is really
working, too?"

"Provided the smart fellow is really working," Frazier
answered, rallying himself with an effort. "Nobody re-
sents the fact that our Planners and Managers could
wear white collars if they wished. But you're quite right:
with adequate cultural design a society might run
smoothly, even though the physical work were not evenly
distributed. It might even be possible, through such engineering, to sustain a small leisure class without serious
danger. A well-organized society is so efficient and productive that a small area of waste is unimportant. A caste
system of brains and brawn could be made to work because it's in the interest of brains to make it fair to
brawn."

"Then why insist upon universal brawn?" said Castle
impatiently.

"Simply because brains and brawn are never exclusive.
No one of us is all brains or all brawn, and our lives must
be adjusted accordingly. It's fatal to forget the minority
element—fatal to treat brawn as if there were no brains,
and perhaps more speedily fatal to treat brains as if there

were no brawn. One or two hours of physical work each day is a health measure. Men have always lived by their muscles—you can tell that from their physiques. We mustn't let our big muscles atrophy just because we've devised superior ways of using the little ones. We haven't yet evolved a pure Man Thinking. Ask any doctor about the occupational diseases of the unoccupied. Because of certain cultural prejudices which Veblen might have noted, the doctor can prescribe nothing more than golf, or a mechanical horse, or chopping wood, provided the patient has no real need for wood. But what the doctor would like to say is 'Go to work!'

"But there's a better reason why brains must not neglect brawn," Frazier continued. "Nowadays it's the smart fellow, the small-muscle user, who finds himself in the position of governor. In Walden Two he makes plans, obtains materials, devises codes, evaluates trends, conducts experiments. In work of this sort the manager must keep an eye on the managed, must understand his needs, must experience his lot. That's why our Planners, Managers, and Scientists are required to work out some of their labor-credits in menial tasks. It's our constitutional guarantee that the problems of the big-muscle user won't be forgotten."

We fell silent. Our reflections in the windows mingled confusingly with the last traces of daylight in the southern sky. Finally Castle roused himself.

"But four hours a day!" he said. "I can't take that seriously. Think of the struggle to get a forty-hour week! What would our industrialists not give for your secret. Or our politicians! Mr. Frazier, we're all compelled to admire the life you are showing us, but I feel somehow as if you were exhibiting a lovely lady floating in midair. You've even passed a hoop about her to emphasize your wizardry. Now, when you pretend to tell us how the trick is done, we're told that the lady is supported by a slender thread. The explanation is as hard to accept as the illusion. Where's your proof?"

"The proof of an accomplished fact? Don't be absurd!

But perhaps I can satisfy you by telling you how we knew it could be done before we tried."

"That would be something," said Castle dryly.

"Very well, then," said Frazier. "Let's take a standard seven-day week of eight hours a day. (The forty-hour week hasn't reached into every walk of life. Many a farmer would call it a vacation.) That's nearly 3000 hours per year. Our plan was to reduce it to 1500. Actually we did better than that, but how were we sure we could cut it in half? Will an answer to that satisfy you?"

"It will astonish me," said Castle.

"Very well, then," said Frazier quickly, as if he had actually been spurred on by Castle's remark. "First of all we have the obvious fact that four is more than half of eight. We work more skillfully and faster during the first four hours of the day. The eventual effect of a four-hour day is enormous, provided the rest of a man's time isn't spent too strenuously. Let's take a conservative estimate, to allow for tasks which can't be speeded up, and say that our four hours are the equivalent of five out of the usual eight. Do you agree?"

"I should be contentious if I didn't," said Castle. "But you're a long way from eight."

"Secondly," said Frazier, with a satisfied smile which promised that eight would be reached in due time, "we have the extra motivation that comes when a man is working for himself instead of for a profit-taking boss. That's a true 'incentive wage' and the effect is prodigious. Waste is avoided, workmanship is better, deliberate slow-downs unheard of. Shall we say that four hours for oneself are worth six out of eight for the other fellow?"

"And I hope you will point out," I said, "that the four are no harder than the six. Loafing doesn't really make a job easier. Boredom's more exhausting than heavy work. But what about the other two?"

"Let me remind you that not all Americans capable of working are now employed," said Frazier. "We're really comparing eight hours a day on the part of *some* with four hours on the part of practically *all*. In Walden

Two we have no leisure class, no prematurely aged or occupationally disabled, no drunkenness, no criminals, far fewer sick. We have no unemployment due to bad planning. No one is paid to sit idle for the sake of maintaining labor standards. Our children work at an early age—moderately, but happily. What will you settle for, Mr. Castle? May I add another hour to my six?"

"I'm afraid I should let you add more than that," said Castle, laughing with surprising good nature.

"But let's be conservative," said Frazier, obviously pleased, "and say that when every potential worker puts in four hours for himself we have the equivalent of perhaps two-thirds of all available workers putting in seven out of eight hours for somebody else. Now, what about those who are actually at work? Are they working to the best advantage? Have they been carefully selected for the work they are doing? Are they making the best use of labor-saving machines and methods? What percentage of the farms in America are mechanized as we are here? Do the workers welcome and improve upon labor-saving devices and methods? How many good workers are free to move on to more productive levels? How much education do workers receive to make them as efficient as possible?"

"I can't let you claim much credit for a better use of manpower," said Castle, "if you give your members a free choice of jobs."

"It's an extravagance, you're right," said Frazier. "In another generation we shall do better; our educational system will see to that. I agree. Add nothing for the waste due to misplaced talents." He was silent a moment, as if calculating whether he could afford to make this concession.

"You still have an hour to account for," I reminded him.

"I know, I know," he said. "Well, how much of the machinery of distribution have we eliminated—with the release of how many men? How many jobs have we simply eliminated? Walk down any city street. How often will you find people really usefully engaged? There's a bank. And beyond it a loan company. And an advertising agency. And over there an insurance office. And another." It was not effective showmanship, but Frazier seemed content to make his point at the cost of some personal dignity. "We have a hard time explaining insurance to our children. Insurance against what? And there's a funeral home—a crematory disposes of our ashes as it sees fit." He threw off this subject with a shake of the head. "And there and there the ubiquitous bars and taverns, equally useless. Drinking isn't prohibited in Walden Two, but we all give it up as soon as we gratify the needs which are responsible for the habit in the world at large."

"If I may be permitted to interrupt this little tour," I said, "what are those needs?"

"Well, why do you drink?" said Frazier.

"I don't—a great deal. But I like a cocktail before dinner. In fact, my company isn't worth much until I've had one."

"On the contrary, I find it delightful," said Frazier.

"It's different here," I said, falling into his trap. Frazier and Castle laughed raucously.

"Of course it's different here!" Frazier shouted. "You need your cocktail to counteract the fatigue and boredom of a mismanaged society. Here we need no antidotes. No opiates. But why else do you drink? Or why does anyone?—since I can see you're not a typical case."

"Why—to forget one's troubles—" I stammered. "Of course, I see what you will say to that. But to get away, let's say, or to get a change—to lower one's inhibitions. You do have inhibitions, don't you? Perhaps someone else can help me out." I turned tactlessly to Barbara, who looked away.

Frazier chuckled quietly for a moment, and struck out again.

"Let me point out a few businesses which we haven't eliminated, but certainly streamlined with respect to manpower," he said. "The big department stores, the meat markets, the corner drugstores, the groceries, the automobile display rooms, the furniture stores, the shoe stores, the candy stores, all staffed with unnecessary people doing unnecessary things. Half the restaurants can be closed for good. And there's a beauty parlor and there a movie palace. And over there a dance hall, and there a bowling alley. And all the time busses and streetcars are whizzing by, carrying people to and fro from one useless spot to another."

It was a bad show but a devastating argument.

"Take your last hour and welcome," said Castle when he saw that Frazier was resting from his labors. "I should have taken your word for it. After all, as you say, it's an accomplished fact."

"Would you like to see me make it *ten* hours?" said Frazier. He smiled boyishly and we all laughed. "I haven't mentioned our most dramatic saving in manpower."

"Then you still have a chance to get away from the book," I said. "I must confess that I'm not quite so impressed as Mr. Castle. Most of what you have said so far is fairly standard criticism of our economic system. You've been pretty close to the professors."

"Of course I have. Even the professors know all this. The economics of a community are child's play."

"What about those two extra hours?" I said, deciding to let the insinuation pass.

Frazier waited a moment, looking from one of us to another.

"*Cherchez la femme!*" he said at last. He stopped to enjoy our puzzlement. "The women! The women! What do you suppose they've been doing all this time? There's our greatest achievement! We have industrialized housewifery!" He pronounced it "huzzifry" again, and this time I got the reference. "Some of our women are still engaged in activities which would have been part of their jobs as housewives, but they work more efficiently and happily. And at least half of them are available for other work."

56

Frazier sat back with evident satisfaction. Castle roused himself.

"I'm worried," he said bluntly. "You've made a four-hour day seem convincing by pointing to a large part of the population not gainfully employed. But many of those people don't live as well as you. Our present average production may need only four hours per day per man—but that won't do. It must be something more than the average. You'd better leave the unproductive sharecropper out of it. He neither produces *nor consumes*—poor devil."

"It's true, we enjoy a high standard of living," said Frazier. "But our personal wealth is actually very small. The goods we consume don't come to much in dollars and cents. We practice the Thoreauvian principle of avoiding unnecessary possessions. Thoreau pointed out that the average Concord laborer worked ten or fifteen years of his life just to have a roof over his head. We could say ten weeks and be on the safe side. Our food is plentiful and healthful, but not expensive. There's little or no spoilage or waste in distribution or storage, and none due to miscalculated needs. The same is true of other staples. We don't feel the pressure of promotional devices which stimulate unnecessary consumption. We have some automobiles and trucks, but far fewer than the hundred family cars and the many business vehicles we should own if we weren't living in a community. Our radio installation is far less expensive than the three or four hundred sets we should otherwise be operating—even if some of us were radioless sharecroppers.

"No, Mr. Castle, we strike for economic freedom at this very point—by devising a very high standard of living with a low consumption of goods. We consume *less* than the average American."

It was now quite dark outside, and very still. Only the faint rhythmic song of frogs and peepers could be heard through the ventilating louvers. The building itself had grown quiet. No one else had been in the lounge for some time, and several of the lights had been frugally turned off. A pleasant drowsiness was creeping over me.

"You know, of course," Frazier said with a frown, "that this is by far the least interesting side of Walden Two." He seemed to have been seized with a sudden fear that we were bored. "And the least important, too—absolutely the least important. How'd we get started on it, anyway?"

"You confessed that you would be paid for talking to us," I said. "And very much underpaid, I may add. I don't know what the dollars-and-cents value of one labor-credit may be, but it's a most inadequate measure of an enjoyable evening."

The others murmured assent, and Frazier smiled with obvious delight.

"While you're in that mood," he said, "I should tell you that you'll be permitted to contribute labor-credits while you're here, too. We ask only two per day, since you're not acquiring a legal interest in the community or clothing yourselves at our expense."

"Fair enough," I said, but rather taken aback.

"We don't begrudge you the food you consume or the space you occupy, nor are we afraid of the effect of idleness upon the morale of our members. We ask you to work because we should feel inhospitable if you didn't. Be frank, now. No matter how warmly we welcomed you, wouldn't you soon feel that you ought to leave? But a couple of hours a day will fully pay for the services the community renders and incidentally do you a lot of good. And you may stay as long as you like with no fear of sponging. And because I receive a credit each day for acting as your guide, you needn't feel that you're imposing on me."

"What's to prevent some visitor—say, a writer—from putting in his two hours and staying on for good?" I asked. "He would find ample time for his trade and buy his own clothes and secure his own future without being a member."

"We've no objection, but we should ask that one half of any money made during his stay be turned over to Walden Two."

"Oh ho!" cried Castle. "Then it would be possible for a member to accumulate a private fortune—by writing books, say, in his spare time."

"Whatever for?" Frazier said. It seemed like genuine surprise, but his tone changed immediately. "As it happens, it isn't possible. *All* money earned by members belongs to the community. Part of our foreign exchange comes from private enterprises of that sort."

"Rather unfair to the member as compared with the guest, isn't it?" said Castle.

"What's unfair about it? What does the member want money for? Remember, the guest doesn't receive medical services, clothing, or security against old age or ill-health."

Frazier had risen as he was speaking, and we all followed his example promptly. It was clear that we had had enough for one day.

"I shouldn't be acting in the interests of the community," said Frazier, "if I kept you from your beds any longer. We expect a full day's work from you tomorrow morning. Can you find your way to your rooms?"

We made arrangements to meet at ten the next day and parted. Castle and I led the way down the silent, dimly lighted Walk. Presently we found that we were alone. Our companions, for reasons best known to themselves, had turned off and gone outside.

"I wonder what their two hours will be worth tomorrow?" said Castle. "Enemies of the people, I suppose you'd call them."

9

I AWOKE next morning with a feeling of timelessness characteristic of new scenes and new schedules. The curtain had been drawn across the window, and the unreal light diffusing into the room might have meant dawn or noonday. It was quiet in the hallway and outside, though I could hear the sheep clearly enough to guess that they had already been brought across the brook.

Eventually my uncertainty forced me down from my bunk. I was surprised to find that my watch was still in my trousers, for I made something of a practice of placing it always in the same position at night. It was still running and said eight-thirty. Castle was asleep.

I slipped into my clothes and went across the hall with my shaving equipment and toothbrush. Ten minutes later I tapped lightly to see if Rodge and Steve were awake. But I had got the wrong room. Mary opened the door, and I caught a glimpse of Barbara asleep in the lower bunk, her face covered by a fan of blond hair.

Mary stepped into the hall and drew the door shut behind her. She was already dressed, and there was a sort of clean shine about her.

"She isn't up," she said softly.

"Neither is mine," I said, pointing to my door. We laughed quietly, like conspirators. "What about the boys?"

Mary shrugged her shoulders. "They ought to be up," she said. "Steve went to bed early."

"All very proper," I hazarded.

"Oh, I didn't mean that!" she said, easily and with a laugh. "Steve and I've been going together for a long time."

"Let's see if they're up," I suggested. I tapped lightly on the door, and we looked at each other inquiringly as we listened. There was no answer.

"Let's play hookey and have breakfast together," I said. "Just the two of us."

Mary gave a quick nod. She seemed rather surprised, but pleased. We climbed the stairs and set out along the Walk, which was deserted, as were most of the common rooms. We saw someone working industriously at a desk, and three women dusting and chatting gaily, but that was all. There was a delicious early-morning air about the place.

"I feel wonderful!" I said, taking a deep breath.

"So do I. It was so *quiet* last night."

"I can't honestly tell you whether I slept or not," I said. "I must have, of course, since it was ten o'clock then and is eight-forty-five now."

This was too strained and academic for Mary, but after a moment she seemed to enjoy it. The remark had probably struck her as unintelligible and she was enjoying the discovery that it was merely unintelligent.

The dining room was not so empty as the Walk. We took trays and stood about near the steam table waiting for service. Presently someone touched my arm. It was a brisk young man grasping a napkin, who seemed to be struggling to suppress a laugh.

"Just help yourselves," he said cordially, with a nod toward the covered dishes. He retreated to a table near the door of the English inn, still smiling to himself.

We helped ourselves to scrambled eggs and bacon, and a cooked cereal of mixed grains—a special product of Walden Two which proved to be delicious. Small glasses of spiced sweet cider or grape juice stood on a near-by table. We found a place under the skylight of one of the modern rooms. Then I realized that we had forgotten coffee.

"Cream and sugar?" I said, starting for the door. Mary jumped up.

"I'll come with you," she said. I started to protest, and she added, "Barbara says no one ever waits on a lady here." I clicked my tongue.

"But I wasn't treating you as a lady," I said. "I could

get two cups this morning, you could get two this noon, and so on. Think of that as a piece of human engineering! I'm sure Mr. Frazier would approve. I wonder how many man-hours per year we'd save?"

"But we aren't going to eat together for a year!" said Mary, puzzled but delighted.

"What a pity! Then all those hours will be wasted."

"And *anyway*," said Mary, with growing animation, "it wouldn't take us that long to learn to get coffee with the rest of our breakfast."

"So it wouldn't! So it wouldn't!" I said, knitting my brow. "How stupid of me!"

"Silly!" she said, handing me a cup.

I was quite pleased with myself. In the short space of five or ten minutes I had overcome a stubborn barrier between myself and this attractive young lady. She was no longer in awe of the professor. Not that we would now speak the same language—God forbid that anyone else should speak the bastard tongue of the academy with which I was damned—but we were no longer on different personal levels.

I wanted to consolidate my gain, to extend our common ground. She had mentioned Barbara, and I guessed that it was a subject on which we saw eye to eye. And I had been curious about the kind of relation that could exist between them.

"So Barbara is a lai-dy," I said as we carried our coffee back to the table.

"She's awfully nice," Mary said. "And she's beautiful, isn't she? I've never known anybody like that."

"Do you like her?"

She nodded energetically. "I like her a lot."

"Rodge seems to be very fond of her," I said.

"He is." I sensed that this was not the whole story.

"When are they getting married?" I said.

"I don't know."

Evidently things were not going well with Rodge and

Barbara, and I wondered whether Walden Two had anything to do with it. I was in the mood for a bit of old-fashioned gossip, but Mary obviously was not, and I could not risk the pleasant atmosphere of our breakfast by pressing her further.

"I wonder what we're all going to do this morning?" I said. "For our labor-credits, I mean."

"How long will it take, I wonder? Steve ought to get up."

"Oh, I imagine there will be plenty of time. Two credits, Frazier said. We'll all do something terribly menial and get it over with in ten minutes."

"I don't think I'd like anything so—hard," said Mary seriously.

"Something about one point zero zero—how would that be?" But Mary was merely puzzled and I felt that the atmosphere was fogging up. Fortunately the situation grew no worse. Through the door of the serving room we saw Rodge and Steve starting toward the steam table with their trays. Mary was unable to keep from joining them. She instructed them to help themselves and put glasses of cider on their trays. I moved what was left of our breakfasts to a larger table and we were all soon chatting merrily. Mary's surprising animation when talking with Steve rather took the edge off my fancied triumph.

It appeared that Steve and Rodge had risen early and had not been in their room when we knocked. They had walked to the ravine and back, by way of the far side of the pond. Barbara and Castle, they reported, were awake and would be coming along soon.

Castle was the first to appear, moving briskly across the serving room with his peculiar bouncing step—a sort of hop, skip, and jump. He waved to us from the coffee urn and presently appeared at the table, clicking his heels together and smiling like the Cheshire cat. We made a place for him and stopped talking to watch him devour his breakfast.

Rodge had left the table when Castle arrived, and we soon discovered him in the serving room helping Barbara with her tray. He followed somewhat behind as she joined us. She greeted us with her smoothest "Good morning" and thanked Rodge rather formally when he put her tray on the table and brought a chair for her.

There was a noticeable lack of spontaneity in the conversation that followed. Barbara made her full contribution, and it was she who greeted Frazier for the whole group when he at last appeared.

When the subject of the day's labor-credit came up, she exclaimed dramatically, "We are your slaves, master. Do with us as you will." Frazier looked at her in surprise, but she stared him down.

After breakfast we reported at the Work Desk in one of the common rooms.

"What have you to offer my friends?" Frazier said to the young woman in charge.

She referred to a box of small cards in a drawer of the desk.

"They'll be staying until Monday noon, is that right? Five days—ten credits. I can give them work at one point two which doesn't call for any particular experience. They could all work together, unless you'd rather have them spread out."

"No, they'll see the rest of the community at their leisure. What have you in mind?"

"The Housekeeper has been asking to have the double glazed windows all along the south side taken apart and washed. It means unscrewing the inner window, washing both surfaces carefully, replacing a drying cartridge, and putting the windows back. If your friends organized as a team, they ought to make good progress. Two hours each day for three days at one point two would give them Sunday off."

Frazier turned to us. "How do you feel about a spot of window-washing?" he asked. We murmured approval.

"Very well, then. Put them down for that. If you'll call the Housekeeper, I'll get them fitted out."

We marched off, feeling, I am afraid, rather like a squad of prisoners. Castle, in particular, fell into line with exaggerated obedience, as if someone might question his good will; and when we turned into the Walk, he swung about in a smartly executed flank movement.

At the far end of the Walk we entered what appeared to be a small clothing store. The attendant gave us zippered coveralls, roughly according to size, and the girls received scarfs for their hair. We returned to our rooms to dress, since the day was warm and we thought it advisable to remove some of our clothes. A few minutes later we reported to the Housekeeper, who turned out to be a man, for instructions and equipment. We then took leave of Frazier after making a date for lunch.

We were to wash all the south windows of the main building, beginning at the west end. In an attempt to get into the spirit of "industrialized housewifery," we organized as follows: Rodge and Steve, as the most agile, were to remove the windows and stand them against the walls on small tarpaulins; Castle and I were then to give them, as well as the outer windows which remained in place, a first cleaning with a sponge and chamois; and Barbara and Mary were to polish them with a special spray and cloth. Rodge and Steve, or perhaps Castle and I, depending upon how our time worked out, were to replace the drying cartridges, which prevented fogging, and set the windows back in place.

We fell to work. Rodge had been given a screw driver which was operated like a crank, and the windows came off quickly. Steve and he worked with beautiful coordination. I was struck by the accuracy with which each anticipated the movements or needs of the other, apparently without signals of any sort. It was rather a different story with the rest of us. Castle struck me as especially amusing. The clothing store attendant had misjudged his size from his rather bulbous face, and his coverall flapped about him as if he were partially deflated. He worked in dead earnest. When the first window came off, he rushed in to help carry it to the neighboring wall, but only succeeded in grasping it in such a way that he was forced to walk backwards in short, rapid steps as if he had been hobbled. He then fell to with pail and sponge, and flooded the tarpaulin so that it was necessary to move the window and clean the floor. We soon settled down to a satisfactory routine, however, and the work proceeded rapidly.

Mary, as one might have expected, was as much at home as Rodge and Steve. She moved quickly and efficiently, and at the same time with a natural ease which was delightful to watch. Barbara had somehow managed to fashion her scarf into a very becoming turban, but she was surprisingly awkward with the spray bottle and polishing cloth. She was uneasy, too, and took refuge in a series of wisecracks which were embarrassingly unsuccessful.

Rodge and Steve soon moved on to the next room and we lost sight of them until noon. Castle and I were also able to forge a room or two ahead of the girls. At this time of day the lounges and reading rooms were not heavily used. An occasional occupant adjusted himself to our operations with invariable good humor and usually with a friendly comment.

At twelve o'clock Rodge and Steve came by, reporting that they had stopped removing windows and were going to replace them at our starting point. Castle and I eventually came to the end of our work also, and we dropped back to give the girls a hand. Rodge and Steve caught up with us just as we were finishing, and we congratulated ourselves on this skillful planning by shaking hands all around.

We went back to our rooms to change. Castle's face was red and he was breathing hard. He dropped into a chair.

"Whoosh!" he said softly.

"But after all," I said, "it's better than grading blue books."

"Or reading term papers," he agreed, giving his brief case, which stood against the wall, a push with his foot. "But somehow I seem to be in better condition for intellectual exercise."

10

"THE SECRET of our economic success," said Frazier as we were having lunch, "is this: we avoid the goat and loom."

"I thought I saw some goats down by the ravine," I said.

"You did," said Frazier, with a quick frown. "And you will see some looms, too. But power-driven."

"I trust the goats are of the usual grass-burning, hand-operated variety," said Castle. His color had subsided, and he was in excellent spirits.

Frazier joined in our laughter, but he was the first to stop.

"The point I wanted to make," he said, "before my figure of speech miscarried so unhappily—is that we avoid the temptation to return to primitive modes of farming and industry. Communities are usually richer in manpower than in materials or cash, and this has often led to the fatal belief that there was manpower to spare."

"I should think that might be the case," I said.

"There's never any *labor* to spare, because it must be kept at a minimum for psychological reasons. But a better way to explain the goat and the loom—if that expression won't be misunderstood by our professors—is that Utopias usually spring from a rejection of modern life. Our point of view here isn't atavistic, however. We look ahead, not backwards, for a better version."

"Haven't you sort of gone back to the farm?" said Rodge.

"We all go back to the farm for food and clothing, or someone goes back for us. We haven't gone back in the course of technical progress. No one is more interested in saving labor than we. No industrialist ever strove harder to get rid of an unnecessary worker. The difference is, we get rid of the work, not the worker."

"But after all, what's wrong with a spot of hard work?" I said. "Why are you so concerned to avoid it?"

"There's nothing wrong with hard work and we aren't concerned to avoid it. We simply avoid uncreative and uninteresting work. If we could satisfy our needs without working that way at all, we'd do so, but it's never been possible except through some form of slavery, and I can't see how it can be done if we're all to work and share alike. What we ask is that a man's work shall not tax his strength or threaten his happiness. Our energies can then be turned toward art, science, play, the exercise of skills, the satisfaction of curiosities, the conquest of nature, the conquest of man—the conquest of man himself, but never of other men. We have created leisure without slavery, a society which neither sponges nor makes war. But we can't stop there. We must live up to our responsibility. Can we build another Golden Age?"

Frazier shook himself, as if the subject were physically painful.

"Let's move along," he said quickly. "We have more immediate questions to answer."

He led us through the kitchen to a room which was windowless and must have been beneath the surface of the hill. It was a sort of giant food locker, which held a year's supply of frozen vegetables and fruits. Many of these were prepared for storage in special ways. For example, ears of fresh corn were "milked" to get out the nutritious parts while leaving the hulls on the cobs.

"The product is delicious," said Frazier. "You must try our corn soufflé. A specialty of the house."

The Manager in charge of food storage, Frazier explained, could commandeer a large force of skilled help to prepare vegetables and fruits at just the right times. This adaptable manpower was also put to another use. An agent of the community kept in touch with the agriculture of the county and frequently found a farmer with a crop which he was not able to harvest. The community would then make a deal to harvest on shares. A fairly stiff bargain could be driven, since the farmer would otherwise lose the crop.

"We send off three or four truckloads of workers in the early morning," said Frazier, "and they come back at noon with a year's supply of cherries, or strawberries, or tomatoes. By evening the whole crop has been prepared and frozen, at very little cost."

"Sounds like a plague of locusts," said Castle. "You allow for this vandalism, I suppose, when proving that four hours a day will suffice?"

Frazier either missed the point or did not care to reply. Instead, he urged us on through a small flour mill to a rear door of the building, where we found two men unloading cans of milk from a truck.

"We can get a ride to the dairy in a moment," said Frazier, "and we may as well start there in our tour of the farm. I had expected Mrs. Meyerson to join us." He looked about from one side to the other as if dramatizing Expectancy.

We climbed onto the platform of the truck and held on desperately as we swayed over the unpaved road which served the kitchen and storehouses.

The dairy was the most modern unit in the Walden Two farm. The cows, like Castle's goats, were of the ordinary grass-burning variety, but they were not handoperated. Butter, cheese, and other products were made in a small creamery near by, and a natural cave on Stone Hill was being used for some experiments in curing special cheeses.

We met the Manager in charge of this part of the farm. Frazier let him take over, and the difference was surprising. Frazier's account had been highly selective. He preferred to talk about his beloved behavioral engineering or of man's triumph over nature—usually his more trivial triumphs at that. The Manager was unfamiliar with general principles. He was dealing with cows and milk and fodder and manure. A cream separator did not save labor or time; it got cream out of whole milk. Cows were not part of the cycle "from-grass-to-cow-to-man-to-grass"; they were Holsteins and Guernseys of certified health, giving so many pounds of butterfat annually. It was refreshing to get some plain facts, and we found ourselves as entranced as if we had been hearing a firsthand account of the Milk of Paradise.

I realized suddenly that Frazier, in a quite literal sense, seldom knew what he was talking about. He could not make a corn soufflé or clear a pond, he probably did not know when peas were ready to be picked or how they should be stored, and I doubted whether he could tell wheat from barley. In all the domestic and rural arts he loved so well, he was a rank amateur. I thought of Emerson at Brook Farm, tilling the soil for the love of it, and I felt a sudden sharp concern that Walden Two might have some fatal flaw. But the professional vigor of this young expert was reassuring. While Frazier dreamt of economic structure and cultural design, he would get out the milk.

Frazier sensed that the Dairy Manager had somehow alienated our interests, and as we crossed the road toward the truck farms, he tried to recover his prestige. He explained that the Managers had been associated in a farmers' cooperative which was on the verge of failure when Walden Two came along to save them. He seemed to realize that his move was too obvious and he cast about quickly for another topic. He pointed to a small building.

"A real achievement in social engineering," he announced, possibly with a touch of irony, but also with satisfaction in finding himself on familiar and favorable ground. "It's impossible to work around cattle or a creamery, or with pigs or poultry, without picking up objectionable odors. Normal cleanliness isn't enough. Our farmers began to suffer a certain ostracism, and the credit value of farm work began to go up too. So—we took the problem seriously." He shrugged his shoulders as if this were as good as solving it.

"This building," he said, "is divided into three parts.

When the farmers come to work, they take off their clothes in the first room. They then walk through to the third room and dress for work. On their return, they remove their work clothes, take a shower in the middle room, and replace their regular clothes."

Castle began a quiet chant:

> " 'Where are you going, my pretty maid?'
> 'To the shower bath,' she said."

"I should explain," said Frazier in great haste, "that there are two series of rooms, one for each sex."

We walked along the edge of the truck gardens, and Frazier pointed out the poultry houses and, farther south, the piggery. We turned about in the direction of the workshops, and Frazier entered upon a discussion of economics. The community was not, of course, completely self-sufficient. It needed certain materials and equipment and had to buy power and pay taxes. Hence it had to create "foreign exchange." At the moment this was apparently not satisfactory. The community had not yet made the best use of its supply of skilled labor. But several small industries were already well established and others were being worked out. The community was paying its way, but Frazier felt that it could be done more efficiently.

I had noticed that Frazier was occasionally glancing in the direction of the main building. As we reached the road in front of the workshops, he dropped upon the grass and invited us to join him.

"Mrs. Meyerson has just left the Hall," he announced. I turned to confirm this but found my view cut off by the pines. I caught Frazier watching me, and he turned away with a suppressed smile. "She will be here in ten minutes," he continued, "and I think we'd better wait."

We grouped ourselves about him as he resumed his analysis of the economics of the community. He appeared to be forcing himself to be interested. He stared at the grass with glassy eyes and repeated one stereotyped phrase after another in a hollow voice. Suddenly, in a gesture of impatience, he threw up a hand and exclaimed, "But this is idiotic! There's no problem here at all! No one can seriously doubt that a well-managed community will get along successfully as an economic unit. A child could prove it. The real problems are psychological. I really shouldn't talk about these details at all. They'll mislead you."

We had walked over some heavy soil in the truck gardens, and Frazier picked up a small stick and began to clean his shoes in silence. Presently Mrs. Meyerson emerged from the strip of pines, walking with a graceful yet rapid and rather military stride. Frazier jumped up quickly and took a few steps to meet her. She gave him her left hand and extended her right to the two girls.

"I'm dreadfully sorry. I hope you haven't waited long," she said. She turned to Frazier and added, "The Bach went badly, and Fergy kept us on and on."

We crossed the road and entered the first of a series of buildings. A single large room contained looms of various sizes, work tables with highly polished tops, and shelves holding bolts of woolens and other supplies. To Frazier's evident surprise, the room was deserted.

"I suppose it's too nice a day for this sort of work," he said. "There's much to be done out of doors at this time of year. In bad weather you would find this place full of life. We make all our woolens, with some to spare. Our looms, you see, are power-driven." He caught himself. "As I believe I've already said," he added, without a smile. "We can't advertise our cloth as hand-woven, but the looms are carefully tended by skilled weavers, and the product is every way as good."

We stopped at a carding machine which contained some reddish-brown wool.

"Did you notice our flock of brown sheep on the far hill?" Frazier asked. "Rather a novelty. We get some fine color mixtures without the use of—"

Mrs. Meyerson broke in to speak to the girls and,

without a word to Frazier, led them away to another building. Frazier watched them in silence and did not return to his sentence. We went on through a passageway to a large wood-working shop. Two men were applying clamps to a piece of furniture under repair, but otherwise the building was also deserted.

"It's the sort of day one likes to work outside," Frazier said uneasily.

A third building of about the same size was a metal-working and machine shop, and a fourth contained many small rooms arranged on both sides of a central hall. Some of these proved to be experimental laboratories.

We went outdoors into the broad area which was enclosed by the buildings we had passed through. From a sawmill we heard the periodic whine of a planer. A mechanical earth-rammer stood under a large shed, amid piles of earth of various colors and finished blocks drying on racks. Several men and women were at work, and I commented on the fact that most of them were surprisingly young.

"Several rooms are being added to one of the personal halls," Frazier said. "These young people will occupy them. There's a certain satisfaction in building your own living quarters. A sort of nesting instinct. It has become part of the process of being in love in Walden Two. Various experienced people supervise the work, of course."

"Not the whole process of being in love, I trust," muttered Castle.

We walked across the area to the clothing shop. As we entered we saw a group of men and women clustered about Mary, who was demonstrating some sort of stitch on a large embroidery frame.

"It's something Mary's grandmother taught her," Barbara explained to Rodge. "It's fascinating!"

Steve worked his way toward Mary and looked at the frame. He murmured deprecatingly, "Sure! Sure!"

It was evident from the general delight that Mary's contribution was appreciated, and I felt rather proud of her. But as the group broke up, I was conscious of the fact that no one thanked her or expressed gratitude in any other way. This, I later discovered, was in accordance with the Walden Two code. What interested me in looking back upon the incident was that Mary clearly expected nothing else. She was quietly pleased, and probably a little proud of herself as she took Steve's arm and whispered something into his ear, but I am sure that any further demonstration would have made her most unhappy.

It was nearly five o'clock, and as we walked toward the pine grove it was evident that we were all a little tired. Frazier suggested that we wait for a truck to take us up to the main building. We stretched out comfortably on the grassy bank beside the road. I was pleasantly drowsy and happy to discover that no further aspects of Walden Two were to be discussed just then.

"So the Bach went badly, Rachel," I heard Frazier say.

"Only at first. It will be worth hearing."

"At eight o'clock?"

"Yes. For about an hour."

"How should we arrange supper, do you think?"

"Why not a late supper, and come directly to the theater? You had a late lunch."

"Will you join us?"

"I think not. I'm going to have high tea with Fergy and the McIntyres, and wait for a bite to eat after the concert."

There was more of this, but I was drugged with fatigue. Later I heard the dull grind of an approaching truck and Frazier stood up to hail it. It proved to be heavily loaded, but we found space, with Rodge and Steve standing on the running boards. We dropped off near our quarters and arranged to meet in the serving room at seven.

Rodge, Steve, and the girls immediately went indoors. I turned to Mrs. Meyerson.

"Was it a Bach chorus you were talking about?"

"Yes," she said, pleased and just a shade surprised.

"We're working on some of the choruses from the *B Minor Mass*."

"Oh, wonderful!" I said. "For some reason I've never heard the *B Minor*."

I began to mention the choral works of Bach with which I was familiar, but at that moment Frazier said to Castle, "Well, what do you think of the Lovely Lady now?"

Mrs. Meyerson lost interest in my musical history and turned slightly in Frazier's direction.

"Are you satisfied she's not really floating in air?" Frazier went on.

I continued my account though I knew my party had been disconnected.

"I'm afraid I preferred her as an illusion," said Castle, "but it has been interesting to see what's underneath."

"What on earth are they talking about?" said Mrs. Meyerson, interrupting me with ill-concealed excitement.

"We prefer the illusion, too, if you wish to call it that," continued Frazier. "We enjoy floating in air. There's enough of the *enfant terrible* in us to wish to violate the inviolable. I confess that I enjoy the Lovely Lady as an illusion. But she's made of solid flesh, pound for pound, and we really obey all the laws."

"Fraze!" said Mrs. Meyerson, her voice pitched very high. "What on earth are you saying?"

"Simply that we're no freer of economic law than the magician's lovely assistant is free of the law of gravitation. But we enjoy seeming to be free. Leisure's our levitation."

"Oh, you are beyond me," said Mrs. Meyerson with a musical laugh. She started to move away. "Coming, Fraze?"

We said good-bye, and Frazier and Mrs. Meyerson strode off across the lawn in the direction of the Ladder, talking and laughing energetically.

"By the way," I said to Castle, as we went indoors, "I think the Lovely Lady's name is Rachel."

It was pseudo-wit. I had no idea what I meant.

11

IN THE walk near the serving room was a bulletin board, arranged like the radio schedules in newspapers. Along the left edge were printed the hours of the day and along the top the names of parts of Walden Two, such as "Theater," "Studio Three," "Lawn," "Radio Lounge," "West Entrance," "English Room," and "Yellow Game Room." Announcements of meetings, parties, concerts, matches, and so on, were caught under clips in their appropriate places. A few which I recall, not all of them intelligible to me, read: "Hedda Gabler," "Curran's Group," "Boston Symphony," "Truck Ride to Canton," "Youngsters' Dance," "AGL," "News Group," "Tap," and "Walden Code."

As Castle and I waited for our group to assemble for supper, I ran my eye down the "Theater" column to "8:00 PM." The notice read:"Bach (Mr. Fergus' group). Three choruses from the *B Minor Mass*. 50 Minutes."

Frazier appeared from one of the lounges.

"Find something to interest you?" he said. "Oh, I see you've spotted our concert."

"There's certainly a great deal going on," I said, indicating the bulletin board with a sweep of my hand.

"There is. Invariably. Much more than you will realize until you've grown accustomed to small print. You must feel a certain lack of excitement in these announcements. No garish posters, no bright lights, none of the paraphernalia with which the entertainment industry whips up a jaded public. But in a day or so these simple notices will begin to take on all the excitement of the shimmering marquee. When there are no signs ten feet high, five feet will do. When there are none five feet high, one foot serves well enough. It isn't the color or brightness or size of a poster which makes it exciting. It's the experiences which have accompanied similar posters in the past. The excitement is a conditioned reflex. Our bulletin board is our Great White Way, and we're dazzled by it."

Frazier scrutinized the notice of the concert.

" 'Fifty minutes,' " he read. "Long enough."

"Are your concerts usually so brief?"

"Usually. There's no sense in a long concert—not here, at any rate."

"What difference does it make whether it's here or elsewhere?"

"In the city a fifty-minute concert would be impossible. No one would get his money's worth."

"If the seats were very reasonable—"

"My dear fellow, the cost of the ticket is only a small part of what one pays for a concert. Think of the transportation, the time consumed, often in bad weather, too. Suppose a stranger asked you to go to a concert hall to pick up a package for him—how much would you charge? If one is to go to all that trouble, nothing short of a two- or three-hour performance will satisfy. But there are only a few works of any importance which require more than forty-five minutes. Some of the operas may be worth hearing all in one piece, and the *Ninth*."

"And the *B Minor Mass*," I said.

"And we shall eventually hear it in one piece, you may depend on Fergy for that. But what else would you care to hear that would last more than an hour, say?"

This struck me as a particularly brazen bit of Philistinism.

"What's wrong with a nicely constructed program? A little variety. The contrast between styles or moods."

"Do you think Beethoven wrote the *Fifth* to be played on the heels of *Til Eulenspiegel?*"

"No, but on the heels of something else, I imagine."

"Only because he had the same trouble with his audiences then. No, a piece of music is an experience to be taken by itself. And we're free to do just that."

I discovered Steve and Mary coming along the Walk with several young people whom I had seen in the dressmaking shop that afternoon. One of them stepped up to Frazier.

"Do you mind if we borrow your friends for the evening? They don't want to hear a Mass."

"How do they know?" said Frazier, scowling at Steve and Mary. "Have they ever heard it?"

"No, but we don't think they'd like it. We're going to the dance."

I caught Mary's eye. She raised her eyebrows to ask if it were all right, and I nodded.

"For supper, too?" asked Frazier.

"If you don't mind."

Frazier dismissed them rather impatiently with a wave of his hand, and they entered the dining room. Presently Rodge and Barbara appeared, walking silently toward us. Rodge allowed Barbara's expansive greeting to serve for both, and we went in to supper.

"Somehow or other," said Frazier, when we had found a table in the Swedish room, "you have avoided the most fatuous of all our visitors' questions. 'If you don't work, then whatever do you do with all your time?' I congratulate you. I'm delighted."

"On the contrary," said Castle. "You've been lying in wait for that question, and are quite disappointed that it hasn't come along. I shall put you to the test. Pardon me for being fatuous, but what *do* you do with all your time?"

"If I've had a plan, it was a mistake to pose the question just yet. I haven't even loaded my gun. When we've had a chance to discuss the psychological management of a community, I can show you how ridiculous it is. But are you asking it seriously?"

"Seriously enough."

"But what about the evidence before your very eyes? Look at our bulletin board."

"I'm not so sure that's evidence," Castle said. " 'Something doing every minute' may be a gesture of despair— or the height of the battle against boredom."

"Bravo!" cried Frazier. "Mr. Castle, you should have been the psychologist, and Burris here, the philosopher.

It might very well be 'the height of the battle against boredom.' A magnificent figure. But let's talk about boredom some other time. I merely wanted to bring up an aspect of Walden Two that you mustn't neglect in evaluating us. I mean our patronage of the arts. This is not a great age in either art or music. But why not? Why shouldn't our civilization produce art as abundantly as it produces science and technology? Obviously because the right conditions are lacking. That's where Walden Two comes in. Here, the right conditions can be achieved."

"What do we really know about those conditions?" I said, a little out of countenance at being called a philosopher.

"Not much, I grant you, but enough. Leisure, for example. A wealthy class to provide leisure for the artist is characteristic of a great age. Artists aren't lazy, but they must be reasonably free of the responsibility of earning a livelihood. Isn't that the very essence of art—that it taps the energies and talents which in a more demanding world go into earning a living?"

"I can show you some exceptions," I said. "Artists who have worked hard, aside from their art."

"But the rule stands," said Frazier dogmatically. "When artists and composers aren't patronized, they generally get a modicum of leisure by becoming irresponsible. Hence their reputation with the public. Irresponsibility or security—the momentary effect is the same. But in the long run a good living is more productive."

"I'm not so sure your conditions are lacking in our present culture," I said. "What about prizes and fellowships?"

"Prizes only scratch the surface. You can't encourage art with money alone. What you need is a culture. You need a real opportunity for young artists. The career must be economically sound and socially acceptable, and prizes won't do that. And you need appreciation—there must be audiences, not to pay the bills, but to enjoy. All in all, we really know a lot about what is needed. We must get to the artist before he has proved his worth. A great productive culture must stimulate large numbers of the young and untried. Philanthropy can't do that. It may produce a few great works of art, but it's only a start. Don't expect a Golden Age."

Frazier swallowed carefully and continued with great deliberation.

"You will grow tired of hearing this," he said, "but I must say it again and again. A Golden Age, whether of art or music or science or peace or plenty, is out of reach of our economic and governmental techniques. Something may be done by accident, as it has from time to time in the past, but not by deliberate intent. At this very moment enormous numbers of intelligent men and women of good will are trying to build a better world. But problems are born faster than they can be solved. Our civilization is running away like a frightened horse, her flanks flashing with sweat, her nostrils breathing a frothy mist; and as she runs, her speed and her panic increase together. As for your politicians, your professors, your writers—let them wave their arms and shout as wildly as they will. They can't bring the frantic beast under control."

"What do *you* do with a runaway?" said Castle.

"Let her run till she drops from exhaustion," said Frazier flatly. "Meanwhile let's see what we can do with her lovely colt." He stopped talking to clean his tray. I found myself silenced by his sudden burst of metaphor, as if I ought not to speak until I could find words similarly exalted. Frazier looked at us once or twice questioningly, but went back to his supper. Finally he put down his fork and wiped his mouth.

"Take music, for example," he resumed. "If you live in Walden Two and like music, you may go as far as you like. I don't mean a few minutes a day—I mean all the time and energy you can give to music and remain healthy. If you want to listen, there's an extensive library of records and, of course, many concerts, some of them quite professional. All the good radio programs are broadcast over the system of loudspeakers that we call the Walden Network, and they are monitored to remove the advertising.

"If you want to perform, you can get instruction on almost any instrument from other members—who get credits for it. If you have any ability, you can soon find an audience. We all go to concerts. We're never too tired, and the night is never too cold or too wet. Even our amateurs are quite popular, though usually with other amateurs—taking in each other's washing, so to speak. There's an atrocious military band with a repertoire in the narrow range between Sousa and von Suppé. But we have excellent string ensembles, and a very good small symphony orchestra.

"Our choruses are especially popular. If you sing, you can shout 'Brennan on the Moor!' to your heart's delight. Or have a go at Gilbert and Sullivan. Or the Bach Cantata Club. And everybody gets a chance. Singers are strangely jealous of each other as a rule, but not here. Here there's no struggle for a few lucrative positions, and no great rivalry for the approval of the public, thanks to a special bit of cultural engineering.

"Think what this means for the young composer! Sometimes his work is performed before it's even finished! Perhaps it's finished for him by enthusiastic friends. And it's talked about by audiences who know him and know music as well. You can have no idea how productive this makes a man until you have seen it in action.

"Lately I have been following a group of young song writers. I remember finding it hard to believe that Schumann could have written three songs in one day, but I believe it now. It's been done here. And very acceptable *Lieder*, too, with a good feeling for modern harmony. And our composers are already entering new territory. That was inevitable. The accelerated tempo alone would have done it. And we aren't held back by commercial standardization. Our audiences grow with our composers. Naturally we will develop our own genre. It's the dawn—the dawn, at least, of a Golden Age . . ." Frazier's voice trailed off, and he echoed himself faintly, "A Golden Age." Then he began again with greater excitement.

"Think of the effect upon our children! Exposed to music in their very cribs—a figure of speech, by the way, since we have replaced the crib with a much more efficient device—given the chance to follow any and every musical inclination, with excellent and enthusiastic teachers, with appreciative and good-humored audiences awaiting their first achievements. What an environment! How could any scrap of musical ability fail to find its fullest possible expression!"

"But a Golden Age from a community of only one thousand!" I said. "How many geniuses can you expect to get from such a limited assortment of genes?"

"Is that a pun? Or do you really think that geniuses come from genes? Well, maybe they do. But how close have we ever got to making the most of our genes? That's the real question. You can't possibly give me an answer, Burris, and you know it. There has been absolutely no way of answering it until now, because it has never been possible to manipulate the environment in the required way."

"What about musical families and musical centers?" I said. "Don't they show that heredity was important?"

"But they were *environments!*" Frazier fairly shouted. "No, history won't give you the answer. History never sets up the experiments the right way. You could draw an opposite conclusion from the very same evidence. Where were the genes before the heyday of the center? How were they brought together? And where did they go when the glory passed?"

Frazier suddenly looked at his wrist watch.

"We shall be late!" he said, in alarm.

We disposed of our trays and started for the theater.

"And remember, we aren't specializing in music, either," Frazier continued, turning halfway about in order to speak to us as he led the way rapidly forward. "We don't specialize in anything. We have time for everything. I could tell you a similar story for painting and sculpture and half a dozen applied arts."

"It's amazing," I said. "Really amazing. I remember the paintings in the Ladder. I have been meaning to go back. Are they all by members of Walden Two?"

Frazier peered back, glowing with delight.

"All of them," he said. "All of them. But it's not amazing. Why amazing?" In his haste he had bumped into several people, and he found it necessary to raise his voice as we became somewhat separated by others moving in the same direction.

"Not amazing at all!" he shouted. "That's just the point. Right conditions, that's all. Right conditions. All you need. (Pardon me.) All you need. Give them a chance, that's all. Leisure. Opportunity. Appreciation."

Suddenly he laughed, and in a burst of good spirits, flushed with his success in astonishing us, he indulged in what seemed like a senseless and manic flight of ideas. Waving his hand above his head, he shouted, *"Liberté! Égalité! Fraternité!"*

The chorus was already on the stage when we filed into the theater. The instrumentalists were taking their places on the near side of the footlights, although there was no orchestra pit. The conductor—Fergy, I presumed —was already on a makeshift podium in the center aisle, directing the arrangement of music stands and chairs.

The room grew quiet as we took our places, and presently some of the lights went off. I found myself staring at Fergy, who was wiping his brow with an enormous handkerchief. Bits of our supper conversation ran through my head—"genius and genes," *"égalité,"* "a Golden Age." It was Frazier's voice, but my own broke through in a violent challenge: *Why not? Why not?*

There was a faint hum in the hushed room, like some sort of premonitory celestial music.

What was a Golden Age, anyway? What distinguished it from any other? The difference might be fantastically slight. Some extra shade of personal stimulation. Time to think. Time to act. Some trivial enlargement of opportunity. Appreciation. Liberty. Equality. And yes, of course, fraternity. A senseless flight of ideas, indeed! Frazier was merely translating!

Fergy raised both fists in the air and looked at the chorus quickly from side to side.

I thought: I must read up on the psychology of artistic creation. It was the kind of thing I should be interested in. I had occasionally given a course in the Aesthetic Experience. The library would have something along that line . . .

I felt a quick flush of shame. How fantastic my academic habits of thought had become! "The library would have something." How very different from the way Frazier would go about it! I sighed heavily. Could I ever escape from the world of books? My eyes ached in vivid reminiscence and I was seized with a violent revulsion, almost a retching. At that moment the opening chorus struck.

Kyrie eleison . . .

I was wholly unprepared for it, and I cowered as if I had received a physical blow. My body stiffened to meet some fancied threat, and my fingers tightened about the arms of my chair.

I cannot remember much of the chorus. I was still in the same position when it came to an end, and too unsure of myself to relax my grip and join in the applause. But I saw Frazier and Castle on either side of me clapping energetically—and Fergy, beaming with pleasure and pride, bowing to right and left and turning to shake his clasped hands at the chorus. Once, as he bowed, he looked straight at me, out over his glasses, like some sort of dream gargoyle, and I imagined that if he could speak to me, it would be in a strange accent, and that his words would be:

"You like it? Our Golden Age? Yes?"

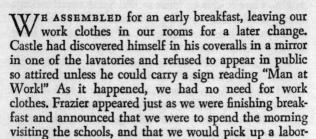

12

W͟E͟ ͟A͟S͟S͟E͟M͟B͟L͟E͟D͟ for an early breakfast, leaving our
work clothes in our rooms for a later change.
Castle had discovered himself in his coveralls in a mirror
in one of the lavatories and refused to appear in public
so attired unless he could carry a sign reading "Man at
Work!" As it happened, we had no need for work
clothes. Frazier appeared just as we were finishing breakfast and announced that we were to spend the morning
visiting the schools, and that we would pick up a labor-
credit or two during the afternoon.

He led the way outdoors and we skirted the flower
beds in a long arc which brought us to the small picnic
tables where we had rested on our first day at Walden
Two. Large sheets of paper were thumbtacked to the
tables, and several students, most of them ten or twelve
years old, but two or three certainly no older than eight,
were drawing what looked like Euclidian constructions
with heavy black pencils. Other children were driving
pegs into the ground and running strings from one peg
to another. Two surveyor's transits and a steel measur-
ing tape were in use. So far as I could see, Euclid was
getting a firsthand experimental check. Or it might have
been trigonometry, I was not sure. Frazier seemed to
know no more about it than the rest of us. He shrugged
off Rodge's hesitant inquiry and pressed forward toward
the nearest wing of the children's building. Perhaps he
merely wanted to take things in order, for this proved to
be the nursery.

A young woman in a white uniform met us in a small
waiting room near the entrance. Frazier addressed her
as Mrs. Nash.

"I hope Mr. Frazier has warned you," she said with
a smile, "that we're going to be rather impolite and
give you only a glimpse of our babies. We try to protect them from infection during the first year. It's especially important when they are cared for as a group."

86

"What about the parents?" said Castle at once. "Don't parents see their babies?"

"Oh, yes, so long as they are in good health. Some parents work in the nursery. Others come around every day or so, for at least a few minutes. They take the baby out for some sunshine, or play with it in a play room." Mrs. Nash smiled at Frazier. "That's the way we build up the baby's resistance," she added.

She opened a door and allowed us to look into a small room, three walls of which were lined with cubicles, each with a large glass window. Behind the windows we could see babies of various ages. None of them wore more than a diaper, and there were no bedclothes. In one cubicle a small red newborn was asleep on its stomach. Some of the older babies were awake and playing with toys. Near the door a baby on all fours pressed its nose against the glass and smiled at us.

"Looks like an aquarium," said Castle.

"And very precious fish they are," said Mrs. Nash, as if the comparison were not unfamiliar.

"Which is yours?" asked Frazier.

"Over there asleep," said Mrs. Nash, pointing to a far corner. "Almost ready to graduate, too. He'll be a year old next month." She drew the door gently shut before we had satisfied our curiosity.

"I can show you one of the units in the isolation room, which isn't being used," she said, leading the way along the corridor. She opened another door and we entered. Two of the cubicles stood against the wall.

"This is a much more efficient way of keeping a baby warm than the usual practice of wrapping it in several layers of cloth," said Mrs. Nash, opening a safety-glass window to permit Barbara and Mary to look inside. "The newborn baby needs moist air at about 88 or 90 degrees. At six months, 80 is about right."

"How do you know that?" said Castle, rather belligerently.

"The baby tells us," said Mrs. Nash pleasantly, as if the question were also familiar.

"You know the story about the bath water, don't you, Mr. Castle?" Frazier interrupted. "The temperature's all right if the baby doesn't turn red or blue."

"But I hope—" Castle began.

"It's only a matter of a degree or two," said Mrs. Nash quickly. "If the baby's too warm, it does turn rather pinkish, and it usually cries. It always stops crying when we lower the temperature." She twisted the dial of a thermostat on the front of a cubicle.

"And I suppose if frost forms around the nose it's too cold," said Castle, getting himself under control.

"The baby turns rather pale," said Mrs. Nash laughing, "and takes a curious posture with its arms along its sides or slightly curled up. With a little practice we can tell at a glance whether the temperature is right or not."

"But why don't you put clothes on them?" said Barbara.

"What for? It would mean laundry for us and discomfort for the child. It's the same with sheets and blankets. Our babies lie on a stretched plastic cloth which doesn't soak up moisture and can be wiped clean in a moment."

"It looks terribly comfortable," I said. "Why don't you all sleep that way?"

"We're working on that," said Frazier, apparently quite seriously. "It would save no end of laundry, and, as you say, it would be comfortable."

"Clothing and blankets are really a great nuisance," said Mrs. Nash. "They keep the baby from exercising, they force it into uncomfortable postures—"

"When a baby graduates from our Lower Nursery," Frazier broke in, "it knows nothing of frustration, anxiety, or fear. It never cries except when sick, which is very seldom, and it has a lively interest in everything."

"But is it prepared for life?" said Castle. "Surely you can't continue to protect it from frustration or frightening situations forever."

"Of course not. But it can be prepared for them. We can build a tolerance for frustration by introducing obstacles gradually as the baby grows strong enough to handle them. But I'm getting ahead of our story. Have you any other point to make, Mrs. Nash?"

"I suppose you'd like to have them know how much work is saved. Since the air is filtered, we only bathe the babies once a week, and we never need to clean their nostrils or eyes. There are no beds to make, of course. And it's easy to prevent infection. The compartments are soundproofed, and the babies sleep well and don't disturb each other. We can keep them on different schedules, so the nursery runs smoothly. Let me see, is there anything else?"

"I think that's quite enough," said Frazier. "We have a lot of ground to cover this morning."

"Not so fast, if you please," said Castle. "I'm not satisfied yet. Aren't you raising a lot of very inadequate organisms? Controlled temperature, noiseless sleep—aren't these babies going to be completely at the mercy of a normal environment? Can you go on coddling them forever?"

"I can answer that, Mrs. Nash," said Frazier. "The answer is *no*. Our babies are especially resistant. It's true that a constant annoyance may develop a tolerance, but the commoner result is that the baby is worn down or enervated. We introduce annoyances slowly, according to the ability of the baby to take them. It's very much like inoculation."

"Another thing," said Castle. "What about mother love?"

Frazier and Mrs. Nash looked at each other and laughed.

"Are you speaking of mother love as an essence, Mr. Castle?" said Frazier.

"I am not!" said Castle, bristling. "I'm speaking of a concrete thing. I mean the love which the mother gives her baby—the affection—well, to be really concrete, the kisses, the fondling, and so on, I suppose you'd say. You can't expect me to give you the physical dimensions of mother love!" He was confused and flushed. "It's real enough to the baby, I'll bet!" he added blackly.

"Very real," said Frazier quietly. "And we supply it in liberal doses. But we don't limit it to mothers. We go in for father love, too—for everybody's love—community love, if you wish. Our children are treated with affection by everyone—and thoughtful affection too, which isn't marred by fits of temper due to overwork or careless handling due to ignorance."

"But the personal relation between the mother and the child—Isn't there some sort of patterning? I thought the whole personality could be shaped in that way?" Castle appealed to me for professional support, but I failed him.

"You mean what the Freudian calls 'identification,' I think," said Frazier. "I agree that it's important, and we use it very effectively in our educational system. But unless you're a strict Freudian, we're talking in the wrong room. Let's wait till we see another age group. Can you come to the Upper Nursery, Mrs. Nash?"

"Let me check my staff," said Mrs. Nash. She disappeared into the "aquarium," returned almost immediately, and led us to another wing.

13

THE QUARTERS for children from one to three consisted of several small playrooms with Lilliputian furniture, a child's lavatory, and a dressing and locker room. Several small sleeping rooms were operated on the same principle as the baby-cubicles. The temperature and the humidity were controlled so that clothes or bedclothing were not needed. The cots were double-decker arrangements of the plastic mattresses we had seen in the cubicles. The children slept unclothed, except for diapers. There were more beds than necessary, so that the children could be grouped according to developmental age or exposure to contagious diseases or need for supervision, or for educational purposes.

We followed Mrs. Nash to a large screened porch on the south side of the building, where several children were playing in sandboxes and on swings and climbing apparatuses. A few wore "training pants"; the rest were naked. Beyond the porch was a grassy play yard enclosed by closely trimmed hedges, where other children, similarly undressed, were at play. Some kind of marching game was in progress.

As we returned, we met two women carrying food hampers. They spoke to Mrs. Nash and followed her to the porch. In a moment five or six children came running into the playrooms and were soon using the lavatory and dressing themselves. Mrs. Nash explained that they were being taken on a picnic.

"What about the children who don't go?" said Castle. "What do you do about the green-eyed monster?"

Mrs. Nash was puzzled.

"Jealousy. Envy," Castle elaborated. "Don't the children who stay home ever feel unhappy about it?"

"I don't understand," said Mrs. Nash.

"And I hope you won't try," said Frazier, with a smile. "I'm afraid we must be moving along."

We said good-bye, and I made an effort to thank Mrs.

Nash, but she seemed to be puzzled by that too, and Frazier frowned as if I had committed some breach of good taste.

"I think Mrs. Nash's puzzlement," said Frazier, as we left the building, "is proof enough that our children are seldom envious or jealous. Mrs. Nash was twelve years old when Walden Two was founded. It was a little late to undo her early training, but I think we were successful. She's a good example of the Walden Two product. She could probably recall the experience of jealousy, but it's not part of her present life."

"Surely that's going too far!" said Castle. "You can't be so godlike as all that! You must be assailed by emotions just as much as the rest of us!"

"We can discuss the question of godlikeness later, if you wish," replied Frazier. "As to emotions—we aren't free of them all, nor should we like to be. But the meaner and more annoying—the emotions which breed unhappiness—are almost unknown here, like unhappiness itself. We don't need them any longer in our struggle for existence, and it's easier on our circulatory system, and certainly pleasanter, to dispense with them."

"If you've discovered how to do that, you are indeed a genius," said Castle. He seemed almost stunned as Frazier nodded assent. "We all know that emotions are useless and bad for our peace of mind and our blood pressure," he went on. "But how arrange things otherwise?"

"We arrange them otherwise here," said Frazier. He was showing a mildness of manner which I was coming to recognize as a sign of confidence.

"But emotions are—fun!" said Barbara. "Life wouldn't be worth living without them."

"Some of them, yes," said Frazier. "The productive and strengthening emotions—joy and love. But sorrow and hate—and the high-voltage excitements of anger, fear, and rage—are out of proportion with the needs of modern life, and they're wasteful and dangerous. Mr. Castle has mentioned jealousy—a minor form of anger,

I think we may call it. Naturally we avoid it. It has served its purpose in the evolution of man; we've no further use for it. If we allowed it to persist, it would only sap the life out of us. In a cooperative society there's no jealousy because there's no need for jealousy."

"That implies that you all get everything you want," said Castle. "But what about social possessions? Last night you mentioned the young man who chose a particular girl or profession. There's still a chance for jealousy there, isn't there?"

"It doesn't imply that we get everything we want," said Frazier. "Of course we don't. But jealousy wouldn't help. In a competitive world there's some point to it. It energizes one to attack a frustrating condition. The impulse and the added energy are an advantage. Indeed, in a competitive world emotions work all too well. Look at the singular lack of success of the complacent man. He enjoys a more serene life, but it's less likely to be a fruitful one. The world isn't ready for simple pacifism or Christian humility, to cite two cases in point. Before you can safely train out the destructive and wasteful emotions, you must make sure they're no longer needed."

"How do you make sure that jealousy isn't needed in Walden Two?" I said.

"In Walden Two problems can't be solved by attacking others," said Frazier with marked finality.

"That's not the same as eliminating jealousy, though," I said.

"Of course it's not. But when a particular emotion is no longer a useful part of a behavioral repertoire, we proceed to eliminate it."

"Yes, but how?"

"It's simply a matter of behavioral engineering," said Frazier.

"Behavioral engineering?"

"You're baiting me, Burris. You know perfectly well what I mean. The techniques have been available for centuries. We use them in education and in the psychological management of the community. But you're forcing my hand," he added. "I was saving that for this evening. But let's strike while the iron is hot."

We had stopped at the door of the large children's building. Frazier shrugged his shoulders, walked to the shade of a large tree, and threw himself on the ground. We arranged ourselves about him and waited.

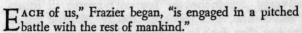

14

"EACH of us," Frazier began, "is engaged in a pitched battle with the rest of mankind."

"A curious premise for a Utopia," said Castle. "Even a pessimist like myself takes a more hopeful view than that."

"You do, you do," said Frazier. "But let's be realistic. Each of us has interests which conflict with the interests of everybody else. That's our original sin, and it can't be helped. Now, 'everybody else' we call 'society.' It's a powerful opponent, and it always wins. Oh, here and there an individual prevails for a while and gets what he wants. Sometimes he storms the culture of a society and changes it slightly to his own advantage. But society wins in the long run, for it has the advantage of numbers and of age. Many prevail against one, and men against a baby. Society attacks early, when the individual is helpless. It enslaves him almost before he has tasted freedom. The 'ologies' will tell you how it's done. Theology calls it building a conscience or developing a spirit of selflessness. Psychology calls it the growth of the super-ego.

"Considering how long society has been at it, you'd expect a better job. But the campaigns have been badly planned and the victory has never been secure. The behavior of the individual has been shaped according to revelations of 'good conduct,' never as the result of experimental study. But why not experiment? The questions are simple enough. What's the best behavior for the individual so far as the group is concerned? And how can the individual be induced to behave in that way? Why not explore these questions in a scientific spirit?

"We could do just that in Walden Two. We had already worked out a code of conduct—subject, of course, to experimental modification. The code would keep things running smoothly if everybody lived up to it.

Our job was to see that everybody did. Now, you can't get people to follow a useful code by making them into so many jacks-in-the-box. You can't foresee all future circumstances, and you can't specify adequate future conduct. You don't know what will be required. Instead you have to set up certain behavioral processes which will lead the individual to design his own 'good' conduct when the time comes. We call that sort of thing 'self-control.' But don't be misled, the control always rests in the last analysis in the hands of society.

"One of our Planners, a young man named Simmons, worked with me. It was the first time in history that the matter was approached in an experimental way. Do you question that statement, Mr. Castle?"

"I'm not sure I know what you are talking about," said Castle.

"Then let me go on. Simmons and I began by studying the great works on morals and ethics—Plato, Aristotle, Confucius, the New Testament, the Puritan divines, Machiavelli, Chesterfield, Freud—there were scores of them. We were looking for any and every method of shaping human behavior by imparting techniques of self-control. Some techniques were obvious enough, for they had marked turning points in human history. 'Love your enemies' is an example—a psychological invention for easing the lot of an oppressed people. The severest trial of oppression is the constant rage which one suffers at the thought of the oppressor. What Jesus discovered was how to avoid these inner devastations. His technique was to *practice the opposite emotion.* If a man can succeed in 'loving his enemies' and 'taking no thought for the morrow,' he will no longer be assailed by hatred of the oppressor or rage at the loss of his freedom or possessions. He may not get his freedom or possessions back, but he's less miserable. It's a difficult lesson. It comes late in our program."

"I thought you were opposed to modifying emotions and instincts until the world was ready for it," said

Castle. "According to you, the principle of 'love your enemies' should have been suicidal."

"It would have been suicidal, except for an entirely unforeseen consequence. Jesus must have been quite astonished at the effect of his discovery. We are only just beginning to understand the power of love because we are just beginning to understand the weakness of force and aggression. But the science of behavior is clear about all that now. Recent discoveries in the analysis of punishment—but I am falling into one digression after another. Let me save my explanation of why the Christian virtues—and I mean merely the Christian techniques of self-control—have not disappeared from the face of the earth, with due recognition of the fact that they suffered a narrow squeak within recent memory.

"When Simmons and I had collected our techniques of control, we had to discover how to teach them. That was more difficult. Current educational practices were of little value, and religious practices scarcely any better. Promising paradise or threatening hell-fire is, we assumed, generally admitted to be unproductive. It is based upon a fundamental fraud which, when discovered, turns the individual against society and nourishes the very thing it tries to stamp out. What Jesus offered in return for loving one's enemies was heaven *on earth*, better known as peace of mind.

"We found a few suggestions worth following in the practices of the clinical psychologist. We undertook to build a tolerance for annoying experiences. The sunshine of midday is extremely painful if you come from a dark room, but take it in easy stages and you can avoid pain altogether. The analogy can be misleading, but in much the same way it's possible to build a tolerance to painful or distasteful stimuli, or to frustration, or to situations which arouse fear, anger or rage. Society and nature throw these annoyances at the individual with no regard for the development of tolerances. Some achieve tolerances, most fail. Where would the science of immunization be if it followed a schedule of accidental dosages?

"Take the principle of 'Get thee behind me, Satan,' for example," Frazier continued. "It's a special case of self-control by altering the environment. Subclass A 3, I believe. We give each child a lollipop which has been dipped in powdered sugar so that a single touch of the tongue can be detected. We tell him he may eat the lollipop later in the day, provided it hasn't already been licked. Since the child is only three or four, it is a fairly diff——"

"Three or four!" Castle exclaimed.

"All our ethical training is completed by the age of six," said Frazier quietly. "A simple principle like putting temptation out of sight would be acquired before four. But at such an early age the problem of not licking the lollipop isn't easy. Now, what would you do, Mr. Castle, in a similar situation?"

"Put the lollipop out of sight as quickly as possible."

"Exactly. I can see you've been well trained. Or perhaps you discovered the principle for yourself. We're in favor of original inquiry wherever possible, but in this case we have a more important goal and we don't hesitate to give verbal help. First of all, the children are urged to examine their own behavior while looking at the lollipops. This helps them to recognize the need for self-control. Then the lollipops are concealed, and the children are asked to notice any gain in happiness or any reduction in tension. Then a strong distraction is arranged—say, an interesting game. Later the children are reminded of the candy and encouraged to examine their reaction. The value of the distraction is generally obvious. Well, need I go on? When the experiment is repeated a day or so later, the children all run with the lollipops to their lockers and do exactly what Mr. Castle would do—a sufficient indication of the success of our training."

"I wish to report an objective observation of my reaction to your story," said Castle, controlling his voice with great precision. "I find myself revolted by this display of sadistic tyranny."

"I don't wish to deny you the exercise of an emotion which you seem to find enjoyable," said Frazier. "So let me go on. Concealing a tempting but forbidden object is a crude solution. For one thing, it's not always feasible. We want a sort of psychological concealment—covering up the candy by paying no attention. In a later experiment the children wear their lollipops like crucifixes for a few hours."

> " 'Instead of the cross, the lollipop,
>   About my neck was hung,' "

said Castle.

"I wish somebody had taught me that, though," said Rodge, with a glance at Barbara.

"Don't we all?" said Frazier. "Some of us learn control, more or less by accident. The rest of us go all our lives not even understanding how it is possible, and blaming our failure on being born the wrong way."

"How do you build up a tolerance to an annoying situation?" I said.

"Oh, for example, by having the children 'take' a more and more painful shock, or drink cocoa with less and less sugar in it until a bitter concoction can be savored without a bitter face."

"But jealousy or envy—you can't administer them in graded doses," I said.

"And why not? Remember, we control the social environment, too, at this age. That's why we get our ethical training in early. Take this case. A group of children arrive home after a long walk tired and hungry. They're expecting supper; they find, instead, that it's time for a lesson in self-control: they must stand for five minutes in front of steaming bowls of soup.

"The assignment is accepted like a problem in arithmetic. Any groaning or complaining is a wrong answer. Instead, the children begin at once to work upon themselves to avoid any unhappiness during the delay. One of them may make a joke of it. We encourage a sense of humor as a good way of not taking an annoyance seriously. The joke won't be much, according to adult standards—perhaps the child will simply pretend to empty the bowl of soup into his upturned mouth. Another may start a song with many verses. The rest join in at once, for they've learned that it's a good way to make time pass."

Frazier glanced uneasily at Castle, who was not to be appeased.

"That also strikes you as a form of torture, Mr. Castle?" he asked.

"I'd rather be put on the rack," said Castle.

"Then you have by no means had the thorough training I supposed. You can't imagine how lightly the children take such an experience. It's a rather severe biological frustration, for the children are tired and hungry and they must stand and look at food; but it's passed off as lightly as a five-minute delay at curtain time. We regard it as a fairly elementary test. Much more difficult problems follow."

"I suspected as much," muttered Castle.

"In a later stage we forbid all social devices. No songs, no jokes—merely silence. Each child is forced back upon his own resources—a very important step."

"I should think so," I said. "And how do you know it's successful. You might produce a lot of silently resentful children. It's certainly a dangerous stage."

"It is, and we follow each child carefully. If he hasn't picked up the necessary techniques, we start back a little. A still more advanced stage"—Frazier glanced again at Castle, who stirred uneasily—"brings me to my point. When it's time to sit down to the soup, the children count off—heads and tails. Then a coin is tossed and if it comes up heads, the 'heads' sit down and eat. The 'tails' remain standing for another five minutes."

Castle groaned.

"And you call that envy?" I asked.

"Perhaps not exactly," said Frazier. "At least there's seldom any aggression against the lucky ones. The emotion, if any, is directed against Lady Luck herself, against the toss of the coin. That, in itself, is a lesson worth learning, for it's the only direction in which emotion has a surviving chance to be useful. And resentment toward things in general, while perhaps just as silly as personal aggression, is more easily controlled. Its expression is not socially objectionable."

Frazier looked nervously from one of us to the other. He seemed to be trying to discover whether we shared Castle's prejudice. I began to realize, also, that he had not really wanted to tell this story. He was vulnerable. He was treading on sanctified ground, and I was pretty sure he had not established the value of most of these practices in an experimental fashion. He could scarcely have done so in the short space of ten years. He was working on faith, and it bothered him.

I tried to bolster his confidence by reminding him that he had a professional colleague among his listeners. "May you not inadvertently teach your children some of the very emotions you're trying to eliminate?" I said. "What's the effect, for example, of finding the anticipation of a warm supper suddenly thwarted? Doesn't that eventually lead to feelings of uncertainty, or even anxiety?"

"It might. We had to discover how often our lessons could be safely administered. But all our schedules are worked out experimentally. We watch for undesired consequences just as any scientist watches for disrupting factors in his experiments.

"After all, it's a simple and sensible program," he went on in a tone of appeasement. "We set up a system of gradually increasing annoyances and frustrations against a background of complete serenity. An easy environment is made more and more difficult as the children acquire the capacity to adjust."

"But *why?*" said Castle. "Why these deliberate unpleasantnesses—to put it mildly? I must say I think you and your friend Simmons are really very subtle sadists."

"You've reversed your position, Mr. Castle," said Frazier in a sudden flash of anger with which I rather sympathized. Castle was calling names, and he was also being unaccountably and perhaps intentionally obtuse. "A while ago you accused me of breeding a race of softies," Frazier continued. "Now you object to toughening them up. But what you don't understand is that these potentially unhappy situations are never very annoying. Our schedules make sure of that. You wouldn't understand, however, because you're not so far advanced as our children."

Castle grew black.

"But what do your children get out of it?" he insisted, apparently trying to press some vague advantage in Frazier's anger.

"What do they get out of it!" exclaimed Frazier, his eyes flashing with a sort of helpless contempt. His lips curled and he dropped his head to look at his fingers, which were crushing a few blades of grass.

"They must get happiness and freedom and strength," I said, putting myself in a ridiculous position in attempting to make peace.

"They don't sound happy or free to me, standing in front of bowls of Forbidden Soup," said Castle, answering me parenthetically while continuing to stare at Frazier.

"If I must spell it out," Frazier began with a deep sigh, "what they get is escape from the petty emotions which eat the heart out of the unprepared. They get the satisfaction of pleasant and profitable social relations on a scale almost undreamed of in the world at large. They get immeasurably increased efficiency, because they can stick to a job without suffering the aches and pains which soon beset most of us. They get new horizons, for they are spared the emotions characteristic of frustration and failure. They get—" His eyes searched the branches of the trees. "Is that enough?" he said at last.

"And the community must gain their loyalty," I said,

"when they discover the fears and jealousies and diffidences in the world at large."

"I'm glad you put it that way," said Frazier. "You might have said that they must feel superior to the miserable products of our public schools. But we're at pains to keep any feeling of superiority or contempt under control, too. Having suffered most acutely from it myself, I put the subject first on our agenda. We carefully avoid any joy in a personal triumph which means the personal failure of somebody else. We take no pleasure in the sophistical, the disputative, the dialectical." He threw a vicious glance at Castle. "We don't use the motive of domination, because we are always thinking of the whole group. We could motivate a few geniuses that way—it was certainly my own motivation —but we'd sacrifice some of the happiness of everyone else. Triumph over nature and over oneself, yes. But over others, never."

"You've taken the mainspring out of the watch," said Castle flatly.

"That's an experimental question, Mr. Castle, and you have the wrong answer."

Frazier was making no effort to conceal his feeling. If he had been riding Castle, he was now using his spurs. Perhaps he sensed that the rest of us had come round and that he could change his tactics with a single holdout. But it was more than strategy, it was genuine feeling. Castle's undeviating skepticism was a growing frustration.

"Are your techniques really so very new?" I said hurriedly. "What about the primitive practice of submitting a boy to various tortures before granting him a place among adults? What about the disciplinary techniques of Puritanism? Or of the modern school, for that matter?"

"In one sense you're right," said Frazier. "And I think you've nicely answered Mr. Castle's tender concern for our little ones. The unhappinesses we deliberately impose are far milder than the normal unhappinesses from which we offer protection. Even at the height of our ethical training, the unhappiness is ridiculously trivial—to the well-trained child.

"But there's a world of difference in the way we use these annoyances," he continued. "For one thing, we don't punish. We never administer an unpleasantness in the hope of repressing or eliminating undesirable behavior. But there's another difference. In most cultures the child meets up with annoyances and reverses of uncontrolled magnitude. Some are imposed in the name of discipline by persons in authority. Some, like hazings, are condoned though not authorized. Others are merely accidental. No one cares to, or is able to, prevent them.

"We all know what happens. A few hardy children emerge, particularly those who have got their unhappiness in doses that could be swallowed. They become brave men. Others become sadists or masochists of varying degrees of pathology. Not having conquered a painful environment, they become preoccupied with pain and make a devious art of it. Others submit—and hope to inherit the earth. The rest—the cravens, the cowards —live in fear for the rest of their lives. And that's only a single field—the reaction to pain. I could cite a dozen parallel cases. The optimist and the pessimist, the contented and the disgruntled, the loved and the unloved, the ambitious and the discouraged—these are only the extreme products of a miserable system.

"Traditional practices are admittedly better than nothing," Frazier went on. "Spartan or Puritan—no one can question the occasional happy result. But the whole system rests upon the wasteful principle of selection. The English public school of the nineteenth century produced brave men—by setting up almost insurmountable barriers and making the most of the few who came over. But selection isn't education. Its crops of brave men will always be small, and the waste enormous. Like all primitive principles, selection serves in place of education only through a profligate use of material. Multiply extravagantly and select with rigor. It's the philosophy of the 'big litter' as an alternative to good child hygiene.

"In Walden Two we have a different objective. We make every man a brave man. They all come over the barriers. Some require more preparation than others, but they all come over. The traditional use of adversity is to select the strong. We control adversity to build strength. And we do it deliberately, no matter how sadistic Mr. Castle may think us, in order to prepare for adversities which are beyond control. Our children eventually experience the 'heartache and the thousand natural shocks that flesh is heir to.' It would be the cruelest possible practice to protect them as long as possible, especially when we *could* protect them so well."

Frazier held out his hands in an exaggerated gesture of appeal.

"What alternative *had* we?" he said, as if he were in pain. "What else could we do? For four or five years we could provide a life in which no important need would go unsatisfied, a life practically free of anxiety or frustration or annoyance. What would *you* do? Would you let the child enjoy this paradise with no thought for the future—like an idolatrous and pampering mother? Or would you relax control of the environment and let the child meet accidental frustrations? *But what is the virtue of accident?* No, there was only one course open to us. We had to *design* a series of adversities, so that the child would develop the greatest possible self-control. Call it deliberate, if you like, and accuse us of sadism; there was no other course." Frazier turned to Castle, but he was scarcely challenging him. He seemed to be waiting, anxiously, for his capitulation. But Castle merely shifted his ground.

"I find it difficult to classify these practices," he said. Frazier emitted a disgruntled "Ha!" and sat back. "Your system seems to have usurped the place as well as the techniques of religion."

"Of religion and family culture," said Frazier wearily. "But I don't call it usurpation. Ethical training belongs to the community. As for techniques, we took every suggestion we could find without prejudice as to the source. But not on faith. We disregarded all claims of revealed truth and put every principle to an experimental test. And by the way, I've very much misrepresented the whole system if you suppose that any of the practices I've described are fixed. We try out many different techniques. Gradually we work toward the best possible set. And we don't pay much attention to the apparent success of a principle in the course of history. History is honored in Walden Two only as entertainment. It isn't taken seriously as food for thought. Which reminds me, very rudely, of our original plan for the morning. Have you had enough of emotion? Shall we turn to intellect?"

Frazier addressed these questions to Castle in a very friendly way and I was glad to see that Castle responded in kind. It was perfectly clear, however, that neither of them had ever worn a lollipop about the neck or faced a bowl of Forbidden Soup.

15

THE LIVING quarters and daily schedules of the older children furnished a particularly good example of behavioral engineering. At first sight they seemed wholly casual, almost haphazard, but as Frazier pointed out their significant features and the consequences of each, I began to make out a comprehensive, almost Machiavellian design.

The children passed smoothly from one age group to another, following a natural process of growth and avoiding the abrupt changes of the home-and-school system. The arrangements were such that each child emulated children slightly older than himself and hence derived motives and patterns for much of his early education without adult aid.

The control of the physical and social environment, of which Frazier had made so much, was progressively relaxed—or, to be more exact, the control was transferred from the authorities to the child himself and to the other members of his group. After spending most of the first year in an air-conditioned cubicle, and the second and third mainly in an air-conditioned room with a minimum of clothing and bedding, the three- or four-year-old was introduced to regular clothes and given the care of a small standard cot in a dormitory. The beds of the five- and six-year-olds were grouped by threes and fours in a series of alcoves furnished like rooms and treated as such by the children. Groups of three or four seven-year-olds occupied small rooms together, and this practice was continued, with frequent change of roommates, until the children were about thirteen, at which time they took temporary rooms in the adult building, usually in pairs. At marriage, or whenever the individual chose, he could participate in building a larger room for himself or refurnishing an old room which might be available.

A similar withdrawal of supervision, proceeding as

rapidly as the child acquired control of himself, could be seen in the dining arrangements. From three through six, the children ate in a small dining room of their own. The older children, as we had observed on our first day at Walden Two, took their meals at specified times in the adult quarters. At thirteen all supervision was abandoned, and the young member was free to eat when and where he pleased.

We visited some of the workshops, laboratories, studies, and reading rooms used in lieu of classrooms. They were occupied, but it was not entirely clear that the children were actually in school. I supposed that the few adults to be seen about the building were teachers, but many of them were men, contrary to my conception of schoolteachers at that age level, and more often than not they were busy with some private business. Since Frazier had requested that we avoid questions or discussions in the presence of the children, we proceeded from one room to another in growing puzzlement. I had to admit that an enormous amount of learning was probably going on, but I had never seen a school like it before.

We inspected a well-equipped gymnasium, a small assembly room, and other facilities. The building was made of rammed earth and very simply decorated, but there was a pleasant "non-institutional" character about it. The doors and many of the windows stood open, and a fair share of the schoolwork, or whatever it was, took place outside. Children were constantly passing in and out. Although there was an obvious excitement about the place, there was little of the boisterous confusion which develops in the ordinary school when discipline is momentarily relaxed. Everyone seemed to be enjoying extraordinary freedom, but the efficiency and comfort of the whole group were preserved.

I was reminded of children on good behavior and was on the point of asking how often the pressure reached the bursting point. But there was a difference, too, and my question slowly evaporated. I could only conclude that this happy and productive atmosphere was probably the usual thing. Here again, so far as I could see, Frazier—or someone—had got things under control.

When we returned to our shade tree, I was primed with questions, and so, I am sure, was Castle. But Frazier had other plans. He had either forgotten how remarkable was the spectacle we had just witnessed, or he was intentionally allowing our wonderment and curiosity to ferment. He began from a very different point of view.

"When we discussed the economics of community life," he said, "I should have mentioned education. Teachers are, of course, workers, and I'm willing to defend all that I said about our economic advantage as specifically applied to education. God knows, the outside world is not exactly profligate in the education of its children. It doesn't spend much on equipment or teachers. Yet in spite of this penny-wise policy, there's still enormous waste. A much better education would cost less if society were better organized.

"We can arrange things more expeditiously here because we don't need to be constantly re-educating. The ordinary teacher spends a good share of her time changing the cultural and intellectual habits which the child acquires from its family and surrounding culture. Or else the teacher duplicates home training, in a complete waste of time. Here we can almost say that the school *is* the family, and vice versa.

"We can adopt the best educational methods and still avoid the administrative machinery which schools need in order to adjust to an unfavorable social structure. We don't have to worry about standardization in order to permit pupils to transfer from one school to another, or to appraise or control the work of particular schools. We don't need 'grades.' Everyone knows that talents and abilities don't develop at the same rate in different children. A fourth-grade reader may be a sixth-grade mathematician. The grade is an administrative device which does violence to the nature of the developmental process. Here the child advances as rapidly as he likes in any field. No time is wasted in forcing him to participate in, or be bored by, activities he has outgrown. And the backward child can be handled more efficiently too.

"We also don't require all our children to develop the same abilities or skills. We don't insist upon a certain set of courses. I don't suppose we have a single child who has had a 'secondary school education,' whatever that means. But they've all developed as rapidly as advisable, and they're well educated in many useful respects. By the same token we don't waste time in teaching the unteachable. The fixed education represented by a diploma is a bit of conspicuous waste which has no place in Walden Two. We don't attach an economic or honorific value to education. It has its own value or none at all.

"Since our children remain happy, energetic, and curious, we don't need to teach 'subjects' at all. We teach only the techniques of learning and thinking. As for geography, literature, the sciences—we give our children opportunity and guidance, and they learn them for themselves. In that way we dispense with half the teachers required under the old system, and the education is incomparably better. Our children aren't neglected, but they're seldom, if ever, *taught* anything.

"Education in Walden Two is part of the life of the community. We don't need to resort to trumped-up life experiences. Our children begin to work at a very early age. It's no hardship; it's accepted as readily as sport or play. And a good share of our education goes on in workshops, laboratories, and fields. It's part of the Walden Two Code to encourage children in all the arts and crafts. We're glad to spend time in instructing them, for we know it's important for the future of Walden Two and our own security."

"What about higher education?" I said.

"We aren't equipped for professional training, of course," said Frazier. "Those who want to go on to graduate study in a university are given special preparation. Entrance requirements are always tyrannical, though perhaps inevitable in a mass-production system. So far, we've been able to find graduate schools that will take our young people as special students, and as they continue to make excellent records, we expect fewer difficulties. If worse comes to worst, we shall organize as a college and get ourselves accredited. But can you imagine the stupid changes we should have to make?" Frazier snorted with impatience. "Oh, well. Tongue in cheek. Tongue in cheek."

"Don't you mean 'chin up'?" I asked.

"We'd have to set up a 'curriculum,' require a 'C average,' a 'foreign language,' 'so many years of residence,' and so on, and so on. It would be most amusing. No, 'tongue in cheek' was what I meant."

"Your people don't go to college, then?"

"We have no more reason to distinguish between college and high school than between high school and grade school. What are these distinctions, anyway, once you have separated education from the administration of education? Are there any natural breaks in a child's development? Many of our children naturally study more and more advanced material as they grow older. We help them in every way short of teaching them. We give them new techniques of acquiring knowledge and thinking. In spite of the beliefs of most educators, our children are taught to think. We give them an excellent survey of the methods and techniques of thinking, taken from logic, statistics, scientific method, psychology, and mathematics. That's all the 'college education' they need. They get the rest by themselves in our libraries and laboratories."

"But what about libraries and laboratories, though?" I said. "What can you actually provide in that line?"

"As to a library, we pride ourselves on having the best books, if not the most. Have you ever spent much time in a large college library? What trash the librarian has saved up in order to report a million volumes in the college catalogue! Bound pamphlets, old journals, ancient junk that even the shoddiest secondhand bookstore would clear from its shelves—all saved on the flimsy pretext that some day someone will want to study the 'history of a field.' Here we have the heart of a great library—not much to please the scholar or specialist, perhaps, but enough to interest the intelligent reader for life. Two or three thousand volumes will do it."

Frazier challenged me with a stare, but I did not wish to fight on such difficult terrain.

"The secret is this," he continued. "We subtract from our shelves as often as we add to them. The result is a collection that never misses fire. We all get something vital every time we take a book from the shelves. If anyone wants to follow a special interest we arrange for loans. If anyone wants to browse, we have half a barnful of discarded volumes.

"Our laboratories are good because they are real. Our workshops are really small engineering laboratories, and anyone with a genuine bent can go farther in them than the college student. We teach anatomy in the slaughterhouse, botany in the field, genetics in the dairy and poultry house, chemistry in the medical building and in the kitchen and dairy laboratory. What more can you ask?"

"And all this is just for the fun of it? You don't feel that some disciplined study is necessary?" said Castle.

"What for?" asked Frazier in unsuccessfully pretended surprise.

"To provide techniques and abilities which will be valuable later," said Castle. "For example, the study of a language."

"Why 'late'? Why not acquire a language *when* it's valuable? We acquire our own tongue that way! Of course, you're thinking of an educational process which comes to a dead stop sometime around the middle of June in one's last year in college. In Walden Two education goes on forever. It's part of our culture. We can acquire a technique whenever we need it.

"As to languages," Frazier continued, "you must know that even in our largest universities a language department considers itself very well off if two or three students at any one time approach fluency. We can do better than that. A member of Walden Two who once lived in France has interested several of our members, from ten to fifty years old, in the language. You may run into them during your stay. I hear them buzzing around the dining room every now and then, and they add a pleasantly cosmopolitan touch. And I'm told they're developing a good feeling for the French language and French literature. They'll never get any grades or credits, but they're getting French. Is there really any choice? Either French is worth learning, *at the time you learn it,* or it's not. And let's be sensible."

"I'm still skeptical," said Castle. "Of course, I'm still at a disadvantage in arguing against an accomplished fact." Frazier nodded his head violently. "But not everything has been accomplished," Castle went on. "Your pleasant schoolrooms, your industrious and contented children—these we must accept. But it would take us a long time to find out how well-educated your children really are according to our standards." Frazier made a move to speak, but Castle hurried on. "I'll admit these standards won't tell us everything. We couldn't ask your children to take our examinations, because they haven't been learning the same things, even in such a field as French. Your students would probably do no better on a second-year French examination than the average Parisian. I'll admit that, and I confess with all the humility I can muster that the kind of learning you've described is the better—if a comparison is possible. It's the ideal which every college teacher glimpses now and then when he looks up from the dance of death in which he has been caught. But I can't swallow the system you've described because I don't see what keeps the motors running. Why do your children learn anything at all? What are your substitutes for our standard motives?"

"Your 'standard motives'—exactly," said Frazier. "And there's the rub. An educational institution spends most of its time, not in presenting facts or imparting techniques of learning, but in trying to make its students learn. It has to create spurious needs. Have you ever stopped to analyze them? What are the 'standard motives,' Mr. Castle?"

"I must admit they're not very attractive," said Castle. "I suppose they consist of fear of one's family in the event of low grades or expulsion, the award of grades and honors, the snob value of a cap and gown, the cash value of a diploma."

"Very good, Mr. Castle," said Frazier. "You're an honest man. And now to answer your question—our substitute is simply the absence of these devices. We have had to *uncover* the worthwhile and truly productive motives —the motives which inspire creative work in science and art outside the academies. No one asks how to motivate a baby. A baby naturally explores everything it can get at, unless restraining forces have already been at work. And this tendency doesn't die out, it's *wiped* out.

"We made a survey of the motives of the unhampered child and found more than we could use. Our engineering job was to *preserve* them by fortifying the child against discouragement. We introduce discouragement as carefully as we introduce any other emotional situation, beginning at about six months. Some of the toys in our air-conditioned cubicles are designed to build perseverance. A bit of a tune from a music box, or a pattern of flashing lights, is arranged to follow an appropriate response—say, pulling on a ring. Later the ring must be pulled twice, later still three or five or ten times. It's possible to build up fantastically perseverative behavior without encountering frustration or rage. It may not surprise you to learn that some of our experiments miscarried; the resistance to discouragement became almost stupid or pathological. One takes some risks in work of this sort, of course. Fortunately, we were able to reverse the process and restore the children to a satisfactory level.

"Building a tolerance for discouraging events proved to be all we needed," Frazier continued. "The motives in education, Mr. Castle, are the motives in all human behavior. Education should be only life itself. We don't need to create motives. We avoid the spurious academic needs you've just listed so frankly, and also the escape from threat so widely used in our civil institutions. We appeal to the curiosity which is characteristic of the unrestrained child, as well as the alert and inquiring adult. We appeal to that drive to control the environment which makes a baby continue to crumple a piece of noisy paper and the scientist continue to press forward with his predictive analyses of nature. We don't need to motivate anyone by creating spurious needs."

"I've known a few men with the kind of motivation you mean," I said.

"The contemporary culture produces a few by accident," said Frazier quickly, "just as it produces a few brave or happy men."

"But I've never understood them," I said rather faintly.

"Why should you, any more than unhappy people can understand the happy ones?"

"But isn't there a real need for the spurious satisfactions?" I said. "Little signs of personal success, money—personal domination, too, if you like. Most of what I do, I do to avoid undesirable consequences, to evade unpleasantnesses, or to reject or attack forces which interfere with my freedom."

"All the unhappy motives," said Frazier.

"Unhappy, perhaps, but powerful. I think the very thing which seems most unpromising in your system is its happiness. Your people are going to be too happy, too successful. But why won't they just go to sleep? Can we expect real achievements from them? Haven't the great men of history been essentially unhappy or maladjusted or neurotic?"

"I have little interest in conclusions drawn from history," said Frazier, "but if you must play that game, I'll play it too. For every genius you cite whose greatness seems to have sprung from a neurosis, I will undertake to cite similar acts of greatness without neurosis. Turn it around and I'll agree. A man with a touch of genius will be so likely to attack existing institutions that he'll be called unbalanced or neurotic. The only geniuses produced by the chaos of society are those who do something about it." Frazier paused, and I wondered if he were thinking of himself. "Chaos breeds geniuses. It offers a man something to be a genius about. But here, we have better things to do."

"But what about the cases where unhappiness has led to artistic or scientific achievement?" I asked.

"Oh, I daresay a few first-rate sonnets would have remained unwritten had the lady yielded," said Frazier. "But not so many, at that. Not many works of art can be traced to the lack of satisfaction of the basic needs. It's not plain sex that gives rise to art, but personal relations which are social or cultural rather than biological. Art deals with something less obvious than the satisfaction to be found in a square meal." Frazier laughed explosively, as if he had perhaps said more than he intended.

"We shall never produce so satisfying a world that there will be no place for art," he continued. "On the contrary, Walden Two has demonstrated very nicely that as soon as the simple necessities of life are obtained with little effort, there's an enormous welling up of artistic interest. And least of all do we need to fear that simple satisfactions will detract from the scientific conquest of the world. What scientist worth the name is engaged, as scientist, in the satisfaction of his own basic needs? He may be thinking of the basic needs of others, but his own motives are clearly cultural. There can be no doubt of the survival value of the inquiring spirit—of curiosity, of exploration, of the need to dominate media, of the urge to control the forces of nature. The world will never be wholly known, and man can't help trying to know more and more of it."

The topic seemed to have grown too vague to stimulate further discussion, but Castle soon offered a substitute.

"I'm torn between two questions which seem incompatible yet equally pressing," he said. "What do you do about differences among your children in intellect and talent? And what do you do to avoid producing a lot of completely standardized young people? Which question should I ask, and what's your answer?"

"They're both good questions," said Frazier, "and quite compatible." I made a move to speak and Frazier said, "I see that Mr. Burris wants to help with the answers."

"My guess is," I said, "that differences are due to environmental and cultural factors and that Mr. Frazier has no great problem to solve. Give all your children the excellent care we have just been witnessing and your differences will be negligible."

"No, you're wrong, Burris," said Frazier. "That's one question we have answered to our satisfaction. Our ten-year-olds have all had the same environment since birth, but the range of their IQ's is almost as great as in the population at large. This seems to be true of other abilities and skills as well."

"And of physical prowess, of course," said Castle.

"Why do you say 'of course'?" said Frazier, with marked interest.

"Why, I suppose because physical differences are generally acknowledged."

"All differences are physical, my dear Mr. Castle. We think with our bodies, too. You might have replied that differences in prowess have always been obvious and impossible to conceal, while other differences have customarily been disguised for the sake of prestige and family pride. We accept our gross physical limitations without protest and are reasonably happy in spite of them, but we may spend a lifetime trying to live up to a wholly false conception of our powers in another field, and suffer the pain of a lingering failure. Here we accept ourselves as we are."

"Aren't the talented going to be unhappy?"

"But we don't go in for personal rivalry; individuals are seldom compared. We never develop a taste much beyond a talent. Our parents have little reason to misrepresent their children's abilities to themselves or others. It's easy for our children to accept their limitations—exactly as they have always accepted the gross differences which Mr. Castle called physical prowess. At the same time our gifted children aren't held back by organized mediocrity. We don't throw our geniuses off balance. The brilliant but unstable type is unfamiliar here. Genius can express itself."

We had shifted our positions from time to time to stay within the shade of our tree. We were now centered due north and crowding the trunk, for it was noon. The schoolwork in the area near the building had gradually come to an end, and the migration toward the dining room had taken place. Frazier stood up and straightened his knees with care. The rest of us also got up—except Castle, who stayed stubbornly in his place.

"I can't believe," he began, looking at the ground and apparently not caring whether he was heard or not, "I can't believe you can really get spontaneity and freedom through a system of tyrannical control. Where does initiative come in? When does the child begin to think of himself as a free agent? What is freedom, anyway, under such a plan?"

"Freedom, freedom," said Frazier, stretching his arms and neck and almost singing the words, as if he were uttering them through a yawn. "Freedom is a question, isn't it? But let's not answer it now. Let's let it ring, shall we? Let's let it ring."

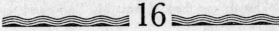

16

Just south of the flower gardens, on a blanket spread out upon the warm grass, lay a naked baby nine or ten months old. A boy and girl were trying to make her crawl toward a rubber doll. We stopped for a moment on our way to the common rooms to enjoy her grotesquely unavailing efforts.

When we resumed our walk, Frazier said casually, "Their first child."

"Good heavens!" I cried. "Do you mean to say those children are the parents of that baby?"

"Why, of course. And a very fine baby it is, too."

"But they can't be more than sixteen or seventeen years old!"

"Probably not."

"But isn't that rather remarkable? It's not the usual thing, I hope." My voice trailed off doubtfully.

"It's not at all unusual with us," Frazier said. "The average age of the Walden Two mother is eighteen at the birth of her first child, and we hope to bring the figure down still further. The war interfered a bit there. I believe the girl you saw was sixteen when her baby was born."

"But why do you encourage *that?*" Barbara said.

"There are a dozen good reasons. There is no excuse for the usual delay in getting married or the still greater delay in bearing children— But shall we save this for luncheon? How about one o'clock in the serving room?"

We reached our quarters, and Frazier took leave of us abruptly. We washed up and met again in front of the building, sitting in a row on a long bench against the wall, partially shaded by the overhanging roof. We were exhausted.

"I want labor-credits for that kind of thing," said Castle, as he dropped onto the bench, "and it will have to be about two point zero zero or I won't play."

"What do you think of what Mr. Frazier said this morning?" Rodge said.

"Well, I can tell you this," Castle said, "I wouldn't sign on the dotted line!"

Rodge, in obvious disappointment, glanced uneasily at Barbara.

"Why not?" I asked, offering whatever support I could.

"Would you?" Castle said.

"Well, I don't know about that. But what Frazier said this morning seemed sound enough. He admitted it was all experimental. If he can really keep himself free to change practices—if he can avoid committing himself stubbornly to some theory—I think he'll come through."

"It's a handy thing, this experimental attitude," said Castle. "The scientist can be sure of himself before he knows anything. We philosophers should have thought of that."

"I suppose you're right," I said. "The scientist may not be sure of the answer, but he's often sure he can find one. And that's a condition which is clearly not enjoyed by philosophy."

"I want to see a few answers—not just the assurance of answers."

"Don't you believe your own eyes?" I said. I was still trying to bolster Rodge's enthusiasm.

"My eyes tell me nothing. Ventures of this sort have often run along very well for a while. What we want to know is whether the thing carries the potentialities of permanence. I want to see more of this wonderful second generation."

"That's curious," I said. "I worry more about the first. I think Frazier is perfectly right about educating people for cooperative living. What bothers me is how to get the first generation safely into their graves, or at least their rocking chairs, when the second are ready to take over. Frazier has promised us more about that this evening."

"There had better be more," said Castle petulantly. "A great deal more."

"Isn't it time to start for lunch?" said Barbara brightly. "Can you imagine having a baby at sixteen?"

We found the dining rooms rather crowded, and we chose a small table in the English inn. Frazier was waiting for us, and we had scarcely picked up our forks before he began to speak, as if he had just broken off.

"No doubt the thought of a girl getting married a year or two after she is ready for childbearing strikes you as something characteristic of primitive cultures or, worse still, backward communities in our own country," he said. "Early marriages are regarded as inadvisable. The figures show they tend to be less successful in the long run, and they are often plainly impossible from an economic point of view. I need scarcely point out, however, that there's no economic obstacle to marriage at any age in Walden Two. The young couple will live quite as well whether married or unmarried. Children are cared for in the same way regardless of the age, experience, or earning power of their parents.

"Certainly most girls are ready for childbearing at fifteen or sixteen. We like to ridicule 'puppy love.' We say it won't last, and judge its depth accordingly. Well, of course it doesn't last! A thousand forces conspire against it. And they are not the forces of nature, either, but of a badly organized society. The boy and girl are ready for love. They will never have the same capacity for love again. And they are ready for marriage and childbearing. It's all part of the same thing. But society never lets them prove it."

"Instead, society makes it into a sex problem," I said.

"Of course!" said Frazier. "Sex is no problem in itself. Here the adolescent finds an immediate and satisfactory expression of his natural impulses. It's a solution which is productive, honorable, and viewed by the community with admiration and pride. How very different from the secrecy and shame which most of us recall in connection with sex at some time or other! Adolescence is seldom pleasant to remember, it's full of unnecessary problems, unnecessary delays. It should be brief and painless, and we make it so in Walden Two.

"All your schemes to keep the adolescent out of trouble—your 'wholesome' substitutes for sex!" Frazier continued. "What is unwholesome about sex? Why must there be a substitute? What's wrong with love, or marriage, or parenthood? You don't solve anything by delay —you make things worse. The more or less pathological aberrations which follow are easily recognized, but there is a great deal more. A normal sexual adjustment is often prevented. And the sportive element in sex is played up —every person of the opposite sex becomes a challenge to seduction. That's a bothersome cultural trait that we're glad to avoid. Promiscuous aggression is no more natural than quarrelsomeness, or an inclination to tease, or jovial backslapping. But if you insist on making sex into a game or hunt before you let it become serious, how can you expect a sane attitude later on?"

"Do girls have babies as easily when they are so young, though?" said Barbara.

"Easier," said Frazier flatly, as if he himself had had several at a tender age. "We make sure, of course, that the girl is capable of normal childbearing, but we should do that at any age."

"How long does she go on having babies?"

"As long as she likes, but generally no longer than usual. If she wants four children, say, she will be finished with childbearing by the time she's twenty-two or -three. That's not too fast, because she is freed of the heavy labor of child care, even though she will probably work in the nursery for her daily stint, and because she gets top medical attention. At twenty-three she will find herself as young in body and spirit as if she had spent the same years unmarried. Her adult life opens up to her with many interesting prospects. For one thing, she is then quite on a par with men. She has made the special contribution which is either the duty or the privilege of woman, and can take her place without distinction of sex. You may have noticed the complete equality of men and women among us. There are scarcely any types of work which are not shared equally."

A remark suddenly struck me with such force that I was surprised to hear myself utter it:

"A 'generation' in Walden Two must mean about twenty years!"

"Instead of the usual thirty," said Frazier, laughing at my astonishment. "We get no end of amusement out of that, at the expense of the 'big litter' people. We don't sacrifice our women to a policy of maximal childbearing, but we equal or exceed their rate of propagation, and with healthy children, too, by the simple expedient of getting three generations for two."

"And a man can be a grandfather at thirty-five," I said, in growing amazement. "And reach three score and ten at about the time the fifth generation is born!"

"One of us may have as many great-grandchildren as one usually has grandchildren at the same age—with fewer children per couple," said Frazier. "And that should be a sufficient answer to the charge that we have somehow interfered with the joy of family or family ties. The average member of Walden Two will see more of his descendants than the very exceptional member of society at large. And every child will have many more living grandparents, great-grandparents, and other relatives, to take an interest in him."

"I should think there might be another advantage," I said. "Young parents should have a fresher memory and a better understanding of the problems of children. They must tend to be more sympathetic and helpful."

"If sympathy and help were needed," said Frazier rather irritably, as if I had suggested that the community was deficient in some respect.

"But isn't there one trouble?" said Barbara. "Do young people really know what kind of person they want to live with for the rest of their lives?"

"They seem to think so," said Frazier.

"But young people grow apart."

"Is that really true?"

"The figures," said Barbara, with obvious pride in talking in Frazier's terms, "show that early marriages tend to be unhappy."

"Because husband and wife grow apart, or because our economic system penalizes early marriage?"

"I don't know."

"Economic hardships could make people grow apart," said Frazier.

"All I know is, the boys I fell for when I was younger wouldn't interest me now," said Barbara, giving up the figures with relief. "I can't imagine what I saw in them."

"I wonder if that wouldn't be true at any age. We grow apart when we live apart."

"I think there may be something in what Miss Macklin says," said Castle. "We are less likely to have fallen into our final life pattern at that age. We're still trying to find ourselves."

"Very well, then. Let that point stand—though I can't see that it makes any difference, since people in Walden Two never stop changing. But at least we can offer some compensating advantages. We can be sure that husband and wife will come from the same economic level, from the same culture, and have the same sort of education. What do the figures show about that?"

Barbara tried to think. "As I remember it, those things are important, too," she said at last.

"Then we are even," said Frazier. "Our boys and girls know each other very well, too. There are no hasty marriages among us."

"The very fact of early marriage itself ought to prevent marriages due to sexual infatuation," I said, "unless you feel I'm spoiling your sympathetic picture of puppy love."

"You aren't spoiling it at all. Puppy love tends not to be overtly sexual at all. It's usually highly idealistic. I wasn't talking about the excitement which springs from the thwarting of natural impulses, but a love which arises spontaneously and with the least possible hindrance and which is therefore its own surest guarantee of success."

"Very romantic and unscientific," I said.

"Then let me add a scientific touch. When a young couple become engaged, they go to our Manager of Marriages. Their interests, school records, and health are examined. If there's any great discrepancy in intellectual ability or temperament they are advised against marrying. The marriage is at least postponed, and that usually means it's abandoned."

"As easy as all that?" I said.

"Usually so. The opportunities for other associations are a great help, just as in the case of personal jealousy."

"But aren't you spoiling some of the best years of a girl's life when you make her marry so young?" said Barbara.

"She is not 'made to marry.' It's all a matter of choice. She skips some of the years in the late teens and early twenties which are romantically painted in our literature. But she gets them back very soon, when her childbearing is over. And they are really better than the years she gave up. For most girls, adolescence is a period of concern over personal success and marriage. For the few happy ones, it's a spurious excitement. The glowing young debutante with a string of devoted swains is an artificial bit of trumpery that civilization can well do without."

"I wonder why your disclosure has been so disconcerting," I said. "Marriage at sixteen or seventeen was not at all uncommon in other times and other cultures. Yet in a way it strikes me as the most radical feature of life at Walden Two."

"I don't think I'd like it," said Barbara.

Frazier gave her a cold glance. "You have made it hard for me to answer Mr. Burris," he said. "I was going to point out that in other times and other cultures there was a much more rapid maturation. One could be an adult at sixteen. I am sure that Miss Macklin has made good use of the years which she values so highly, but that's not the universal case. At least half of the high-school years are a total waste—and half of college, too, as our more emancipated educators are beginning to discover. Whatever their age, young members of Walden Two don't marry before they are mature. They have much better control of themselves than youngsters of the same age elsewhere, and they are much less likely to mis-understand their own emotions or the motives of others. The 'best years of one's life,' Miss Macklin, are reached after the problems of adolescence have been solved or passed by. We multiply them many fold."

"I'm afraid the birth control people aren't going to thank you for your early marriages," I said. "Malthus must have taken an extra turn in his grave."

"It's no solution of the Malthusian problem to lower the birth rate of those who understand it. On the contrary, we need to expand the culture which recognizes the need for birth control. If you argue that we should set an example, you must prove to me that we shall not all be extinguished before the example is followed. No, our genetic program is a vital one. We don't worry about our birth rate, or its consequences."

"Are you conducting any genetic experiments?" I said.

"No," said Frazier, but he sat straight up as if the subject were especially interesting. "We discourage child-bearing by the unfit, of course, but that's all. You must remember that we've only recently reached our present size, and even so, we aren't large enough for serious experimentation. Later, perhaps, something can be done. The weakening of the family structure will make experimental breeding possible."

Frazier smiled quietly.

"I have been waiting for that one!" said Castle explosively. "What about the 'weakening of the family structure,' Mr. Frazier?"

"The all-absorbing concern of the outside world," he said, "is what happens to the family in Walden Two. The family is the frailest of modern institutions. Its weakness is evident to everyone. Will it survive as the culture changes? We watch it with all the panic which besets a mother as her backward child steps to the platform and begins to speak a piece. Well, a great deal happens to the family in Walden Two, Mr. Castle, I can tell you that."

We had finished our lunch, but the dining rooms had become less crowded and we had therefore kept our table. Frazier, with a demonstrative gesture of discomfort, suggested that we find a more comfortable spot for a few minutes before getting our work assignments. The nearer lounges were occupied, but we found an empty studio. A number of leather cushions were scattered on the floor, and we arranged ourselves on them, feeling very Bohemian and therefore very objective with respect to the subject under discussion.

17

"The significant history of our times," Frazier began, "is the story of the growing weakness of the family. The decline of the home as a medium for perpetuating a culture, the struggle for equality for women, including their right to select professions other than housewife or nursemaid, the extraordinary consequences of birth control and the practical separation of sex and parenthood, the social recognition of divorce, the critical issue of blood relationship or race—all these are parts of the same field. And you can hardly call it quiescent.

"A community must solve the problem of the family by revising certain established practices. That's absolutely inevitable. The family is an ancient form of community, and the customs and habits which have been set up to perpetuate it are out of place in a society which isn't based on blood ties. Walden Two replaces the family, not only as an economic unit, but to some extent as a social and psychological unit as well. What survives is an experimental question."

"What answer have you reached?" said Castle.

"No definite answer yet. But I can describe some of the family practices which were part of the plan of Walden Two and tell you the consequences to date. A few experimental questions have been answered to our satisfaction."

"Such as?"

"Oh, the advisability of separate rooms for husband and wife, for example. We don't insist on it, but in the long run there's a more satisfactory relation when a single room isn't shared. Many of our visitors suppose that a community means a sacrifice of privacy. On the contrary, we've carefully provided for much more personal privacy than is likely to be found in the world at large. You may be alone here whenever you wish. A man's room is his castle. And a woman's, too."

"But how could you *prove* that separate rooms were advisable?" said Castle.

"Very simply. We asked all husbands and wives who were willing to do so to accept separate or common rooms on the basis of a drawing of lots. That was in the early days. We did the same thing with new members. Our psychologists kept in close touch with all personal problems and at the end of eight years the troubles and satisfactions of our members were analyzed with respect to the factor of separate or common rooms. It's the sort of experiment that would be impossible, or next to impossible, anywhere except in Walden Two. The result was clear-cut. Living in a separate room not only made the individual happier and better adjusted, it tended to strengthen the love and affection of husband and wife. Most of our married couples have now changed to separate rooms. It's difficult to explain the advantages to the newly married, and I suspect it will become a sort of tradition to room together until the period of childbearing is over. But the later advantages in point of health, convenience, and personal freedom are too great to be overlooked."

"But aren't you leaving the door wide open to promiscuity?" said Castle.

"On the contrary, we are perpetuating loyalty and affection. We can be sure that any continuing affection is genuine, and not the result of a police system, and hence it's something in which we take pride. We place abiding affection on a very high plane.

"The simple fact is, there's no more promiscuity in Walden Two than in society at large. There's probably less. For one thing, we encourage simple friendship between the sexes. The world at large all but forbids it. What might have been a satisfying friendship must become a clandestine affair. Here we give friendship every support. We don't practice 'free love,' but we have a great deal of 'free affection.' And that goes a long way toward satisfying the needs which lead to promiscuity elsewhere. We have successfully established the principle of 'Seduction not expected.' When a man strikes up an acquaintanceship with a woman, he does not worry about failing to make advances, and the woman isn't hurt if advances aren't made. We recognize that sort of sexual play for what it is—a sign, not of potency, but of malaise or instability.

"I don't mean that no one in Walden Two has fallen in love 'illicitly,'" Frazier continued, "but I'm sure there has been a minimum of mere sex without love. We don't regard extramarital love as wholly justifiable or without its difficulties. The problem of the deserted mate always remains. But we've done all we can to avoid unhappiness. It's part of the Walden Two Code to avoid gossip about personal ties, and a slight disturbance often works itself out quietly. Our vastly extended opportunities for affection also help. No one really feels very much deserted. There's not much wounded pride.

"At the moment that's the best we can do. It's not a final solution, but it's an improvement. Remember that many cultures condone the occasional reassortment of mates—look at the frequent divorces among those who can afford them. We haven't gone that far here and we shan't. Economically we could dispense with permanent marriage altogether, but we don't. Abiding personal affection is more than a romantic rationalization of a crude economic unit."

"Have you found it necessary," I said, "to conceal or misrepresent your practices to avoid unfavorable gossip or even legal action?"

"Not at all. We follow the legal practices of the state. But these are always subject to local interpretation, and Walden Two is no exception. We make a great deal of the 'engagement.' In the world at large this is a statement of intention and a period of trial. It's that with us. The young couple receive medical and psychological counsel during this period. Long engagements are not encouraged and, of course, are unnecessary for economic reasons. Our marriage ceremony is unambiguous, and

I'm sure it's entered into in good faith. If in the course of time extramarital friendships weaken the original tie, we try to avoid an open break. A disinterested person, usually one of our psychologists, gives immediate counsel and guidance. Frequently the matter straightens itself out, and the original tie is preserved. But if the old affection is quite dead and the new one genuine, a divorce is carried through.

"It will be hard for you to understand how simple this is, because you can't quite appreciate our triumph over emotions like jealousy or wounded pride. Here the whole community works toward making a personal readjustment as easy as possible, instead of converting it into stock for the scandalmonger."

There was a slight flash of anger in Frazier's eyes as he said this, and he shifted his position on his cushion impatiently. I suddenly realized that he had been exceptionally unemotional up to this point. There had been no sign of his usual aggression. He was showing a beneficent, almost fatherly concern for the problem of marriage. I was inclined to interpret this again as merely a sign of confidence, but there was a suggestion of tenderness—of sentimentality—which almost astonished me. His manner became even softer as the conversation proceeded.

"What about the children?" I said. "The group care we saw this morning must also weaken the relation between parent and child."

"It does. By design. We have to attenuate the child-parent relation for several reasons. Group care is better than parental care. In the old pre-scientific days the early education of the child could be left to the parents, and indeed almost certainly had to be left to them. But with the rise of a science of behavior all is changed. The bad repute into which scientific child care has fallen is no reflection upon our technical knowledge of what should be done. The requirements of good child care are well established. Where we have failed is in getting good care in the average home. We have failed to teach the average parent even the simplest scientific principles. And that's not surprising. The control of behavior is an intricate science, into which the average mother could not be initiated without years of training. But the fact that most children today are badly raised isn't all the fault of a lack of technical skill, either. Even when the mother knows the right thing to do, she often can't do it in a household which is busy with other affairs. Home is not the place to raise children.

"Even when our young mothers and fathers become skilled nursery-school workers, we avoid a strong personal dependency. Our goal is to have every adult member of Walden Two regard all our children as his own, and to have every child think of every adult as his parent. To this end we have made it bad taste to single out one's own child for special favors. If you want to take your child on a picnic, the correct thing is to take several of his friends as well. If you want to give him a little present for his birthday, you are expected to give similar presents to the guests at his party. You may spend as much time as you like with your children, but to do so exclusively is taboo. The result is that a child never gets from its parents any services or favors which it does not also frequently get from others. We have untied the apron strings."

Frazier was still having trouble with his cushion. He tried several positions and eventually assumed a Buddha-like posture from which he seemed to speak with even greater oracular authority.

"Think what this means to the child who has no mother or father! There is no occasion to envy companions who are not so deprived, because there is little or no practical difference. It's true he may not call anyone 'Mother' or 'Father,' but we discourage this anyway, in favor of given names. And he frequently receives presents and attentions from many adults and may find among them one or more for whom he will develop deep affection.

"And think what it means, too, for the childless! They

can express their natural affection toward children in spite of the biological or social accident which deprived them of parenthood. No sensible person will suppose that love or affection has anything to do with blood. One's love for one's wife is required by law to be free of a close blood connection. Foster children and stepchildren are loved as dearly as one's own. Love and affection are psychological and cultural, and blood relationships can be happily forgotten."

"Don't many parents resent sharing their children?" I said.

"Why should they? What are they actually sharing? They see more of their children than the typical mother in most upper-class households—where the arrangement is also, by the way, from choice. And much more than the average father. Many parents are glad to be relieved of the awful responsibility of being a child's only source of affection and help. Here it's impossible to be an inadequate or unskillful parent, and the vigorous, happy growth of our children is enough to remove any last suspicion that we have been deprived of anything.

"The weakening of the relation between parent and child is valuable in other ways," Frazier continued, with sustained gentleness. "When divorce cannot be avoided, the children are not embarrassed by severe changes in their way of life or their behavior toward their parents. It's also easy to induce the unfit or unwell to forego parenthood. No stigma attaches to being childless, and no lack of affection. That's what I meant when I said that experiments in selective breeding would eventually be possible in Walden Two. The hereditary connection will be minimized to the point of being forgotten. Long before that, it will be possible to breed through artificial insemination without altering the personal relation of husband and wife. Our people will marry as they wish, but have children according to a genetic plan."

"It seems to me," said Castle, "that you're flying in the face of strong natural forces, just the same."

"What would you have said if I had proposed killing

unwanted female babies?" said Frazier. "Yet that practice is condoned in some cultures. What do we really know about the *nature* of the parental relation? Anything? I doubt it."

"I'm reminded," I said, "of an earlier question of Mr. Castle's. What happens to 'identification'? Have you any substitute for the parent as a pattern for the child? If your boys don't want to 'be like Daddy' or, less happily, 'like Mama,' how are their personalities built up?"

"We know very little about what happens in identification," Frazier said. "No one has ever made a careful scientific analysis. The evidence isn't truly experimental. We have seen the process at work only in our standard family structure. The Freudian pattern may be due to the peculiarities of that structure or even the eccentricities of the members of the family. All we really know is that children tend to imitate adults, in gestures and mannerisms, and in personal attitudes and relations. They do that here, too, but since the family structure is changed, the effect is very different.

"Our children are cared for by many different people. It isn't institutional care, but genuine affection. Our members aren't overworked, and they haven't been forced into a job for which they have no talent or inclination. What the child imitates is a sort of essential happy adult. He can avoid the idiosyncrasies of a single parent. Identification is easy and valuable.

"Remember that the adults who care for our children are of both sexes. We have broken down prejudices regarding the occupations of the sexes, and we have worked particularly hard to keep a balance in the nursery and school system. There's no stigma attached to such work, and many men find it satisfying. The work in the nursery is very close to that of a highly skilled laboratory technician. By balancing the sexes we eliminate all the Freudian problems which arise from the asymmetrical relations to the female parent. But that's a technical problem which you and I can discuss some other time."

"But as the child grows older," I said, "doesn't he

naturally single out particular individuals as objects of interest and affection?"

"That's exactly what we intend," said Frazier. "It may happen because of common interests: the artistically inclined will naturally be attracted to artists, the potential farmer will like to hang around the dairy. Or it may arise from a similarity of character or personality. In the family, identification is usually confined to one parent or the other, but neither one may have characteristics suitable to the child's developing personality. It's a sort of coerced identification, which we are glad to avoid."

"Don't these attenuated personal ties lead to feelings of insecurity?" said Castle.

"Who is insecure? And about what? Not our children, certainly. They have every chance in the world of getting affection and help from hundreds of adults. You will find your insecure child in the care of an overworked or emotional mother, or living with quarrelsome parents, or sent to school unprepared for needed adjustments, or left to get along with children from different cultural levels. We have *increased* the feeling of security of our children."

"I was thinking more of the women," Castle said, "the wives and mothers. Don't they feel that they are less necessary to their families?"

"Of course they do, and they ought to. You are talking about a tradition of slavery, and of the sentiments which have preserved it for thousands of years. The world has made some progress in the emancipation of women, but equality is still a long way off. There are few cultures today in which the rights of women are respected at all. America is one of perhaps three or four nations in which some progress has been made. Yet very few American women have the economic independence and cultural freedom of American men.

"Feelings of insecurity!" Frazier continued with increasing warmth. "The marriage system trades on them! What does the ordinary middle-class marriage amount to? Well, it's agreed that the husband will provide shelter, clothing, food, and perhaps some amusement, while the wife will work as a cook and cleaning woman and bear and raise children. The man is reasonably free to select or change his work; the woman has no choice, except between accepting and neglecting her lot. She has a legal claim for support, he has a claim for a certain type of labor.

"To make matters worse, we educate our women as if they were equal, and promise them equality. Is it any wonder they are soon disillusioned? The current remedy is to revive the slogans and sentiments which have made the system work in the past. The good wife is told to consider it an honor and a privilege to work in the kitchen, to make the beds every day, to watch the children. She is made to believe that she is *necessary*, that she has the care of her husband's happiness and health and also her children's. That's the stock treatment of the neurotic housewife: reconcile her to her lot! But the intelligent woman sees through it at once, no matter how hard she wants to believe. She knows very well that someone else could make the beds and get the meals and wash the clothes, and her family wouldn't know the difference. The role of mother she wants to play herself, but that has no more connection with her daily work than the role of father with his work in the office or factory or field.

"Here, there's no reason to feel that anyone is necessary to anyone else. Each of us is necessary in the same amount, which is very little. The community would go on just as smoothly tomorrow if any one of us died tonight. We cannot, therefore, get much satisfaction out of feeling important. But there are compensating satisfactions. Each of us is necessary as a person to the extent that he is loved as a person. No woman gets much satisfaction out of feeling that she will be missed as one misses a departed cook or scrub woman; she wants to be missed as a wife and mother. By providing good care for everyone as a matter of course, we emphasize the personal need. When a mother feels she is losing the affection of her child, she is more likely to discover the true reason.

She will not try to make herself necessary by making her child more helpless. That's impossible. Her only recourse is to win back the affection of her child, and she is likely to do it if she understands the problem.

"The community, as a revised family, has changed the place of women more radically than that of men. Some women feel momentarily insecure for that reason. But their new position is more dignified, more enjoyable, and more healthful, and the whole question of security eventually vanishes. In a world of complete economic equality, you get and keep the affections you deserve. You can't buy love with gifts or favors, you can't hold love by raising an inadequate child, and you can't be secure in love by serving as a good scrub woman or a good provider."

"But I suspect you find it hardest to convince women of the advantages of community life," I said.

"Naturally! Those who stand to gain most are always the hardest to convince. That's true of the exploited worker, too—and for the same reason. They have both been kept in their places, not by external force, but much more subtly by a system of beliefs implanted within their skins. It's sometimes an almost hopeless task to take the shackles off their souls, but it can be done. But, speaking of shackles, I mustn't keep you any longer from your work."

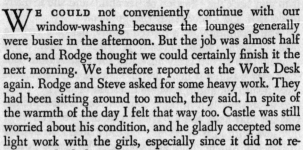

18

W<small>E COULD</small> not conveniently continue with our window-washing because the lounges generally were busier in the afternoon. But the job was almost half done, and Rodge thought we could certainly finish it the next morning. We therefore reported at the Work Desk again. Rodge and Steve asked for some heavy work. They had been sitting around too much, they said. In spite of the warmth of the day I felt that way too. Castle was still worried about his condition, and he gladly accepted some light work with the girls, especially since it did not require work clothes.

Rodge, Steve, and I changed into shorts and reported to the space behind the theater. Here we found a large pile of firewood in two-foot lengths. It had been dumped into the area from a truck and our job was to pile it against the blank wall of the theater. The present pile was twenty or thirty feet from the wall. Steve suggested that we first throw a few hundred pieces toward the wall, to save the labor of walking back and forth. This might have been an excellent idea for anyone under thirty years of age, but I was soon aware that it was too much for me. I offered to begin stacking if I could be protected from flying logs. I laid careful plans for a well-stacked pile, but made little actual progress, and presently Rodge joined me.

A quarter of an hour later we stopped for a short rest, sitting on top of the pile we had made. Steve disdained rest and kept up a rhythmic bombardment.

"Well, what do you think of it all?" I said.

Rodge glanced at me, almost fearfully.

"It's everything Steve and I used to dream about, sir. And more." There was effort behind the assertion, as if it were an unpleasant duty.

"Quite remarkable, isn't it?" I agreed.

"And Mr. Frazier—the first real genius I've ever known."

"Brilliant chap, all right. And he has been clever enough to get excellent people to help him. The whole managerial staff seems very capable. Frazier would be the first to admit their contribution."

"But he's a genius, just the same. To plan such a thing all by himself."

"I don't believe he would claim that," I said. "There were other Planners."

"But the main idea—that was his, wasn't it?"

"Perhaps it was. But many of the details had already been worked out. Some had even been tried."

"Well, I don't know how it was, and I don't care. But look at the way he has made it work! Why, these people are happy! All of them! And they aren't depending on anybody else, either. Oh, there're so damned many wonderful things about it that nobody has even mentioned!" He almost groaned, and he shook his head slowly. "How could anybody want a better life, sir? Why doesn't everybody just go and do the same thing?"

"It isn't a life that would satisfy everybody," I said. "Not by any means. I'm fairly sure Frazier can keep his second generation in line, but a lot of people haven't had the right history."

"I know," said Rodge.

We were silent for a few moments as Steve, with a pretended complaint at our idleness, began to roll logs up to our very feet.

"Some people," Rodge continued, "don't even see why anybody would want to do this. They don't see the point."

He looked at me, but I said nothing.

"They don't seem to realize," he continued, "how almost any other kind of life means unhappiness for somebody somewhere. Just so long as they're happy, they don't care. They don't seem to see the trouble coming."

I remained silent.

"What would you say to somebody who felt that way, sir?" Rodge said, appealing to me desperately.

"I'm afraid just saying something wouldn't do much

good. It's a long, slow process—giving anyone a social conscience. It's hard to see our own life in relation to the whole world. We learn about the two things in different ways."

"I ought to know that," said Rodge. "I was one of the happy ones myself a few years ago. I was in line for a pretty satisfactory life, and it wasn't far off, either. A home, a good-looking wife, kids maybe, a car, more money than most people. That's not a bad life."

"Not a bad life at all."

We slipped off the pile and began to stack logs again.

"And I didn't think I was imposing on anybody, either," Rodge went on. "I always paid for what I got, and everybody treated me in a friendly way. I was the sort of fellow most people liked, I guess."

"What made you see through it? Two or three years in the Pacific?"

"Right, sir! It made me see through that and a lot of other things, too." He threw a particularly heavy log into place with a crash.

"Well, I'd call myself lucky, then. You're still young, and you can do something about it. About your own life, and maybe the other fellow's too."

"The trouble is, not everybody has been through the same thing. A lot of people still don't see the way things are. The old life seems all right. They really aren't hurting anybody, at least anybody they know. And it doesn't seem to matter to them whether it's a kind of life that can go on very much longer." Rodge threw another log into place.

"I take it one of 'them' is—"

"Barbara. Yes."

"Walden Two isn't for her?"

"God, no! She 'loathes' it! Can't see any reason for being so—queer. It's funny, sir. She's an intelligent girl, too, I think. I used to think so, anyway. But she's so blind about some things. You called it a social conscience. Well, she hasn't got any."

"She might get one in time. Have you talked with her about it?"

"Not much. But it's—hopeless. For instance, she doesn't see why a man as bright as Mr. Frazier didn't just go out and earn a lot of money and buy the kind of life he wanted, all by himself."

"She does rather miss the point, doesn't she?"

"It just isn't her line. She wants a home and children. And a maid, of course. She wants to entertain her friends. And have a car."

"How about you?"

"If I had only myself to think about, I'd never leave. I don't know what my father would say. He'd be on Barbara's side, at first. But after all, he wouldn't have to come here with me, and I'm not so sure he wouldn't have a pretty good idea why I might want to try it. A few things he's said since I came back—"

"So it's up to Barbara, then?"

"Oh, I don't know. It's hard to decide. She's changed a lot." Another vicious pitch, and I began to wonder about the strength of rammed-earth walls.

"I think you've done the changing, Rodge."

"Of course that's right, sir, but it comes to the same thing: we don't agree. And I don't think it would be fair to hold out for my side of the argument. After all, I could adjust to her kind of life well enough."

"Do you think you could? Or isn't it too late?"

"I don't know, sir, I really don't. I don't know what it's all about, to tell you the truth. I've never been in a spot like this, not even in the service. What's the matter with me anyway? What would a psychologist say?"

"I can tell you, but you may not want to hear it."

"Go ahead. I can take it."

"It's none of my business, but I think you're having lollipop trouble."

19

THE BOYS were right about a spot of heavy work: it was just what I needed. A shower and a change put me in the pink. After lunch I could have enjoyed a nap, and I had rather planned to rest later in the afternoon. But a couple of hours on the woodpile had cleared my head after the strenuous discussion of the morning, and I was ready for more.

Castle had not yet turned up, and I recalled with some satisfaction that the credit value of piling wood had been slightly higher than his work with the girls. I decided to indulge myself in a private survey of the art of Walden Two. In addition to the Ladder gallery I had noticed many pictures in the lounges and reading rooms, some on a fairly ambitious scale. There were also many small sculptures. I had learned that most of the personal rooms contained pictures or sculptures on loan from a common collection.

My tour proved to be more convenient and in many ways more enjoyable than a visit to a museum. It was usually possible to draw up a chair if I wanted to spend any time on a particular work, and somehow I took additional pleasure from the fact that the rooms were lived in. Nothing seemed to be merely on display.

After about an hour I began to feel tired. I drew a chair close to one of the windows overlooking the Walden Two landscape, and sat down. I was near the serving room, where we had agreed to meet at half-past six, and I decided to relax for a while before supper.

I was awakened at seven o'clock by a group of people returning from the dining rooms. In a panic, which was quite out of the spirit of Walden Two, I dashed into the hallway to look for my party. They were not in sight, but I found them in animated conversation in the Swedish Room. It appeared that they had been constructing theories to explain my disappearance, the most promising of which they communicated to me as soon as I had filled my tray.

There was a great deal more laughter than I thought the situation called for, but I was still groggy from my long nap and may have misjudged them. Their theories were highly improbable, but seemed to be amusing. Someone had suggested that I was in reality a spy engaged in sabotage at that moment teaching the sheep to nibble on the unelectrified fence. Frazier's theory—he suspected me of Freudian sympathies—was that I had moved into one of the baby cubicles and had hung up a shingle reading "A Womb with a View." When I tried to explain where I had actually been, they stubbornly refused to believe a word of it, and they seemed to find this very funny, too.

I began to shake off the effects of my nap, and the conversation veered round to more serious matters. In some connection or other I said, "But how do you explain the invariable failure of communities in the past?"

Frazier placed his knife and fork carefully on the table but kept hold of them, staring at me with a blank expression which I could not for a moment interpret. He looked like some trained animal holding its paws awkwardly in place for a trick photograph. Gradually a mixture of anger and contempt displayed itself.

"I find it difficult," he said at last, with exaggerated control, "to answer a question of that sort with equanimity. Why should I be asked to explain it?"

"It's commonly supposed that a man profits from experience," I said, hoping to show that I was not cowed. "I should think the failure of similar attempts in the past would have some bearing upon Walden Two."

"Similar! Similar!" Frazier sang, making it sound a little like *Figaro! Figaro!* "The song the sirens sing to all historians. What do we really know about it? *How* similar? *How* similar?"

"Oh, come, come," I said, resolving to be undismayed, though I saw the line he was going to take and feared that I was lost. "I think you can make out a fair case for a considerable similarity. A group of people decide to live cooperatively and independently of the outside world—"

"And on the strength of *that*," he said, with pure contempt, "you predict the failure of Walden Two."

"Well, no, not on the strength of that alone. And I don't predict failure. But we know something about the living conditions in these old communities, their customs—"

"We know that they ate and drank and performed the other alimentary functions, worked a good deal, believed in God—most of them—had children—some of them—made money or didn't, and disbanded. We know what their buildings looked like to second-rate artists, and what they wrote about themselves when literate."

"You amaze me, Mr. Frazier," said Castle. "I expected you to have the greatest respect for these pioneers in community living."

"I have the greatest respect for them, as I *believe* them to have been. But I know nothing about them, really, except for their literary remains, and most of them were rather uncommunicative souls. What I am perhaps not altogether unemotional about is the assumption that the historical account has the status of a body of facts, from which we can make predictions about the success of a contemporary venture."

"You admit the relevancy of their writing," I said faintly.

"I do. And also that most of the communities are no longer in existence. But prediction in the field of the social sciences is very doubtful even when we know what we are talking about, and we know scarcely anything about the actual conditions in these so-called experiments. Most of them were economically successful. Some of them broke up because the members couldn't resist the temptation to divide the loot, and a few still survive. But the crucial thing is the psychological management, and of this we know very little. A few facts, yes, but an adequate picture, no."

"It seems to me they conducted some fairly important psychological experiments," I said.

"But we don't really know what was done and, hence, why they failed. On the other hand, we do know why the right thing was probably not done. The cultural pattern was usually a matter of revealed truth and not open to experimental modification—except when conspicuously unsuccessful. The community wasn't set up as a real experiment, but to put certain principles into practice. These principles, when not revealed by God, flowed from a philosophy of perfectionism. Generally the plan was to get away from government and to allow the natural virtue of man to assert itself. What more can you ask for as an explanation of failure?"

"Well, you might have said that in the first place!" I exclaimed, trying to laugh off Frazier's evident feeling.

"Perhaps I misunderstood you," he said, without laughing. "But at any rate we have got started on the crucial point in the whole venture. We ought to make ourselves more comfortable."

20

FRAZIER led us in the direction of the personal rooms, and I hoped that we might be going to his own quarters, which I was curious to see. But we turned and climbed a low ramp to the roof of the common rooms. Many members were sitting up here in the early twilight. It was a part of Walden Two of which I had had no hint.

There was a pleasant breeze, and the sky was almost uniformly pink in a curious sort of early sunset. We collected a few deck and beach chairs and two or three leather cushions and arranged ourselves to enjoy both the evening and the conversation.

Frazier turned first to Castle.

"Have you ever taught a course in ethics, Mr. Castle?" he said.

"I have taught a course in ethics every year for thirteen years," said Castle in his most precise manner.

"Then you can tell us what the Good Life consists of," said Frazier.

"Oh, no, I can't," said Castle, "not by any means. You are thirteen years too late."

Frazier was delighted.

"Then let me tell you," he said.

"By all means," said Castle jovially. "But I must inform you that everything you say will be taken down and may be used against you. I've been waiting for this. Unless you *can* show me what the Good Life consists of, and that you can achieve it in Walden Two, I shall tell you to take your power looms and your food lockers and your glass trays and I'll go back to the Square Deal Pants Store and the Hamburgteria."

"Of course, I know nothing about your course in ethics," Frazier said, "but the philosopher in search of a rational basis for deciding what is good has always reminded me of the centipede trying to decide how to walk. Simply go ahead and walk! We all know what's good, until we stop to think about it. For example, is there any doubt that health is better than sickness?"

"There might be a time when a man would choose ill-health or death, even," said Castle. "And we might applaud his decision."

"Yes, but you're moving the wrong foot. Try the one on the opposite side." This was not playing fair, and Castle obviously resented it. He had made a friendly gesture and Frazier was taking advantage of it. *"Other things being equal,* we choose health," Frazier continued. "The technical problem is simple enough. Perhaps we can find time tomorrow to visit our medical building.

"Secondly, can anyone doubt that an absolute minimum of unpleasant labor is part of the Good Life?" Frazier turned again to Castle, but he was greeted with a sullen silence.

"That's the millionaire's idea, anyway," I said.

"I mean the minimum which is possible without imposing on anyone. We must always think of the whole group. I don't mean that we want to be inactive—we have proved that idleness doesn't follow. But painful or uninteresting work is a threat to both physical and psychological health. Our plan was to reduce unwanted work to a minimum, but we wiped it out. Even hard work is fun if it's not beyond our strength and we don't have too much of it. A strong man rejoices to run a race or split wood or build a wall. When we're not being imposed on, when we choose our work freely, then we *want* to work. We may even search for work when a scarcity threatens. William Morris, you remember, tried to make that state of affairs plausible in *News from Nowhere,* but without success, I think. Imagine our surprise to find we had made him a true prophet!"

I mentioned my pleasant stint on the woodpile and said I was willing to accept the point without further proof.

"But I don't think a labor leader would be anxious to agree with you," I added.

"He might want to, in the long run," said Frazier, "but

he can't afford to agree just now. That's the fatal flaw in labor reform. The program calls for a long, dreary campaign in which the leaders not only keep their men dissatisfied but stir up additional and often spurious grounds for dissatisfaction. So long as reform remains a battle between labor and capital, the labor leader must 'increase the misery' to heighten the morale of his troops. No one knows how much heavier the lot of the worker is made by the very people who are trying to make it lighter. Here, there's no battle. We can freely admit that we like to work. Can you believe that we don't need to keep an accurate account of each man's contribution? Or that most of us have stored up enough spare credits to take a long vacation if we liked? But let me go on.

"The Good Life also means a chance to exercise talents and abilities. And we have let it be so. We have time for sports, hobbies, arts and crafts, and most important of all, the expression of that interest in the world which is *science* in the deepest sense. It may be a casual interest in current affairs or in literature or the controlled and creative efforts of the laboratory—in any case it represents the unnecessary and pleasurably selective exploration of nature.

"And we need intimate and satisfying personal contacts. We must have the best possible chance of finding congenial spirits. Our Social Manager sees to that with many ingenious devices. And we don't restrict personal relations to conform to outmoded customs. We discourage attitudes of domination and criticism. Our goal is a general tolerance and affection.

"Last of all, the Good Life means relaxation and rest. We get that in Walden Two almost as a matter of course, but not merely because we have reduced our hours of work. In the world at large the leisure class is perhaps the least relaxed. The important thing is to satisfy our needs. Then we can give up the blind struggle to 'have a good time' or 'get what we want.' We have achieved a true leisure.

"And that's all, Mr. Castle—absolutely all. I can't give

you a rational justification for any of it. I can't reduce it to any principle of 'the greatest good.' This *is* the Good Life. We know it. It's a fact, not a theory. It has an experimental justification, not a rational one. As for your conflict of principles, that's an experimental question, too. We don't puzzle our little minds over the outcome of Love versus Duty. We simply arrange a world in which serious conflicts occur as seldom as possible or, with a little luck, not at all."

Castle was gazing steadily across the evening landscape. There was no sign that he was listening. Frazier was not to be refused.

"Do you agree, Professor?" he said. There was obvious contempt for the honorific title.

"I don't think you and I are interested in the same thing," said Castle.

"Well, that's what *we* are interested in, and I think we've turned the trick," said Frazier, obviously disappointed. "Things are going well, at least."

"As I remember it, you made short shrift of perfectionism," I said. "Aren't you adopting a sort of perfectionist view yourself? You seem to imply that people will naturally be happy, active, affectionate, and so on, if you simply give them the chance. How do you keep these conditions in force?"

"There is no perfec— *In force!* Now there's an illuminating expression! You can't *enforce* happiness. You can't in the long run enforce anything. We don't *use* force! All we need is adequate behavioral engineering."

"Now we're getting somewhere," said Castle, looking up but still rather glum.

"I'll admit there's a special problem in the case of members who come to us as adults," said Frazier. "It's easier with members who are born into the community and pass through our school system. With new adult members we have to appeal to something like conversion."

"I should think so!" said Castle.

"It's not so difficult," said Frazier suspiciously. "The new member simply agrees to follow the customs of the community in return for the advantages of living among us. He may still thrive on motives which we carefully avoid in the design of our children. He may be the victim of emotions which we dispense with. But he agrees to hold himself in check, to live up to certain specifications, for the sake of the consequences. For example, he may be motivated very largely by a rejection of the outside world, a motive which is quite lacking in our children. But he agrees not to spend much time in invidious comparisons. Eventually, the adult members become very much like our properly educated second generation."

"That's all very fine as a program," said Castle. "It's more than that, it's beautiful. But here's the crux of the whole question of community life: how can you put such a program into effect?"

"It's really not so hard as the Philistines have supposed," said Frazier. "We have certain rules of conduct, the Walden Code, which are changed from time to time as experience suggests. Some of these, like the Ten Commandments, are rather fundamental, but many may seem trivial. Each member agrees to abide by the Code when he accepts membership. That's what he gives in return for his constitutional guarantee of a share in the wealth and life of the community. The Code acts as a memory aid until good behavior becomes habitual."

"Can you give us an example of a trivial rule?" I asked.

"Let's see. One is: 'Don't talk to outsiders about the affairs of the community.' Planners are exempt, and others are allowed to violate the rule in certain cases." Frazier turned to Steve and Mary. "What did you find out about us at the dance last night?"

"Not a thing," said Steve. "We noticed that."

"You can see why we have the rule. Our Manager of Public Relations would have a bad time of it if visitors were misled by remarks which might be misinterpreted. We aren't quite sure of ourselves in the eyes of the world, and must take precautions. Another rule is: 'Explain your work to any member who is interested'. That's the 'Apprenticeship Rule.' It makes for a much more informed and capable membership, as well as a fairer assignment of credit values to various kinds of work. Another is: 'Don't gossip about the personal relations of members.' It was hard to put that into practice, but I think we've really done it. A very valuable rule, of course, in easing personal difficulties.

"The Code even descends to the level of the social graces," Frazier continued. "We've tried a number of experiments to expedite and improve personal relations. For example, introductions in Walden Two are solely for the purpose of communicating information; we don't wait to be introduced before speaking to a stranger, nor do we bother to make introductions if no relevant information is to be communicated. The average American may stand about uneasily without speaking, or he may regard us as forward if we speak without an introduction. But the custom is familiar to the English and causes no embarrassment or comment.

"A similar rule permits the ready expression of boredom. We had to use some rather drastic measures to introduce this and it's only occasionally used. But it's perfectly good form among us to say 'You've told me that before,' or 'I'm fairly well acquainted with that subject,' or 'That's something which I don't find very interesting.' The result is, we spare ourselves many an hour of boredom. If you stop to recall that a community multiplies social contacts many fold, you'll appreciate the value of the rule."

"The speaker doesn't take offense?" I said.

"Not when the practice is fully accepted as part of the culture. It's just a matter of getting used to it. Many characteristic American remarks are rude in other cultures. And remember, too, that the speaker gains just as much as the listener. He doesn't need to ask the listener to stop him if he's 'heard it before,' and he need never fear that he's being a bore."

"But why do you all continue to observe the Code?" I said. "Isn't there a natural drift away from it? Or simple disagreement?"

"As to disagreement, anyone may examine the evidence upon which a rule was introduced into the Code. He may argue against its inclusion and may present his own evidence. If the Managers refuse to change the rule, he may appeal to the Planners. But in no case must he argue about the Code with the members at large. There's a rule against that."

"I would certainly argue against the inclusion of *that* rule," said Castle. "Simple democracy requires public discussion of so fundamental a matter as a code."

"You won't find very much 'simple democracy' here," said Frazier casually, and he resumed his discussion as if he had referred to the absence of white flour in the Walden Two bread. "As to any drifting away from the Code, that's prevented by the very techniques which the Managers use to gain observance in the first place. The rules are frequently brought to the attention of the members. Groups of rules are discussed from time to time in our weekly meetings. The advantages for the community are pointed out and specific applications are described. In some cases simple rules are appropriately posted."

"I noticed one over the bathtub," said Castle.

"What were the 'drastic measures' used to put over the rule about boredom?" I asked.

"You will find an account of that bit of social engineering in a manuscript in one of the libraries," said Frazier. "It's called 'The Bore War.' The rule was regarded as a doubtful experiment, but it was put over quite successfully. It was announced and explained at a weekly meeting. There was a good deal of intentional joking about it. In a severe change of custom it's important to invoke a sense of humor. Each member was asked to exercise the rule at least once a day, even if it meant finding a trivial instance. Little cards appeared on the dining-room tables reading 'Have you been bored today? If not, why not?' Some one complained to the Manager that the cards themselves were boring, and they were immediately taken away to prove the value of the rule. One member wrote a play called *The Man Who Bored Everybody*. He got one point zero zero for his time, too. The play considers the dilemma of a man who never opens his mouth without being told that he's boring. He eventually capitalizes on his idiosyncrasy by making public appearances as the World's Greatest Bore, but the police close the show because the crowds which swarm to see him prove that boredom can't be genuine if it's that interesting.

"My synopsis doesn't do justice to the funny situations which the author managed to develop, but it doesn't matter. Thanks to all this publicity, a custom of expressing a lack of interest became quite commonplace and wasn't resented. The advantages to both speaker and hearer alike have been enough to keep the rule in operation."

"You used the word 'publicity,'" I said. "I was going to ask you whether your techniques aren't already familiar to advertisers, politicians, and other kinds of applied psychologists. Is there anything very original about them?"

"Nothing original whatever. That's the point. Society already possesses the psychological techniques needed to obtain universal observance of a code—a code which would guarantee the success of a community or state. The difficulty is that these techniques are in the hands of the wrong people—or, rather, there aren't any right people. Our government won't accept the responsibility of building the sort of behavior needed for a happy state. In Walden Two we have merely created an agency to get these things done."

Castle had not been following much of this. As Frazier paused, he adopted a complete change of posture in his apparently uncomfortable deck chair and made several rustling noises preparatory to speaking.

"I am not satisfied with your Good Life," he said at last with a direct look at Frazier.

"You're not?"

"No. There's something lacking."

"Not the greatest good for the greatest number!" said Frazier.

"No. Something necessary to keep your exceptional people exceptional. Life here wouldn't challenge me— and I suspect it wouldn't challenge the dozen first-rate men who have gone through my classes during the past decade. As I remember them, they weren't interested in momentary tasks. They would have cared very little for something that could be finished tomorrow. What you lack, compared with the world at large, is the opportunity to make long-term plans. The scientist has them. An experiment which answers an isolated question is of little interest. Even the artist has them. If he's a good artist or a good composer, he isn't concerned with the single picture on his easel or the composition on his piano. He wants to feel that all his pictures or compositions are saying something—are all part of a broader movement. The mere joy in running a race, or painting a picture, or weaving a rug, isn't enough. Your good man must be working on a theory or a new style or an improved technique."

"But don't think we all live from day to day!" said Frazier. "I can see why you might, because you have seen only our day-to-day life. We may seem to have some abiding preoccupation with the momentary enjoyment of happiness. That's by no means the case. But let me clear up another point first. You mentioned a dozen students who would be dissatisfied. What about the others?"

"Oh, you could take care of them well enough!" said Castle. "And you're welcome to do so."

"The difference between us, Mr. Castle, is greater than I supposed," said Frazier. "We not only have use for these people, we have respect. Most people do live from day to day, or, if they have any long-time plan it's little more than the anticipation of some natural course—they look forward to having children, to seeing the children grow up, and so on. The majority of people don't want to plan. They want to be free of the responsibility of planning. What they ask is merely some assurance that they will be decently provided for. The rest is a day-to-day enjoyment of life. That's the explanation of your Father

Divines; people naturally flock to anyone they can trust for the necessities of life. People of that sort are completely happy here. And they pay their way. They aren't spongers and I don't see why you view them with contempt. They are the backbone of a community—solid, trustworthy, essential. But what about the highly intelligent few who must have distant and magnificent goals? In what sense would we interfere with their dreams?"

"It's just a feeling I have that these students would be quite out of water here. One of them might be interested in a social problem, for example."

"But do you think we have no social problems? Wouldn't your young friend enjoy a few months of apprenticeship with our Manager of Personal Behavior or Cultural Behavior or Public Relations? Wouldn't he find long-term ideas worth working for in educating our young —perhaps ways of interesting them in the very problems he holds so dear? Wouldn't he be an enthusiastic member of our newly formed Office of Information, which is to give an account of our experiment to the world? No, indeed, I don't think your young friend would lack distant goals. And the important thing is, we could show him how to *reach* these goals, or most of them, within a reasonable time. What can you do along that line?"

"Not much, I confess."

"Of course not. Because there are a thousand forces which prevent you and all the other men of good will from even starting toward your goal. What your young friend has, I'll wager, is a true spirit of experimentation, but like thousands of others he has no laboratory and no techniques. Shall we try an experiment right now? Send him here and let's see whether he will lack distant goals!"

This was not very subtle, and the excitement in Frazier's manner less so. But I could not tell whether he was simply out to recruit new material or whether he sincerely wanted to refute Castle's charge in the only way he knew—with a practical proof that Walden Two would challenge a good man.

"I wasn't thinking of any one man in particular," said

Castle. "Merely of a certain type. Your answer is reasonable, but I happened to hit upon an easy case. What about the boy who wants to make a name for himself in some business? Let's say he has discovered some new process and wants to set up an industry."

"What does 'making a name for himself' mean?" asked Frazier. "Do you mean making a fortune? We have no need for fortunes, and until you can show me how a fortune can be made without making a few paupers in the bargain, it's one goal we're glad to do without."

"I suppose I was thinking more of fame than fortune," said Castle.

"Fame is also won at the expense of others. Even the well-deserved honors of the scientist or man of learning are unfair to many persons of equal achievement who get none. When one man gets a place in the sun, others are put in a denser shade. From the point of view of the whole group there's no gain whatsoever, and perhaps a loss."

"But is there anything wrong with admiring exceptional achievements, or being pleased to receive recognition?" I said.

"Yes," said Frazier flatly. "If it points up the unexceptional achievements of others, it's wrong. We are opposed to personal competition. We don't encourage competitive games, for example, with the exception of tennis or chess, where the exercise of skill is as important as the outcome of the game; and we never have tournaments, even so. We never mark any member for special approbation. There must be some other source of satisfaction in one's work or play, or we regard an achievement as quite trivial. A triumph over another man is never a laudable act. Our decision to eliminate personal aggrandizement arose quite naturally from the fact that we were thinking about the whole group. We could not see how the group could gain from individual glory."

"But do you exclude simple personal gratitude?" asked Castle. "Suppose one of your doctors worked out a system of sanitation or medication so that none of you ever had colds. Wouldn't you want to honor him and wouldn't he want to be honored?"

"We don't need to talk about hypothetical cases," said Frazier. "Our people are constantly making contributions to the health, leisure, happiness, comfort, and amusement of the community. That's where your young friend with the new industrial process would find himself. But to single anyone out for citation would be to neglect all the others. Gratitude itself isn't wrong, it's the ingratitude or lack of gratitude which it involves."

"So you have just stopped being grateful," said Castle.

"On the contrary, we're all extraordinarily grateful. We overflow with gratitude—but to no one in particular. We are grateful to all and to none. We feel a sort of generalized gratitude toward the whole community— very much as one gives thanks to God for blessings which are more immediately due to a next-door neighbor or even the sweat of one's own brow."

"How is your generalized gratitude expressed?" I said.

"Well, what's gratitude, anyway?" said Frazier. He waited for an answer, but none came, and he went on. "Isn't it a readiness to do return favors? At least that's the sense in which we're all grateful here. There isn't one of us who wouldn't willingly enter upon the most difficult assignment if the need arose. We're ready to do something for all in return for what we've received from all."

"In other words, you get the effect of gratitude without the unfairness of oversights," I said.

"That may be," said Frazier doubtfully, "although I don't think we care very much about the unfairness. It's a practical matter. Things run more smoothly if we don't hand out tokens of gratitude and if we conceal personal contributions."

"It must be difficult, though," said Castle. "Don't tell me a patient doesn't show gratitude for the shot of morphine which relieves his pain!"

"Why should he? Think of the plumber who gets out of bed in the middle of the night to correct some trouble in the water supply—perhaps with more far-reaching effects upon the comfort and health of the community than one shot of morphine. Where's the gratitude there?"

"Couldn't you explain the plumber's achievement to the community and make some public acknowledgment?" I said.

"No one would feel sillier than the plumber if we did that. And what about the cooks, the dairymen, and all the other workers in the community? Where should we stop? As close to the beginning as possible, I say. Eliminate expressions of personal gratitude altogether. After all, the community paid for the morphine and the training which enabled the doctor to administer it."

"You accept medical care without so much as a 'thank you'?" I said.

"Particularly without a 'thank you,'" said Frazier. "The deliberate expression of thanks is prohibited by the Code. A casual 'thank you' for the sake of social articulation is allowed, but it has about as much meaning as 'How do you do?' or 'Excuse me.' We may say 'Excuse me' to call the attention of someone who's in our way, but it isn't regarded as a petition for pardon."

"That explains the puzzlement of the charming young lady in the aquarium," I said. "I tried to thank her."

"I saw that," said Frazier. "You put her on the spot. In her position as nurse, or as an authorized member speaking to guests, it was her job to explain her work. She didn't expect thanks from you, nor will the plumber expect you to call at his shop and thank him for the facilities you've used during your stay. Mrs. Nash was aware of the outside practice, but you put her in an embarrassing position nevertheless. It's as if you had handed her a certain amount of money which belonged to the whole community."

"I find that very hard to believe," I said.

"Naturally. A cultural fact is hard to *see*, let alone

158

understand. It's impossible for you to know how 'Thank you' sounds to anyone who has lived for a few months in Walden Two. A psychological change has to take place—"

I regretted having opened that line again, and interrupted Frazier as soon as I could think of something to say.

"What's left to motivate your workers?" I said. "Take a Manager, for example. He doesn't work for money—that's out. He doesn't work for personal acclaim—that's forbidden. What's left? I suppose you'd say he works to avoid the consequences of failure. He has to keep going or he'll be held responsible for the resulting mess."

"I wouldn't say that. We don't condemn a man for poor work. After all, if we don't praise him, it would be unfair to blame him."

"You mean you would let an incompetent man continue to do a poor job?" said Castle.

"By no means. He would be given other work, and a competent man brought in. But he wouldn't be blamed."

"For heaven's sake, why not?" said Castle.

"Do you blame a man for getting sick?"

"Of course not."

"But poor work by a capable man is a form of illness."

"That sounds like *Erewhon*," said Castle, "and I confess that I find it absurd."

"I found *Erewhon* absurd when I first read it, too," said Frazier, and as Castle made a gesture of impatience he hastened to add, "I'm sorry. I didn't mean to imply that you hadn't thought the thing out. But you can't think these things all the way out; you have to *work* them out. 'Experience is the mother of all certainty.' We had no expectation of seeing Butler's little flight of fancy so beautifully confirmed. And, incidentally, we haven't confirmed his companion piece of cultural engineering. We don't throw a man into prison for illness. Butler was carried away by the Principle of Upside Down. A moral or ethical lapse, whether in explicit violation of the Code or not, needs treatment, not punishment."

"You merely offer your condolences for a mild case of larceny?" said Castle.

"No, condolences are out too. The doctor seldom expresses sympathy for his patient—and wisely, I think. We simply treat the illness as an objective fact."

"How do you treat a man for a bad case of 'poor work'?" I asked.

"With common sense! Take him off the job. If the boy who has charge of collecting eggs breaks too many, give him other work. And the same with a Manager. But why condemn him? Or blame him?"

"I should think you might encourage a sort of malingering," I said. "Wouldn't a man be tempted to do poor work in order to get an easier job?—Oh, well. Forgive me. I see the answer to that: you have no easier jobs, of course. And he could change jobs freely anyway. I'm sorry."

"But what if a man did poor work, or none at all, in every job you put him on?" said Castle.

"The disease would be judged quite serious, and the man would be sent to one of our psychologists. It's more likely that he would long since have gone of his own accord. This would happen before any very critical condition developed, and a cure would be quite possible. But compare the situation in the outside world. There the man would have stuck to his job in spite of his indisposition—that is, in spite of his desire not to work or work well—because he needed the wages, or was afraid of censure, or because another job wasn't available. The condition would have become critical. I think it's that kind of ultimate violent revolt that you're thinking about. It's quite unlikely here."

"But what would you do if it occurred?" Castle insisted. "Certainly you can conceive of a member refusing to work."

"We should deal with it somehow. I don't know. You might as well ask what we should do if leprosy broke out. We'd think of something. We aren't helpless."

"It's a curious thing," I said, and I was rather surprised

to note that I was trying to get Frazier out of a hole, "how accurately Butler predicted the modern change in attitude toward criminal and moral lapses."

"And it's a change I deplore," said Castle sharply. "It has left the individual with no responsibility, no choice. 'Society is to blame. It's all the working of natural law.' But what happens to the individual under such a view? Where is personal initiative? Have 'right' and 'wrong' no longer any meaning?"

"I'm sure I don't know," said Frazier. "Do you? But what amazes me, Mr. Castle, is your unwillingness to put these cherished concepts to an experimental test. Does it strike you as in any sense relevant to ask which view will be most helpful in eliminating 'moral' lapses? Certainly you can't say much for the old notion of personal responsibility. At least it led to very little progress."

"I'm not going to be trapped into taking a pragmatic view of morals," said Castle. "Moral law would be moral law even if a mechanistic view of human behavior proved to be more expeditious in achieving the Good Life. I'll take my stand on that."

"I show you a community," said Frazier, speaking slowly and precisely, "in which there's no crime and very few petty lapses, and you condemn it because none of its members have heard about, or care about, moral law. Isn't our Code enough?"

"Your Code is far from enough. Why, you change it from time to time! What sort of moral law is that?"

"But can't you conceive of an experimental ethics? Aren't you willing to profit from experience in working out an agreement for the common good?"

"I'm afraid not. That position leads to too many completely impossible consequences regarding man's place in the world and among men. I need an ethics that will be logically satisfying."

"Even if you must contemplate it forever from a world of moral chaos?"

"Even so."

Frazier sighed.

"I suppose," he said, "it's because you're temperamentally not an experimentalist. I wish I could convince you of the simplicity and the adequacy of the experimental point of view. The problems are clear enough. What is the 'original nature of man'? I mean, what are the basic psychological characteristics of human behavior—the inherited characteristics, if any, and the possibilities of modifying them and creating others? That's certainly an experimental question—for a science of behavior to answer. And what are the techniques, the engineering practices, which will shape the behavior of the members of a group so that they will function smoothly for the benefit of all? That's also an experimental question, Mr. Castle—to be answered by a behavioral technology. It requires all the techniques of applied psychology, from the various ways of keeping in touch with opinions and attitudes to the educational and persuasive practices which shape the individual from the cubicle to the grave. Experimentation, Mr. Castle, not reason. Experimentation with life—could anything be more fascinating?"

"You use the word 'experiment' a great deal," I said, "but do you really experiment at all? Isn't one feature of good scientific practice missing from all the cases you have described?"

"You mean the 'control,'" said Frazier.

"Yes," I said, rather surprised to have him get my point so quickly. "How do you know that the ethical training you give your young people is really responsible for their equanimity and happiness? Might these not be due to some of the other experimental conditions which you have set up? Why don't you divide your children into two groups? One could receive an ethical training, the other not."

"Probably," said Frazier, "because I am not offering Walden Two 'in partial fulfillment of the requirements for the degree of Doctor of Philosophy.' Besides, it wouldn't work. There would be too many cross-influences. We're too small to keep two groups of children separate. Some day it may be possible—we shall have controls to satisfy the most academic statistician. And by that time they may be necessary, too, for we shall have reached the point of dealing with very subtle differences. At present they aren't necessary. To go to all the trouble of running controls would be to make a fetish of scientific method. Even in the exact sciences we frequently don't ask for controls. If I touch a match to a mixture of chemicals and an explosion occurs, I don't set a second mixture aside to see if it will blow up without the help of the match. The effect of the match is obvious."

"The mixture might have been on the point of blowing up just as you applied the match," I said, with a caution born of academic carping.

"But it's a slim chance, and I'm willing to run a chance of the same magnitude that I'm wrong. I have other things to do. Anyway, I'll find out soon enough, if I continue to work in the field."

"But your example isn't quite applicable," I insisted. "Here you are dealing with many factors—many forces all acting at once. You need a control group to be sure of anything."

"The number of forces is beside the point," said Frazier. "Let's say a man comes into a doctor's office suffering from fallen arches, eyestrain, and dandruff. The doctor prescribes arch supports, glasses, and a hair lotion. A month later the patient returns quite cured. Now, the doctor is in no doubt whatsoever as to what cured what. He entertains no suspicion whatsoever that the glasses or the hair lotion cured the fallen arches, he has no reason to believe that the arch supports or the eyeglasses . . ."

Frazier seldom said "and so forth." A thought was a thought and needed to come out in one piece. I permitted him to give a slow birth to all the conclusions to which the doctor would not come, and then said:

"But you have taken an example in which your factors are all clearly separated. The analogy isn't good. It's by no means so simple to show that adult happiness is related to self-control acquired before the age of seven. So many other aspects of the life in Walden Two could lead to the same result."

"Yes, it's remarkable, isn't it?" he said.

"But wait a minute! What about my point? Are your problems all as separate as fallen arches and dandruff, or aren't they?"

"My dear fellow," said Frazier, "of course they're not. It's not the separation that counts, but whether the relation between cause and effect is obvious. The happiness and equanimity of our people are *obviously* related to the self-control they have acquired."

My head was spinning like Alice's in this logical wonderland. I could not see how Frazier had been so successful if these were really the principles he practiced and not something he had cooked up to annoy me. Later, when I was still puzzling over the question, I realized that the history of science had known many comparable cases. Often they are attributed to genius—to the art of experimental design—to the gift of the good hunch. I could see one chance of explaining them otherwise. In the early days of any science, it may be possible to make extraordinary speed without elaborate statistical control. A new technique may permit a straightforward observation which is sometimes as direct as our sensory contact with nature. But I hoped that Frazier's emotional rejection of academic rigor would not be allowed to prevail in the later stages of the Walden Two experiment.

I cannot recall that evening without remembering the grandeur of the slowly changing sky. It was not a picturesque sunset, for there were no clouds, but a strange pink light surrounded us, as if we were indeed looking at the world through rose-colored glasses. Eventually the sky faded and then darkened, and the stars came out.

It was now fairly late, as hours at Walden Two went. Most of the other occupants of the roof had gone, and the frogs and peepers had taken over all conversations but our own. Frazier indulged in a most conspicuous yawn.

"I find myself reminded of our cardinal piece of personal engineering," he said when he had composed his face again. He turned to me. "Have you ever studied sleep?"

"Not beyond the usual textbooks," I said. "It seems to be important in avoiding behavioral disorders in children."

"In adults, too," said Frazier. "It makes an enormous difference with me. I can take any frustration in my stride if I've had enough sleep. And give me a good night's sleep and I can do a day's work in a couple of hours."

"I thought that was the usual thing," said Castle.

"I mean intellectual work. Nowadays I can do more creative thinking or writing in a couple of hours than I used to do in a whole day, when I forced myself to keep going in spite of a distracting weariness. What folly that was! What an inefficient use of Man Thinking!"

"I'm sure many people never know what it's like to be rested," I said.

"Of course they don't," said Frazier, in exceptionally cordial agreement. "They never have a chance to discover how tired they really are, or how well they could work otherwise, or what brilliant flashes they might have."

"I get a glimpse of it at vacation time," I said.

"I dare say you do. But not the usual vacationer. He's so accustomed to a fast pace that he immediately looks about for something to do. Even the lucky ones who can relax, who don't feel that time is wasted if they sleep it away, seldom get beyond the drugged stage. The simple fact is, our civilization puts no value on rest.

"I'm sure it has a bearing on longevity, too," Frazier continued. "Many parts of *News from Nowhere* are ridiculous, but if Morris could convince me that he knew how to achieve his 'epoch of leisure,' I would grant him the fabulous youthfulness of his people." He rose and started to fold his chair. "Let us rejuvenate for a few hours," he said.

We rose and carried our chairs and cushions to neat piles along the rear edge of the roof.

"I suspect that 'Return your chairs' is to be found somewhere in the Code," I said.

Frazier smiled but said nothing. He led us down the ramp, saw us off safely in the direction of the Walk, and turned toward his room.

Castle and I were again soon deserted. We reached the hallway in front of our room and stood talking for a few moments as I indicated my intention of going outside. Castle was engaged in a bitter struggle with himself. He would clench his fist and slap it into the palm of his hand, and shake his head with an exaggerated sweep from side to side, in no apparent connection with our remarks. "Not for me!" he would interject. "Not for me!" I said that I could see no fundamental flaw in Frazier's program and pointed to the apparently successful accomplished fact before our eyes. This was not exactly fair, for I was still in conflict myself, but I enjoyed Castle's struggle. And I was on Frazier's side on the main issue.

Finally, with a "Good night" which was less a farewell than a paraphrase of "The jig is up," Castle strode into our room and slammed the door.

21

I HAD decided to walk down to the gardens and have a cigarette.

Very few people smoked in Walden Two—Frazier not at all, so far as I could tell, though I remembered him as a heavy pipe-smoker in graduate school. In such company my own consumption of tobacco had fallen off. At first this was because I had felt conspicuous when smoking, and rather guilty, although not the slightest objection was made or implied. Later I found that my interest had weakened. I was surprised to note that I was still on the pack of cigarettes I had slipped into my pocket Wednesday morning. I had smoked only twice since breakfast. I began to wonder whether I might not be able to give it up, after all. As I wandered slowly in the direction of the flower beds, I found myself taking deeper and deeper drags, and with mixed joy and alarm saw that I was getting nothing out of it. I had heard that smoking in the dark was unsatisfactory, but I had never noticed it before. I had a flash of Hans Castorp on his magic mountain; he had had cigar trouble under similar circumstances, I remembered. What was the psychology of smoking, anyway? Adult thumb-sucking, I used to tell my classes, but I had never meant it.

I heard footsteps in the dewy grass, and discovered Steve and Mary quite near me. I cupped my hand over my cigarette, intending to let the "maid and her wight go whispering by." I suspected they would find it hard to take their leave if we once spoke, and I did not want to interfere with their evening together.

"Professor?"

It was Steve. They had been looking for me, and Castle had put them on my trail.

"I wonder if we could ask you a couple of questions, Professor."

"Anything you like, Steve. Shall we go inside?"

"Let's stay here," said Mary.

We began to walk down the slope, and I waited for Steve to speak.

"Professor, what do you think of all this?" he said at last.

"You mean Walden Two?"

"Yes."

"What do I think of it? Well, I can't say—in a single word. I don't know whether I think anything just now. It's a pretty big dish."

"Do you think it's all straight? I mean, is it all the way Mr. Frazier says?"

"If you mean, is Frazier telling the truth—yes, I think he is. And I'm sure he's giving us a complete picture. He's not the sort to cover his mistakes."

"We think so, too," said Mary. "Steve didn't mean—"

"The only thing is—we can't believe it," said Steve. "I mean, we can't believe we've got it straight. For instance, is this right: if Mary and I joined up tomorrow —if they'd take us—does that mean we could go on eating in those dining rooms from now on till we *die?*"

"I guess it does."

"Another thing. Could we get married right away?"

"So far as I know, you could."

"And have a room of our own, and use all the other rooms like everybody else? And go to the movies and dances and things like that?"

"Right."

"And our kids—would they live in that nursery we saw? And go through that school just like all the others?"

"That's right."

"*Exactly* like the others? The same kind of clothes and everything?"

"That's right."

"And they'd be friends with kids like the kids we saw?"

"Yes."

"But how would we pay for all that?" Steve said, with an agonized stress. "Things like that aren't free. There must be some catch."

"No," I said. "You and Mary would give your four labor-credits each day."

"I'd give them the biggest goddamn labor-credits they ever saw," said Steve, and he pulled up a few blades of grass and walked a little away from us.

"I don't think you know what this means," said Mary. "Do you know what we've got to go back to in the city?"

"I've a pretty good idea, I think."

"We couldn't get married till Steve got a job. And it wouldn't be much of a job. And we'd get a couple of rooms somewhere across the tracks. And our babies would be born at home and they would grow up like all the other kids over there—in the streets most of the time. And the school—Steve and I both went there—the kids get knocked around, and they fight. They pick on the Jews or the Irish or the Italians. It's awful."

"You and Steve might be able to get away from that," I said.

"We'd *want* to get away, and we'd try. But we wouldn't. Steve and I know that. My sister tried, and she couldn't. She was a lot smarter, too."

She had begun to cry, and I found myself at a loss. But Steve came back shortly and put his arm around Mary, and we walked on in silence.

"What are we waiting for, Professor?" he said at last. "Can you tell me that?"

"I suppose it's taking a little time to sink in," I said.

"You mean—?"

"If I were you, yes. You've nothing to lose and everything to gain."

"Will they take us, d'you think?"

"I don't think there's any question. If I know Frazier, you're in right now."

We had stopped. Steve took Mary in his arms and held her for a long time. I seemed to have been forgotten, and walked on a few steps. Presently they joined me.

"Could we get it settled tonight?" Steve said.

"I wouldn't bother Frazier, if I were you. You haven't

169

a thing to worry about. See him in the morning. I suppose you'll have to get a physical checkup, but that shouldn't take long."

Steve and Mary tried to kiss again as they walked, but they soon fell behind. Later I heard them whispering and laughing excitedly.

"I think I'll turn back now," I called, trying not to sound too obviously tactful. "Eight o'clock for breakfast. Right?"

"Eight o'clock, Professor," Steve called.

I said good night and turned up the slope. A moment later Steve called again, and they came up to me as I waited.

"We forgot to say thank you," Steve said.

"We'll always be saying thank you," said Mary. "You've been wonderful."

I felt it necessary to deny this, for I had done very little; but it was nice to hear, and I could not get the words out of my head as I walked back to our room. They awakened a strange conflict of feelings, and as I undressed in the dark to avoid waking Castle, though I was pretty sure he was not asleep, I tried to analyze them.

I saw no way to avoid the conclusion that I was jealous of Frazier. In confessing that it was he who deserved the full measure of Mary's gratitude, I gained a sudden insight into the profound satisfaction which he must constantly feel, and it set my head spinning with envy. The episode I had just witnessed must have been repeated in its essentials hundreds of times during the past ten years. What more could one man ask? But my present emotion was more than jealousy.

As I climbed into my bunk, I reflected that if I were living in Walden Two, I would be seeing Mary—and Steve, of course—from time to time. It was an idle thought, but I seized upon it in an attempt to explain my uneasiness. It offered two plausible clues. In the first place it seemed to show that I was growing fond of Mary. That, of course, was silly. I scarcely knew her, and no one could have shared fewer of my interests. Doubtless I was suffering from some vague sexual attraction.

The second and more astonishing clue was embedded in the words "if I were living in Walden Two." Was I actually thinking of joining up?

I decided not to be a damn fool and went to sleep.

22

C ASTLE was still fulminating when I found him in the washroom at eight-thirty.

"Well, how does it look this morning?" I said, as I unwound the cord of my razor.

"I've decided the whole thing's a hoax," he said.

"No!"

"Well, not exactly. But a very skillful fake." He was drawing his chin out of shape to accommodate his razor, and his words were not clear.

"Did you say 'fake'? What's fake about it?"

"I don't think it works the way Frazier says. It's like that old automatic chess player. The audience sees a lot of dummy gears and levers, but all the while some midget chess champion is lurking in one corner of the machine."

"Who's the midget?"

"Frazier."

"Frazier!"

"Yes. It's nothing more or less than personal magnetism. The Führer principle. He's got these people hypnotized. Makes them work like sin. Keeps them smiling for the sake of appearances."

"You're not serious!" I said, over the hum of my razor.

"I suppose not. But it's as good a theory as any. There must be *something* back of it."

"Why not take it at its face value?"

Castle was wiping his chin and did not answer.

"Anyway, the hypnotist has two more victims in his power this morning," I said. Castle stopped still.

"Who?"

"Steve and Mary. They've decided to sign up."

Castle shook his head slowly. Then he grasped the plunger which opened the drain in his washbowl and gave it a tug upward. It came loose in his hand. He looked at it for a moment and sniffed in disgust, as if he were offended by the poor quality of the fixture. He stuck the piece back into the hole and withdrew it again. Then he put it back and left it. After he had gathered up his shaving equipment, he tried it again, withdrawing the plunger gently, as if he hoped it might somehow have knitted itself into the rest of the mechanism, like a broken bone.

"What am I supposed to do with this, I wonder?" he said, waving the plunger in the air. "What do you suppose the Code says about broken washbowls?"

From the serving room I caught a glimpse of Rodge and Barbara, already at breakfast and arguing in lowered voices.

As Castle and I joined them, Barbara exclaimed, "Steve and Mary are joining Walden Two. Isn't it wonderful?"

Rodge's glance of surprise suggested that she had been expressing a different view.

"I think it's a fine thing," I said, feeling that some solid opinion should be put forth in unmistakable terms. "They'll find a much happier life here than they were likely to get back home. Has it been settled?"

"They've gone to see Mr. Frazier," said Barbara. "It seems so strange, though, don't you think? Actually *living* here!"

"It will be a very fine life," I said.

A few minutes later Steve and Mary appeared in the serving room with two members of Walden Two whom we had not seen before. Frazier was with them. They took a table in one of the other rooms, and I was unable to learn what was going on. In about a quarter of an hour, however, Steve and Mary joined us, just as we were carrying our trays to the utility window. Frazier and the other members had left.

"Well, are you in?" I said, to relieve their apparent embarrassment.

"We don't know," said Steve. "They asked us a lot of questions, and we gave them all the answers. Didn't we?"

He gave Mary a squeeze. "We can be married next week —if we get in."

"How wonderful!" said Barbara.

"That's great!" said Rodge, with an earnestness which seemed intended to emphasize that he meant what he said. "I'm glad things have worked out."

"It sure is wonderful!" said Steve. "For us, anyway." He grasped Rodge's extended hand, which he had not at first noticed, and shook it jerkily. Barbara gave Mary a little peck of a kiss, as if some sort of formal announcement had just been made. Rodge saw it and drew his face into a pathetic wince. I had never seen an unhappier man.

"Let's get to work!" I said desperately. "We've got to get those windows washed for Mrs. Jamnik!" It was a feeble gesture and it did not wholly ease the strain, but I think it helped. At any rate, something had to be said and quickly, and it was the best I could do. Steve, who was perhaps least out of control at the moment, seemed to understand my motive and backed me up.

"And no loafing, you fellows!" he said. "We don't stand for that around here."

We started down the Walk toward our rooms to change into our work clothes, but we ran into Frazier coming out of one of the lounges. He was beaming, and he glanced at Castle and me with a clear look of triumph. Somehow or other he maneuvered himself between Steve and Mary and put his arms on their shoulders.

"All you have to do is pass the medical," he said, looking from one to the other. "And Mr. Meyerson can see you around twelve o'clock. I don't think you'll have any trouble."

"I'm strong as a horse," said Steve in a rough voice. He looked helplessly at Mary.

"I congratulate you, Frazier," I said, "and I congratulate them, too. And I just want to say we all think it's a fine thing." This was not strictly true, since we were about evenly divided, but I was talking again just to make a noise. It was apparently the right thing to say, for it steadied Steve and Mary, and Frazier was extravagantly pleased.

"I thought I could count on you to see that," he said, grasping my hand.

No one came to my rescue, and there were a few awkward moments. Eventually we began to move along the Walk again, and Frazier took his leave, calling back in a gently paternal tone to remind Steve and Mary of their appointment with Mr. Meyerson at twelve.

It was nearly ten o'clock when we set to work at the windows, but we finished them before noon. We had obviously acquired the knack. In two days we had disposed of what the girl at the Work Desk had taken to be a three-day job.

After a change of clothes we went out of doors and turned up the hill, circling the personal rooms in order to reach the medical building, which was on a sort of ledge or plateau above the Ladder. On our way we passed a new wing which was under construction. Nothing had been completed except the concrete floor on which the rammed-earth walls would be erected, and the plumbing and wiring which protruded from conduits. Steve pointed it out to Mary and explained to us that their room would probably be built here. We all climbed upon the concrete block and turned to inspect the view. Below us lay the common rooms and one wing of personal rooms; beyond them almost the whole of the Walden Two valley could be seen.

It was a delightful spot, but it was now past twelve and Steve urged us uneasily forward to the medical building. Mr. Meyerson was waiting at the door and greeted us cordially.

"My wife has been telling me about you," he said. "She hoped you would *all* be staying on with us."

I said it was certainly a very tempting thought, but that unfortunately we had other matters to attend to. I saw that the remark was fatuous, but only after it was beyond recall. There had been no introductions, of course, but I indicated that Steve and Mary were the lucky couple. Mr. Meyerson turned them over to a very professional-looking nurse.

"Would you by any chance care to see our medical center?" he said to the rest of us, as if he were asking a great favor.

"We've been looking forward to it," I said.

"It may just be worth your while," he said. "At the moment it's a rather unique institution, though we hope it won't be long before many millions of people are similarly cared for.

"My colleagues and I are responsible for the health of Walden Two," he continued as we moved slowly down a central hallway, "and we couldn't accept that rare responsibility without asking for extraordinary powers. We can place the whole community in quarantine with respect to the outside world, for example. And we can ask for personal examinations of the members as often as we like, and I'm delighted to say we can get them. We can control their diet, in collaboration with our very good dietitians, and of course, we supervise all sanitation. Our patients automatically get regular exercise, fresh air, sunshine, and rest as part of their lives at Walden Two. It's a beautiful situation from the point of view of preventive medicine."

We had stopped in front of a small dental office.

"Our dentists will tell you how good the situation really is," Mr. Meyerson continued, raising his voice to reach a young woman in a white coat who was washing her hands and who turned and smiled at us. "Miss Ely is one of them. She can tell you of their unbelievably clever scheme which has reduced their working hours to the point where we're ready to let one of them go." This seemed to be a standing joke.

"As soon as the dentists were given extraordinary powers," Mr. Meyerson explained, "they set to work to eliminate every cavity and bad tooth in the community. A checkup is required of each member every three months. The predictable result is that very few conditions ever become critical. Our dentists do nothing except put in an occasional filling the size of the head of a pin." Mr. Meyerson scowled at Miss Ely, who laughed gaily. "I must say, though, that our consumption of amalgam has fallen off. Our foreign exchange has benefited extraordinarily."

We walked on, past three small hospital bedrooms, only one of which was occupied. A young man, his leg suspended and under traction, was enjoying a rather gay party with three or four visitors. In the rear of the building several young people were at work in a large and well-equipped laboratory.

"It's a more interesting situation than military or institutional medicine in every way," said Mr. Meyerson, looking fondly over the glistening equipment. "Our patients lead normal lives, and they're representative of people in general. And we have their intelligent cooperation in our rather extensive experiments."

"Are some of your dentists really unemployed?" I said, as I saw Miss Ely leaving the building. Mr. Meyerson laughed at length.

"Unemployed? Oh, by no means," he said. "You can't keep a good man unemployed. They spend a lot of time in the laboratory—preventive dentistry, you know. They're trying fluorine in our nursery now, I believe. If they're *quite* successful, we shall have practically no use for dentists at all in another generation. But now I see that I'm wanted in the examination room. We must get your young friends out of here in time for a bit of lunch."

We looked about the center a little longer without a guide. There was an elaborate records office, a small kitchen, and other facilities.

"Rather more doctors and dentists than a thousand people get in the world at large," said Castle. "I wonder how they justify that?"

"Does it need to be justified?" I said. "It's no more than a thousand people need, certainly—if you're going to give the doctor a four-hour day too. Anyway, I suspect the community will produce more doctors than it uses."

"I think they may be sponging on our medical schools," Castle insisted. "Their training must be financed by foundations or by the state, you see, but the state doesn't get the doctors. I must ask Frazier how he justifies that."

23

WE RETURNED to the dining rooms by way of a kitchen door. Frazier came up as we were being served, and pointed to the large central table in one of the modern rooms, to which he had just moved his tray.

"Well," he said, as we began to eat, "there isn't much left to show you. We've shot our bolt. I'm curious to know whether you've been properly impressed?"

" 'Impressed' is scarcely the word," I said. "It's the most soul-shaking experience of my life."

"A very interesting experiment, there's no doubt about that," said Castle. "Utopia come to life, apparently."

"Utopia, indeed," said Frazier. "And do you know what single fact I find most incredible?" He looked eagerly from one of us to the other, particularly at Rodge, and I began to wonder whether he was not satisfied with two converts out of six.

"The fact that it's been a success, I should imagine," I said.

"What's incredible about that? How could it possibly have failed? No, I'm referring to a detail which distinguishes Walden Two from all the imaginary Utopias ever dreamed of. And a very simple thing, too." He continued to look at us, but we were completely at sea.

"Why, the fact that it exists right here and now!" he announced at last. "In the very midst of modern civilization!" He watched for the effect upon us, but it could not have been very marked.

"The Utopias *have* tended to be a bit out of things," said Castle at last, a little doubtfully, but beginning to get the point.

"Out of things! I should say! Why, 'Utopia' is Greek for 'nowhere,' and Butler spelled 'nowhere' backwards! Bacon chose a lost Atlantis, and Shangri-La is cut off by the highest mountains in the world. Bellamy and Morris felt it necessary to get away by a century or two in the dimension of time. Out of things, indeed! It's the first rule of the Utopian romance: 'Get away from life as we know it, either in space or time, or no one will believe you!'

"The one fact that I would cry from every housetop is this: the Good Life is waiting for us—here and now!" he continued. I almost fancied I heard a Salvation Army drum throbbing in the distance. "It doesn't depend on a change in government or on the machinations of world politics. It doesn't wait upon an improvement in human nature. At this very moment we have the necessary techniques, both material and psychological, to create a full and satisfying life for everyone."

"The trick is to put those techniques into effect," said Castle. "You still have to solve the practical problems of government and politics."

"Government and politics! It's not a problem of government and politics at all. That's the first plank in the Walden Two platform. You can't make progress toward the Good Life by political action! Not under *any* current form of government! You must operate upon another level entirely. What you need is a sort of Nonpolitical Action Committee: keep out of politics and away from government except for practical and temporary purposes. It's not the place for men of good will or vision.

"As we use the term these days, government means power—mainly the power to compel obedience," Frazier went on. "The techniques of government are what you would expect—they use force or the threat of force. But that's incompatible with permanent happiness—we know enough about human nature to be sure of that. You can't force a man to be happy. He isn't even likely to be happy if he's *forced* to follow a supposedly happy pattern. He must be led into it in a different way if it's to be satisfying."

"But there have certainly been many happy men under governments of one sort or another," I objected.

"Not *because* of government—in *spite* of it. Some philosophies of life have made men happy, yes, because they have set forth principles which I want to see taken seriously as principles of government. But these philosophies have come from rebels. Governments which use force are based upon bad principles of human engineering. Nor are they able to improve upon these principles, or discover their inadequacy, because they aren't able to accumulate any body of knowledge approaching a science. All that can ever be done by way of 'improvement' is to wrest power from one group and transfer it to another. It's never possible to plan and carry out experiments to investigate the better use of power or how to dispense with it altogether. That would be fatal. Governments must always be right—they can't experiment because they can't admit doubt or question.

"Once in a while a new government initiates a program to put power to better use, but its success or failure never really proves anything. In science, experiments are designed, checked, altered, repeated—but not in politics. Hence our extraordinarily slow progress toward a science of government. We have no real *cumulative* knowledge. History tells us nothing. That's the tragedy of the political reformer. He has nothing to work with but a spurious science of history. He has no real facts—no real laws. A pathetic figure!"

"He's fighting against tremendous odds," I said.

"But that isn't the pathetic thing. I dare say we ought to admire David as he goes forth to meet Goliath, but the pathetic thing is—he wants to be Goliath. He has no better program than to put himself in power. Your liberals and radicals all want to govern. They want to try it their way—to show that people will be happier if the power is wielded in a different way or for different purposes. But how do they know? Have they ever tried it? No, it's merely their guess. And we know it's a bad guess, because if they were right, they wouldn't want power at all.

"How sincere are these liberals, anyway?" Frazier went on. "Why don't they build a world to their liking without trying to seize power? It simply isn't true that all governments persecute everyone who succeeds in being happy! On the contrary, any group of men of good will

181

can work out a satisfactory life within the existing political structures of half a dozen modern governments."

"Aren't you possibly overlooking a certain altruism?" I said. "Perhaps your liberals want to improve the lot of men in general—not just work out a better life for themselves."

"But do they know how to get what they want? Do they know what sort of world will satisfy 'men in general'? No. They are only guessing again. Anyone can suggest changes that would almost certainly be improvements, but that's patchwork. An efficient state culture must be discovered by experimentation."

"It sounds a little like the old program of anarchy," said Castle.

"By no means. I'm not arguing for no government at all, but only for none of the existing forms. We want a government based upon a science of human behavior. Nothing short of that will produce a permanent social structure. For the first time in history we're ready for it, because we can now deal with human behavior in accordance with simple scientific principles. The trouble with the program of anarchy was that it placed too much faith in human nature. It was an offshoot of the philosophy of perfectionism."

"But you yourself seem to have unbounded faith in human nature," I said.

"I have none at all," said Frazier bluntly, "if you mean that men are naturally good or naturally prepared to get along with each other. We have no truck with philosophies of innate goodness—or evil, either, for that matter. But we do have faith in our power to change human behavior. We can *make* men adequate for group living—to the satisfaction of everybody. That was our faith, but it's now a fact."

"I'm not at all easy, though, about your relation to the existing government," said Castle. "What sort of deal can you make with it?"

"All we ask is to be let alone," said Frazier quietly.

"But will you be let alone?" said Castle. "You mentioned taxes, and I can see that you're able to meet that demand as well as anyone. But what about the draft of men in time of war, for example?"

"We're no worse off than anyone else in that respect, either. On the contrary, our young men left their wives and children in a secure and normal environment, and they suffered no doubts about the world to which they would return."

"But do you feel you have accepted the full responsibility of citizenship?" I insisted.

"In what way can we possibly be deficient as citizens?"

"Do you all vote? Do you take an interest in politics, local or national?"

"We go in for politics for immediate practical purposes. We all vote but we don't all take an interest. We have a Political Manager, who informs himself of the qualifications of the candidates in local and state elections. With the help of the Planners he draws up what we call the 'Walden Ticket,' and we all go to the polls and vote it straight."

"Most of your members merely vote as they are told?" said Castle.

"And why not?" said Frazier. "Do you think we'd be so foolish as to vote half one way and half the other? We might as well stay home. Remember that our interests are all alike, and our Political Manager is in the best possible position to tell us what candidates will act in those interests. Why should our members take the time—and it does take time—to inform themselves on so complex a matter?"

"But free suffrage—" Castle began.

"Free fiddlesticks!" said Frazier. "We all know what we want so far as the local government is concerned, and we know how to get it—by voting the Walden Ticket."

"I imagine you get it, all right," I said. "You must throw quite a bit of weight around with—what?—six or seven hundred votes?"

"We do, indeed. We've cleaned up the township and are in a fair way to cleaning up the county. A lot of sensible people hereabouts know what we're doing and ask for the Walden Ticket when they go to the polls. They know it's an honest selection. The candidates know we have a long memory, too, and they remember their commitments. And we've been able, through promise of support, to induce better men to run for office. Free suffrage, my hat!"

"I'm not sure the end justifies the means," said Castle, but he seemed to lack conviction. "You're perverting the democratic process, no matter how desirable the result may be."

I stepped in to avoid hearing Frazier's answer. I was aware of a sort of vicarious shame whenever he hinted at certain antidemocratic principles, and the only course open to me at the moment was simple suppression.

"But aren't you playing with dynamite when you dabble in politics?" I said. "You must have alienated the local forces of graft and corruption. Won't their allies in the rest of the state be out to 'get' you before your influence spreads too far?"

"Now you are recommending that we *shirk* the responsibilities of citizenship," said Frazier with a mock sigh.

"But aren't you afraid of that?"

"How could they possibly 'get' us?"

"They might pass laws limiting your activities or levying confiscatory taxes."

"You'll have to ask our lawyers," said Frazier, "but my hunch is that any law of that sort would hurt some pretty powerful people. Religious organizations, for example. Or cooperatives, which are fairly powerful in the state."

"The forces of corruption," said Castle, "wouldn't be so straightforward as to go to the legislature. They would be spreading stories of free love or multiple marriages or atheism at Walden Two."

"Don't think we haven't thought of that! And we're not just sitting around waiting for it to happen, either. Our Manager of Public Relations sees that the surrounding areas get a good report of us. Some of his present practices I don't approve of, because I'm opposed to anything beyond the truth by way of propaganda, but I've been overruled by the rest of the Planners and we now stretch a point, particularly in regard to religion. It's a sort of anticipatory counterpropaganda."

"I have been meaning to ask about religious practices," I said. "Is there any reason why you can't describe—"

"Not at all. Walden Two isn't a religious community. It differs in that respect from all other reasonably permanent communities of the past. We don't give our children any religious training, though parents are free to do so if they wish. Our conception of man is not taken from theology but from a scientific examination of man himself. And we recognize no revealed truths about good or evil or the laws or codes of a successful society.

"The simple fact is, the religious practices which our members brought to Walden Two have fallen away little by little, like drinking and smoking. It would take me a long time to describe, and I'm not sure I could explain, how religious faith becomes irrelevant when the fears which nourish it are allayed and the hopes fulfilled— here on earth. We have no need for formal religion, either as ritual or philosophy. But I think we're a devout people in the best sense of that word, and we're far better behaved than any thousand church members taken at random.

"We've borrowed some of the practices of organized religion—to inspire group loyalty and strengthen the observance of the Code. I believe I've mentioned our Sunday meetings. There's usually some sort of music, sometimes religious. And a philosophical, poetic, or religious work is read or acted out. We like the effect of this upon the speech of the community. It gives us a common stock of literary allusions. Then there's a brief 'lesson'—of the utmost importance in maintaining an observance of the Code. Usually items are chosen for discussion which deal with self-control and certain kinds of social articulation.

"There's nothing spurious about this—it's not an imitation church service, and our members aren't fooled. The music serves the same purpose as in a church—it makes the service enjoyable and establishes a mood. The weekly lesson is a sort of group therapy. And it seems to be all we need. If the Code is too difficult for anyone or doesn't seem to be working to his advantage, he seeks the help of our psychologists. They're our 'priests,' if you like. The treatments prescribed are very much like those of the psychological clinic except that the disorders are almost always comparatively minor and the therapy therefore usually successful.

"So much for our services. No ritual, no dalliance with the supernatural. Just an enjoyable experience, in part aesthetic, in part intellectual. Now, what else does organized religion provide? Aid to the sick and needy? I shan't insult you by pointing out our practices in that respect there. Comfort in time of loss? But why a professional comforter? Isn't that something we've outgrown, like professional mourners? Here, we offer genuine comfort—the sympathy and affection of many friends. Hope for a better world in the future? We like it well enough here on earth. We don't ask to be consoled for a vale of tears by promises of heaven."

"What did you mean," I said, "when you spoke of going beyond the truth in propagandizing in the surrounding country?"

"Our services are sometimes misrepresented. Our Public Relations man insists that we invite each clergyman in the neighboring towns to late Sunday dinner, with his family, perhaps once a year. We feed them well, and they always accept readily. They usually attend one of our services. We read from the Bible that day, since they all seem to regard Confucius as a heathen, and our chorus sticks to Bach or Handel. I call it deception, but I've been overruled. The argument is that we're fighting bigotry, and must meet it on its own terms.

"Another little trick I don't like is putting into the hands of these clergymen some tracts which we prepared for our ten-year-olds. They're small pamphlets dealing with gluttony, jealousy, theft, lying—a sort of ethical refresher course. The clergymen are led to believe they're prepared for our adult members. I suppose there's some justification, since our adults use them frequently, especially when recommended by our psychologists. I consulted one of them just the other day, myself. I'd just read an article that I'd always meant to write, and I was quite unhappy. But the tracts on Jealousy cured me immediately. They're little masterpieces of behavioral engineering. As a matter of fact, I wrote them."

"Have you really avoided prejudice on the score of religion?" I asked.

"I think we have. At least we've not yet been attacked. The Manager has done a good job, I confess, in spite of his methods. Of course, he's resorted to other measures too. Whenever we have an excess of perishable food, we manage to drop a basket off at the poorer parsonages hereabouts, and we take Christmas baskets around as a regular thing. At one time we also sent members to attend church once or twice a month—gave them point seven five, too—but that's no longer felt to be necessary. We have some things in our favor, of course. Our court and police records are clean. We have fewer divorces than an average community of this size, and no bastardy.

"I should add that our relations with the more intelligent clergy are excellent. Some of our most interesting visitors have been churchmen, and they have in general approved of what we're doing. The real test will come when we expand and they begin to feel the threat. What sort of treatment we get then will, I suppose, depend on their intellectual integrity, which I have no way of evaluating."

"I'm glad to see that you have scruples about these practices," said Castle, "for I find them quite objectionable. I don't know how much good your Sunday services can do by way of ethical training when they're so obviously fraudulent."

"'Fraud' is a strong word, Mr. Castle," said Frazier. "We need these services. I object to unnecessary misrep-

187

resentation. The truth would have sufficed. I think our Manager of Public Relations is being scared by a bogeyman. But it's his job. I may be wrong."

"I can see how these techniques may work for the surrounding countryside," I said. "If you face the problem of public relations squarely, I think you can avoid trouble. But what about your relation to the whole country?"

"It will be some time yet before we need to butter up the country as a whole," said Frazier.

"But what about your responsibilities as citizens of the United States? What interest do you take in national affairs?"

"We vote for president because we happen to be at the polls anyway in connection with local affairs, and our Political Manager makes a recommendation. But for us, as for everyone else, it is six of one, half a dozen of the other. No one of us believes that his weight will be felt in a national election."

"But after all," said Castle, "the national government isn't exactly unimportant. It's protecting you from invaders who would destroy every trace of Walden Two if they could get at it, as well as from aggression by citizens of your own country. Incidentally, isn't that something you forgot when you were talking about self-sufficiency?"

"Not at all. We pay for these services exactly like other taxpayers. We make only a partial use of the services we pay for, in fact. We ask no help for unemployed, for example."

"But you do seem to avoid thinking of yourselves as part of the nation, I think," said Castle.

"Quite so. We have a much better conception of government than the politicians and have, therefore, no interest in what they're doing. The very threats of invasion you were just talking about are only due to governments throwing their weight about."

"But isn't that just the point?" said Castle. "Aren't you really neglecting important problems in world politics? Haven't you any interest in world peace?"

"As much as anyone else," said Frazier. "But we have

a more realistic view of the techniques of achieving peace. And even so, most of us are willing to leave the matter to specialists. Nothing comes from a general frothing at the mouth."

"But are you taking any active step toward world peace?" said Castle.

"Any active step!" cried Frazier. "Just this: we aren't making war! We have no imperialist policy—no designs on the possessions of others—no interest in foreign trade except to encourage happiness and self-sufficiency. What is Walden Two but a grand experiment in the structure of a peaceful world? Point to any internationalist who really *knows* what sort of society or culture or government will make for peace. He *doesn't* know! He's only guessing! Through the machinations of power politics he may, if he's lucky, get an experimental test under way, but almost certainly in such a form that the outcome will prove nothing. He may, through some colossal accident, achieve world peace, perhaps permanently. But the chance is negligible. World politics won't yield the kind of data necessary for a scientific solution of the basic problems. What do people want? What will satisfy them? How can they be made to want what they can get? Or how can they get what they want without taking it away from anyone else? I could go on asking questions like that all day. And who has the answer to one of them? Not the politicians!"

"But are you being realistic?" Castle said. "Suppose the whole country converted itself into communities like this. How would you make war if attacked? Where would your heavy industry be? A couple of days ago you said that the world wasn't ready for Christian humility or pacifism. Aren't you being inconsistent?"

"There are many things to say to that, but I'm not sure I could really convince you. I could argue that we'd have, not a reduced, but a greatly increased military strength. We would still have heavy industries, but they would be so distributed that atomic bombing would be difficult. Large centers of population are an anachronism, you must admit. And our usable manpower would be two or three times as great as in the last war because we'd develop every last grain of physical and psychological strength.

"But that line doesn't appeal to me," he continued. "For a different approach I could cite authorities from Jesus Christ to Henry David Thoreau, and review the techniques of civil disobedience and passive resistance. Or I might argue that America couldn't be converted to this way of life without having a tremendous effect upon the rest of the world—which would wipe out all threat of aggression.

"I don't really want to argue the matter one way or the other because the issue can't be decided by argument. But let me ask you to compare what I am doing for world peace with what you are doing as a 'good citizen.' What are your techniques? What progress are you making toward a peaceful life?"

"All right. All right," Castle said with a laugh. "You asked to be let alone. I will oblige."

24

"THERE'S another way in which the outside world must threaten you," I said, after we had left the dining room and were moving by tacit agreement toward one of the front doors. "It must draw your young people away from you. After all, an enormous amount of talent and skill have gone into making modern life attractive. How do you protect yourselves? By indoctrination, I suppose."

We stepped outside and, for want of a better plan, sat down on the partially shaded benches along the wall.

"Indoctrination is a hard word," said Frazier. "We don't propagandize in favor of our way of life, except to present what we think is a fair comparison of other types of society. We don't use emotional or motivational devices to establish a favorable attitude toward Walden Two or against the world at large. We have no songs which glorify the group. We don't poke fun at the rest of mankind or laugh at their stupid economic or social practices. All we use is unbiased information."

"But is that enough? Do you mean to say your bright young fifteen-year-olds aren't impressed by the movie palaces in the city or by night clubs or fancy restaurants? Can they drive along the wealthiest street in town without experiencing a bit of envy or wondering whether Walden Two is really the best world after all? You can't very well keep them ignorant of such things, can you? You have movies here, for I saw one announced on the bulletin board. Your children must know about the outside world. How can you avoid the ravages of envy or doubt?"

"Of course our children know about the outside world! We simply make sure they know the whole truth! Nothing more is needed. We take them to the city from time to time, and they see the movie palaces, the churches, the museums, the fine residences. But they also see the other side of the tracks—the city hospital, the missions, the home for indigents, the saloons, the jails. We can usually find someone in the slums who will let us pass through her filthy flat in return for the price of a drink. That in itself would be enough.

"Once in a while we give a group of children a sort of detective assignment. The game is to establish a connection in the shortest possible time between any given bit of luxury and some piece of poverty or depravity. The children may start with a fine residence, for example. By going in the service drive they may be able to speak to a black laundress hanging out clothes. They induce her to let them drive her home. That's enough. Or they pick out some shabby figure leaving a cathedral and follow him to the less exalted surroundings in which he spends most of his day.

"We do something of the sort with our magazines and movies. We explain why advertisements almost always show pleasant and attractive people, and interesting and beautiful landscapes, beaches, and homes. And we explain that these have never been available to many except at the expense of poverty, disease, and filth for many more. Our more intelligent young people are naturally challenged by the problem. They want to find out why the poverty has been necessary. They're the ones in whom we worry least about defection."

"Why don't you indoctrinate, though?" I said. "Wouldn't that be the safest way of assuring the success of the community?"

"It would be the safest way of assuring failure," said Frazier with some warmth. "It would be a fatal mistake. Nothing but the truth, that's our rule. No one can doubt the possibility of raising loyal members of almost any sort of community. The techniques have long since proved their worth. Look at the religious cultures which have perpetuated themselves for centuries by rearing children to ways of life which seem to us to violate every human instinct. Look at the monasteries, lamaseries, and other forms of unnatural societies. No, the potency of behavioral engineering can scarcely be overestimated. It makes one wonder why the techniques haven't been put to better use long before this. We could teach our children to be satisfied with a very limited and rigorous existence, to despise other forms of society, and to turn from the pleasures of the flesh. We might make such a society last for many years."

"Why not forever?" said Castle. "Why prefer one society to another? What's wrong with a Tibetan lamasery or an Amish community in Pennsylvania or a monastery in Sicily? If survival is your touchstone, can you choose? I suppose you will argue that some forms are happier than others."

"Happiness is not the deciding factor," said Frazier. "All the communities you mention might yield the same amount of happiness, though I think you can argue for an extra modicum when the basic needs are satisfied."

"But a modicum isn't enough to justify all this," said Castle, excitedly waving his hand across the Walden Two landscape.

"Of course it isn't. We aren't satisfied to produce merely a happy people. Our technology is powerful enough to make men happy under many conditions of life."

"Then how can you possibly decide when you have been successful?" Castle shouted, jumping up from the bench like an excited ballplayer.

"Are you quite sure about this?" I said. "I thought that happiness, the greatest good for the greatest number—"

"Then I've been a bad expositor, indeed," said Frazier. "Can't you see what's wrong with the indoctrinated communities you've just mentioned? What's their most conspicuous characteristic? Isn't it simply that they don't change? They've been the way they are now for centuries."

"But if you have a happy life, why change?" said Castle, moving restlessly about in front of us.

"Isn't their permanence the best proof of their success?" I added, also getting up, on the pretext of picking up a scrap of paper.

Frazier was undisturbed.

"I'm talking about permanence of another sort," he said. "If these communities have survived, it's only because the competition hasn't been keen. It's obvious to everyone that civilization has left them behind. They haven't kept up with human progress, and they will eventually fail in fact as they have already failed in principle. Their weakness is proved by their inability to expand in competition with other forms of society. They have fatal defects, and I submit that the defects have not been seen because of overpropagandizing."

"How can a failure to keep up with civilization be related to propaganda?" I said. I sat down again, but Castle was describing a circle perhaps twenty feet in diameter out across the lawn and back.

"It's directly related," said Frazier. "Nothing could be more direct." He spoke slowly to give Castle time to swim into our ken again. "It's directly related in this way: in order to make such a culture acceptable it's necessary to suppress some of the most powerful human emotions and motives. Intellect is stultified or diverted into hypnotic meditations, ritualistic incantations, et cetera. The basic needs are sublimated. False needs are created to absorb the energies. Look at India—do you need any clearer proof of the interchangeability of propaganda and progress?

"What we are trying to achieve through our cultural experiments in Walden Two is a way of life which will be satisfying without propaganda and for which, therefore, we won't have to pay the price of personal stultification. Happiness is our first goal, but an alert and active drive toward the future is our second. We'll settle for the degree of happiness which has been achieved in other communities or cultures, but we'll be satisfied with nothing short of the most alert and active group-intelligence yet to appear on the face of the earth."

"'A drive toward the future,'" Castle mumbled,

clearly disappointed with the turn of events. "What's that? Where does that come in? How can we keep up with you when you keep springing something new? How do you know there *is* any future? How can the future play a part in a culture here and now?"

"It doesn't," said Frazier. "I am not going to talk about destiny, any more than about history. The past and the future are both irrelevant. We don't act because of a future, nor because we know there's going to be one. But man changes. It's characteristic of him to discover and to control, and the world doesn't long remain the same once he sets to work. Look at what he has done in spite of the political and economic chaos in which he has always lived. And that characteristic will survive in a successful community. It must survive or less efficient cultures will somehow come out on top."

"You're still saying you avoid propaganda because you seek permanence," I said. "But you haven't proved the connection."

"We should ruin our whole experiment if we over-doctrinated," said Frazier. "You can't propagandize and experiment at the same time. To engineer an attitude in favor of Walden Two would conceal symptoms which are absolutely essential to our psychologists. Happiness is one of our indicators, and we couldn't evaluate an experimental culture if the indicator is loaded with propaganda. It's no mean achievement to build satisfaction in any way whatsoever; but we want the real thing. Walden Two must be *naturally* satisfying."

"I can't see how you can be exactly neutral," I said. "You do point out the advantages of life at Walden Two, I trust. How do you know when to stop? You might as well argue that you ought to propagandize *against* the community."

"We may do so!" said Frazier quickly. "As a means of testing a culture. We should do so with care, of course, but if we could show that our members preferred life in Walden Two in the face of a considerable indoctrination against it, it would be the best possible evidence that we had reached a safe and productive social structure. We'd discontinue the counterpropaganda, of course, after the test was completed."

Castle jarred the bench as he sat down. He was obviously a disturbed and unhappy man. I was a little off balance, too, for this was a new line that I needed time to think over. None of us wanted to continue the discussion, and presently Frazier stood up. At the same moment Steve and Mary appeared around the west end of the building, walking rapidly, arm in arm. They waved their free hands, and the message they were bringing was plain to see. They were in.

25

I WAS constantly amazed by the pleasant atmosphere which prevailed in Walden Two. Superficially, the place resembled a big summer hotel. A large number of people, without homes in the usual sense, with few responsibilities and a good deal of leisure, were brought into contact with each other during a great part of each day. But I remembered the dreary routine of vacation hotel life, the straining after excitement, the desperate struggles with which professional hostesses warded off an ever threatening monotony. None of this was evident in Walden Two. But why not?

I decided to make a little investigation. It was just possible that we were being deceived by a series of conducted tours. We had been invited to wander about the community at will, but most of our time had actually been carefully accounted for. Might there not be some side of Walden Two that we had not been allowed to see? I decided to mingle among the members at tea time and make an impartial sampling of their behavior.

I began at the foot of the Ladder at four o'clock. We were all to meet for dinner and had presumably gone to our rooms to rest. My plan was to stand casually on each stage for exactly five minutes and to eavesdrop upon the occupants. By glancing at my watch from time to time I hoped to convey the impression that I was waiting for someone. I could also time my visit at each stage accurately. This may seem unimportant to the nonprofessional reader, but an objective sampling procedure was practically a compulsion with me.

I would make a very bad detective. I could not shadow a man for ten minutes without collecting a retinue of followers curious to see what I was up to. Just standing around doesn't come natural. I do not claim, therefore, to have been wholly inconspicuous on my little voyage of exploration. But the members of Walden Two are extraordinarily cordial and seem to view the personal idiosyncrasies of others without suspicion. I am satisfied that they did not appreciably alter their conduct because I was shuffling aimlessly about, just a few feet away.

In the first alcove I found a group of men and women in their late forties who could be described with only one word: jolly. Their conversation was a sort of non-malignant gossip—amusing stories of their friends, a convulsing reminiscence of precommunity life, plans for the evening, comment on a young girl who had made her debut in a one-act play in the theater, and so on.

On the second stage, four young men were engaged in an earnest analysis of army discipline and distinction in rank. One of them kept referring to the organization of a Chinese guerrilla army into which he had literally dropped from the skies. My five minutes were up before the superior efficiency of a totally democratic army was explained.

On the third stage all was quiet, except for the story of the Chinese guerrillas, which floated gently over the flowers. Several tea drinkers were watching a game of chess between a young man and a somewhat older woman. Before it was time for me to leave, the woman carefully moved a piece. The young man looked at the board, then at his opponent. He said "Hm" and returned to the board with a deep frown. One of the onlookers conveyed to another his opinion of the best next move, using a sort of sign language which I could not interpret.

On the fourth stage a woman was reading to three little girls who were sipping drinks through straws. A man, sitting with his back to the reader, looking out over the lawn, occasionally turned his head as if he were following the story with great interest. I learned, at the conclusion of the chapter, that he was the author and that later chapters were still to be written. When the reading had come to an end, the children pointed out a section of the flower garden which was the special care of a group to which they belonged. The man and woman commented upon the straightness of the rows and the clever pattern of color.

On the fifth stage I thought I detected a note of discord.

"It's plain luck!" a man was saying. "A heavy rain and the whole thing would've been washed into the pond."

"Why didn't you speak to the Manager?" someone asked.

"I did. And he told me the fellow who had charge of it would be glad to get my advice. But you know those young ones. No telling them anything."

"It came out all right, didn't it?"

"Yes, but that's no way to do, just the same. A heavy rain— It was just plain luck."

"Well, it was your luck, too, wasn't it? You're eating the strawberries."

This remark was greeted with laughter all around, and the conversation which followed was disgustingly jovial.

The next stage was empty. On the next, three attractive young ladies were sipping tea. Speaking without the slightest embarrassment, they asked me to join them. I explained that I had an appointment in five minutes, but would be happy to sit down for a moment. They quickly learned that I was a college professor and began to ask me about my work. Frazier's confounded system of education must have included a study of the techniques of conversation, for they drew me out deftly and began to bear down with a series of embarrassing questions. Why did colleges make their students take examinations, and why did they give grades? What did a grade really mean? When a student "studied" did he do anything more than read and think—or was there something special which no one at Walden Two would know about? Why did the professors lecture to the students? Were the students never expected to do anything except answer questions? Was it true that students were made to read books they were not interested in?

I escaped before my five minutes were up and hurried past the next two stages to make my departure seem convincing. I stopped at an alcove in which a rather large group of tea-drinkers were discussing an article in a news magazine, which had apparently just been read, and was in part occasionally reread, by one of the group.

Impatient with my progress in ferreting out signs of psychological insufficiency, I decided to skip the other stages and have a look at the lounges and reading rooms, which in spite of the fine weather were in use. In the lounges I saw groups similar to those in the Ladder. In one of the reading rooms I became so absorbed in a shelf of books that I forgot my mission. It was a remarkable reference library of technical books, formularies, and so on, apparently for the use of the various Managers and applied scientists. I was quite unaware of such a literature, having supposed that that sort of knowledge existed only in the heads of craftsmen, who imparted it to apprentices.

I recalled the business at hand, and realizing that I had wasted valuable time, I tried to add to my data as rapidly as possible by surveying the Walden Two landscape from one of the windows. In every direction it was possible to find a group or a single individual engaged in some apparently profitable or enjoyable activity. I thought I detected a general homeward movement.

I was without further plans. But I was wholly dissatisfied, and I began to wander aimlessly about. From one of the music rooms came the strains of an excellent string quartet, and eventually I turned in that direction. As I approached, I heard the strong opening chords of the Schumann *Piano Quintet*. I stood for a few moments, with my head bent close to the door.

I was caught unawares as the door opened and several young people came out. One of them, supposing that I had been on the verge of entering, left the door ajar. Inside I could see a number of leather cushions scattered on the floor and other people sprawled about, reading or merely listening. There was a clear space near the door, and I accepted the implied invitation and slipped into the room, dropping upon a cushion as unobtrusively as I could.

The string players were all surprisingly young, but they showed both competence and poise. From where I sat I could see only the feet of the pianist, but it was obvious that he was rather less skillful than his companions. I knew the piano score well enough to detect some clever faking. The total effect was spirited and thoroughly enjoyable. As the end of the first movement approached, the pianist's left foot stamped out the missing accents, the volume mounted, and the tempo, I am bound to record, was accelerated. The end came in a thumping *fortissimo*.

There was a burst of applause, mostly from the players themselves. The pianist threw both hands in the air, jumped to his feet, and shouted "Bravo!"

It was Frazier.

"Thank you! Thank you!" he shouted to the other players. "You're angels! Angels!" He grabbed the pigtail of the second violinist and kissed it with a ceremonious bow. "You were wonderful!" He began to collect the parts. "*Please* let me play it again soon," he said in a childish tone. "If you only knew how much it means to me! And I promise to practice that *bitchy* part in the middle!"

There was a burst of laughter at this bit of verbal license. Frazier tucked the parts into the piano score, climbed over the cello and between the stands, and started for the door. I drew myself down among the cushions, hoping to escape notice.

"Good-bye, good-bye," he called back, as the players began to arrange other music on their stands. Then, dropping his voice, he added, "Hello, Burris. I saw you come in."

I scrambled hastily to my feet and said sheepishly, "Nice going, Frazier. I didn't know you played."

"Rank amateur," he said, shrugging his shoulders and preceding me through the door. "Rank amateur! There are fifty pianists in Walden Two who can play it better. And do, damn them. And do."

On MY way back to my room, walking along the wall of the main building above the flower beds, I came upon a woman of perhaps fifty-five or sixty, sitting in a light deck chair. She wore a plain house dress, and her graying hair was drawn straight back in a simple "bun." Her hands were folded comfortably across her stomach, and she was gazing peacefully across the valley. There was nothing unusual about her appearance, but I stopped in my tracks as if she were a ghost. She had come straight out of my imagination! I actually believed for a moment that I was suffering a hallucination, and I am afraid I also considered the possibility that Frazier was in league with the Prince of Darkness and had materialized my thoughts in some kind of ghastly joke.

What I had been thinking was this: my survey had failed, but perhaps it had not been conducted in the right way. After all, I had made my little expedition at just the time of day when people ought to be happy. There was always the chance that, like the dial, I had recorded only the sunny hours. What should happen if I carried out what was fashionably called a "longitudinal" study—followed some member round the clock?

I had, by now, no illusions regarding my objectivity. I was not out to get the facts; I wanted desperately to find something wrong. Otherwise, I was caught in an intolerable position. I was not ready to subscribe to the Walden Two program, but what was wrong with it? I had to find something. The economics were sound enough, I conceded that. But there was a possibility that the weak point in the whole venture might be too much leisure. The arts and crafts and sports which Frazier had reviewed would supply avocations for many members, particularly those of talent. But what about a typical middle-class housewife? What would she do with eight or ten hours of leisure every day? Would she not be bored? Or restless and ill at ease?

And now, there she sat—the very case I had in mind! And there I stood, transfixed. She was the first to move. She turned and smiled.

"This is my favorite spot," she said. "I love flowers."

"It's a beautiful spot," I agreed.

"I'm glad you like it. You're visiting, aren't you?"

"Yes, we're guests of Mr. Frazier."

"Frazier? Oh, yes. I know who he is. Has a little goatee. A thin man. He thinks too much."

I sat down on the grass, hugging my knees and looking at the flowers.

"What do you think of Walden?" she asked. Like many of the members, she omitted the "Two."

"I think it's fine," I said. "A beautiful spot. And everyone so perfectly happy." My face burned with shame at this obvious maneuver.

"Happy?" she said with evident surprise.

I looked up. Perhaps I had struck something.

"Why, yes. You all seem very happy. Aren't you?"

"It's a funny thing," she said. "I haven't thought about that for a good many years. Why do you ask?"

"Why do I ask? Well, if seems to me it's a pretty important thing to know if you're going to size a place up."

"Why didn't you ask me if we were all well-fed? *There's* something I could of told you. Or whether we were healthy? Though it all comes to the same thing!"

"Why, I can see that you're well-fed and healthy," I said. "I don't need to ask."

"Don't we look happy?"

"But you can't always tell," I said.

"You're kind of a gloomy fellow, aren't you? If you'll pardon me saying so."

"Why do you say that?"

"Oh, wondering are we happy—and things like that.

You're a little like that What-do-you-call-'im—the young
man who comes around to see if you're satisfied with
everything."

"Is there someone who does that?"

"Oh, yes, about once a year maybe. It was a new fellow last time. I had a bit of fun with him."

"What did you do?"

"Well, I shouldn't be telling you this, but he says,
'Have you got any complaints, Mrs. Olson?' and I said,
'If I had, I know where to take them.' The Kitchen
Manager, you know—the woman I work for. 'Well,' he
says, 'is there anything you'd like that you haven't got?'
and I said, 'To tell you the truth, there is.' So he got
out his little black book"—Mrs. Olson laughed explosively—"and he wrote down my name and then he
said, 'Now, Mrs. Olson, tell me what it is.' 'Well,' I
said, 'I've always wanted to look like Greta Garbo!' "
Another explosive laugh. " 'Well,' he said, 'I guess that's
a little out of my line.' He took it fine, I must say."

"What sort of work do you do?" I said.

"Cook. Pastry. Couldn't you tell?"

"What labor-credits do they give you for that kind
of work?"

"Oh, I don't know. I just get out the pies and cakes.
Have some good girls to help me. Mr. Engelbaum,
too."

"What does Mr. Engelbaum do?" I asked.

"Makes pies."

"How long do you work?"

"Oh, till I get the pies and cakes out. Mornings."

"Doesn't that give you a lot of time with nothing
to do?"

"I almost never do nothing. I wasn't doing nothing
when you came up. I was sort of resting."

"What else do you do with your time?"

"Oh, there's my daughter's children and their little
friends. I spend a lot of time with them. I'm teaching
them to cook, just now. Pies and cakes. Watch them

swim, too. Then I have a flower garden this time of year. I love flowers. You can't see my plot from here. I always take one farther down. I like to sit up here in my chair, and I wouldn't want people to think I was sitting and looking at my own garden."

"What else do you do?"

"Well, there's our pinochle club. And sometimes, when we can't go out, we set up the tapestry frame. Beautiful thing. Seven of us working on it. One of the young artist people drew the picture. We use a funny kind of stitch. Never saw anything just like it. Lovely, though."

"You all just sit around and sew on this tapestry?"

"Sewing isn't *all* we do! We talk. There isn't much we don't know about. We get the news quicker than that little paper the young ones publish."

"Is that enough to keep you busy?"

"It doesn't keep me *busy*. I haven't been busy for years. I can come out here any time I like. It's a nice spot, isn't it?"

"It is," I said. "And you're one of the nicest things about it."

She smiled broadly.

"Why don't you come in with us permanent?" she said. "The boys would make you one of these chairs if you asked them to. You could leave it up against the wall there, when you weren't using it, the same as I do. I like to talk to you. And maybe you wouldn't be so gloomy after a little."

I said I could think of nothing nicer and took my leave. My heart had gone out of my longitudinal study. True enough, one case proved nothing. But, damn it all, it was obvious that people could be happy with "nothing to do." Before I reached my room I was quite violent about it. What extraordinary cynicism—this view that nothing but hard labor could prevent boredom! What did we actually know about happiness anyway? Had there ever been enough of it in the world in any one spot and at any one time to suffice for a decent experiment?

Experiment!

Apprehensively I threw open the door of my room. Frazier was not there, but I fancied I smelled brimstone.

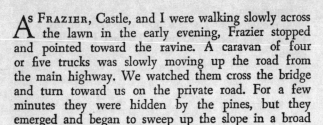

27

As Frazier, Castle, and I were walking slowly across the lawn in the early evening, Frazier stopped and pointed toward the ravine. A caravan of four or five trucks was slowly moving up the road from the main highway. We watched them cross the bridge and turn toward us on the private road. For a few minutes they were hidden by the pines, but they emerged and began to sweep up the slope in a broad arc.

At the same time a group of perhaps a hundred members of Walden Two who had been waiting near the west end of the building swarmed down the road. The trucks slackened speed when they met, and the members ran alongside and exchanged greetings with the dozens of men and women, young and old, who were on board. Many of the latter jumped to the ground, and there were many affectionate embraces.

"The advance guard of Walden Six," said Frazier with calculated casualness. "Here to spend Sunday."

"You mean there's another— Is there a Walden Six?" I said, with all the confusion Frazier could have desired.

"Not a full-fledged community yet," said Frazier. "But it will be, shortly. Walden Two has grown too big, and we're about to undergo fission."

"But 'Six'—do you mean you've already subdivided several times?"

"Unfortunately not. We haven't grown that rapidly. And I'm not sure we could have properly engineered a more rapid growth. We haven't any connection with Waldens Three, Four, or Five, except that they're patterned after our model. Four was founded by one of our members, but it wasn't a case of fission."

"Did you have other Waldens in mind when you started?" I asked.

"Only 'Walden One.' We chose our name in honor

of Thoreau's experiment, which was in many ways like our own. It was an experiment in living, and it sprang from a similar doctrine of our relation to the state. Several ambiguities in the name amused us. Thoreau's was not only the first of the Waldens, it was an experiment with *one* life, and social questions were neglected. Our problem was to build a 'Walden for Two.' There's also a pun on t-double-o—'All this and Walden, too.' " Frazier brushed this nonsense aside with a laugh and continued in all seriousness.

"Four years ago a man on the West Coast started a similar venture and asked if he could call it Walden Three. We could hardly monopolize a borrowed name and, of course, agreed. Walden Three is doing very well, though it has, I think, only two or three hundred members. One of our first Planners started Walden Four not far from the old Oneida country. The Walden Five people heard about the community in the west and asked if they could be 'Four.' We assigned them 'Five.' Somehow we've become proprietors of the system."

"Why don't you set up some overall organization?" said Castle. "A sort of United Communities."

"It might be possible. A planning committee has been suggested to guide us in choosing industries so that we can exchange goods."

"Then you'll have to face the problem of transportation, which you were boasting you had avoided," said Castle, and his triumphant smile made me suspect that his first suggestion had been a trap.

"Quite right," Frazier readily agreed. "Walden Six is only seventy miles away, but the other Waldens are too far apart to make barter worth while."

"Who are these people who've just arrived?" I said.

"They're members of Walden Two who have been working 'on location' since early spring. They're putting up enough buildings to take a skeleton crew through the winter. A year from now, Walden Six will be on its own."

"You mean a new generation moves on to another community, like the birds and bees?" I said.

"Not at all. That would be disastrous. We need members of all ages in each group—to provide for the security of the older members. The cleavage takes place vertically. We haven't worked out the details, but the general plan is clear. The Assistant Managers in Walden Two will become the Managers of Walden Six. Even our Board of Planners will subdivide, and we're adding four new members this fall with that in mind.—But I wanted you to meet our architects. They should have been on the trucks."

We had walked more or less in the direction of the west end of the building, and two or three newcomers approached to shake hands with Frazier. He asked for the architects and was told they had gone to the common rooms. We found them in one of the larger lounges, where they had set up a portable three-dimensional map of Walden Six. They were describing the progress they had made since their last visit. One of them, an attractive young woman with a slight accent which I took to be Viennese, was reporting on a new method of construction.

"It was wonderful," she said. She made a little ring with her thumb and forefinger and held it near her eye. "Everything worked out just right."

Here for the first time in Walden Two we saw a crowd. The room was packed. Frazier tried to force his way toward the architects. When that failed, he tapped one of the listeners on the shoulder and asked him to pass a message along to them. But it was lost en route. Someone turned and shook his head in vague puzzlement. Frazier shrugged his shoulders and walked off toward another lounge. He was out of countenance and remained moodily silent. I tried to come to his rescue.

"Aren't you going to break up a lot of families when you subdivide?" I said as we sat down.

"Not husbands and wives, probably, or parents and young children," he said without enthusiasm. "But otherwise we'll try to break as many as possible. We must soon think about the problem of inbreeding. A few large families in each community wouldn't be advisable from a genetic point of view."

"I should think such separation would be a strong count against your system," said Castle. "Isn't it going to mean plenty of unhappiness?"

"Why should it? After all, the 'Sixers' are only going seventy miles away. Families are separated more than that in the world at large. And we're looking forward to the time when members will move about a good deal from one community to another. That can be easily arranged, because our people are skillful at many jobs and fit in anywhere."

"Won't you be seriously undermanned after subdividing?" I said.

"We may be spread a little thin for a time, but new people will be coming in."

"How fast can you assimilate them?" I said. "Two young people like Steve and Mary will soon be observing the Code like anybody else, but suppose you take in a large crowd at once. What then? Suppose you've just subdivided so that your influence is attenuated. Can you educate and convert fast enough, or will the whole cultural structure slip?"

"That's an experimental question," said Frazier. "We shan't risk the whole venture by trying any large-scale additions—not just yet. We'll probably step up our rate as time goes on. Our psychologists will make a special survey of cultural changes and it won't be difficult to spot trouble long before it has reached serious proportions. We might have to stop immigration for a time. We can accept new members or not, as we like."

"It seems to me that a serious condition might arise without warning," I insisted. "Suppose you take in a family with a fourteen-year-old boy who is an aggressive sexual problem. Meanwhile, you've raised a lot of balanced young people with a healthy attitude toward sex. Isn't the boy going to cause trouble?"

"How? By seducing our girls?"

"Well, yes. Or telling dirty stories, and so on."

Frazier laughed convulsively.

"You put me in a curious position," he said at last. "I must now prove that Virtue is a shield and a buckler. Of course, we shouldn't accept an actual criminal. We can't undertake to act as a reform school. Society has made the criminal and must take care of him. But the usual sexual aggressiveness of the fourteen-year-old is no problem at all. He's immediately thrown on his own and his ties with his family are broken. That removes part of the exciting condition. He finds himself among boys of his own age who are a couple of years more mature. They're more accomplished in the arts and sciences, as well as in the social graces. And they've never found sex amusing or secretly exciting. They know the bodily functions of both sexes, and they're looking forward to marriage within a couple of years. They have brothers and sisters and friends scarcely older than themselves who are married and having children. The first attempt at sexual humor on the part of the new arrival will be the conspicuous failure it deserves to be. It won't cause surprise, because our fourteen-year-olds have been told of the sexual practices of children in society at large. It will simply be classified as a shortcoming—like poor grammar; and a good deal of countereducation will come from the boys themselves."

"What about your girls, though? Aren't you really afraid they'll be harmed by obscenities or attempted seduction?" I insisted.

Frazier laughed again. "You're forgetting the position of the sexes in Walden Two. The fourteen-year-old girl is rather more mature than the boy of the same age. The sexual interest of the newcomer wouldn't surprise or disturb her in the least."

Frazier was unpleasantly self-assured in all this, as

if to compensate for his earlier moodiness, and I has-
tended to change the subject.

"How do you take in a new member? Is there some
sort of legal contract?"

"There's an agreement which guarantees certain rights
to the individual as long as he stays in Walden Two,"
said Frazier, transferring his jauntiness without any difficulty. "In return, the member agrees to work according
to our schedules and not to claim any share in the fruits
of his labor. He may leave at any time, and take with
him the personal possessions he brought. He can't take
anything he has produced in the community. He may
share in that only by staying with us, which he has a
right to do even after he's no longer a productive member."

Suddenly a great many people began to pass the door
of the lounge, and I caught sight of the portable map of
Walden Six as it was carried by. Frazier jumped up
and rushed to the door. He stopped a young woman and
questioned her in a lowered voice. She shook her head,
pointed along the Walk, and hurried on.

"I only wanted them to meet some friends of mine,"
Frazier called after her. He got no answer and returned
to his chair, flushed with embarrassment. This time
Castle came to his rescue.

"I want to hear more about your plans for the future,"
he said. "After all, I've got to look out for the form of
society I prefer. Are you really a threat?"

"I think we'll be a threat, if you look at it in that
light, before many years have passed," said Frazier, again
without enthusiasm. "We'll expand just as fast as we
can assimilate new members and build new plants. If
we required fifteen hundred labor-credits a year, instead
of twelve hundred, we could build new communities
very rapidly. But why should we sacrifice 'the very thing
we're fighting for'?"

"That's a curious statement," said Castle. "I took you
to be a more aggressive reformer."

"I'm aggressive enough," said Frazier, warming up.

"Suppose it's possible to grow and subdivide once every two years. Then in ten years Waldens Two and Six will give birth to some sixty-odd communities."

"Very odd communities," I said, but nobody laughed and Frazier glared at me.

"In *thirty* years," he continued, with increasing determination, "we could absorb the whole country many times over. Evidently you haven't thought through the dynamics of reform, Mr. Castle. Of course, limiting factors will appear. Predictions of that sort are always optimistic. But I see nothing to stop us in the long run. We're using the only technique of conquest which has ever given permanent results: we set an example. We offer a full and happy life to all who go and do likewise.

"The prospect is almost frightening," he continued, "because we may not be ready for the future. We must control the rate at which the idea spreads. Our Office of Information was set up, not to create, but to control publicity. A glowing story of Walden Two would lead to frightful confusion. We couldn't assimilate the converts, and they would get into trouble if they tried to go ahead without the benefit of our scientific practices. Our plan is to stimulate just enough interest to keep new members coming at the right rate. We shall publish a full account of Walden Two in about six months, but it won't be widely circulated until more communities have been established."

"You are unduly optimistic," I said. "Publicity is certainly one thing you can't control. Just let a news magazine get hold of you, and see where your publicity goes."

"We've been afraid of that, but we've managed to avoid it so far. Anyway, it's unlikely that publicity not under our control will be wholly favorable, and hence it won't embarrass us with a flood of converts. Give us five or ten years more and it won't matter. We'll be ready for anything."

"Aren't you confessing to an inner weakness?" said Castle. "After all, the Church managed to set up new groups of believers by sending out single missionaries. It must have meant a more complete conversion than you need here. Why couldn't one person establish 'Walden N'?"

"One could and did, but not as a general rule. One man can't pass along the technical information and skill needed in all our departments. As the science of behavioral engineering advances, less and less is left to personal judgment. More training and apprenticeship are needed. At present we must proceed carefully and train a complete crew of competent managers for each new Walden."

"That sort of compound-interest growth always runs into the problem of crowding," I said. "You will have to start your communities farther and farther apart if they are also to subdivide freely."

"But that will be possible."

"You may not be able to get the land, at least as rapidly as you get the people."

"The real estate problem of a large-scale expansion is interesting," said Frazier fondly. "We don't use a great deal of land per person as agricultural areas go, but you're quite right, we may run into trouble. Farm land is usually passed on from one generation to another. Farmers don't like to sell and seldom are in sufficiently desperate need to do so. We might be forced into offering exorbitant prices, and that would slow down our expansion. But by the time a shortage of land threatens us in any locality, we'll be in a position to exert pressure. If we buy up half the farms which do business in a particular town, we control the town. The feed dealers, hardware stores, and farm machinery salesmen depend on us. We can put them out of business or control them through our trade. The real estate values in the town can be manipulated at will, and the town itself gradually wiped out. We can always use second-hand brick and lumber. Then we can make the area very uncomfortable for noncooperative landowners, because they have lost their channels of supply and distribution. In the long run any increase in the value of the land to us will mean a decrease in the value to anyone else. It's a very different case from the usual real estate boom. We shan't worry about a few stubborn holdouts. We don't need all the land."

"Oh, ho! Oh, ho!" cried Castle. "So you aren't making war! I submit that no monopolist ever had a more ruthless program!"

Frazier was embarrassed. He had been carried away by his dreams, and Castle had caught him off guard.

"It will all depend," he stammered, "on how the program is carried out. We wouldn't deal unfairly with anyone."

"Wait a minute. Wait a minute!" cried Castle. "That's what the Nazis said! Hitler wasn't going to deal unfairly with Poland. Eliminating several million undesirables was all for her greater glory, you remember. The zealot always thinks he knows what's fair, and justifies his aggression accordingly. But ask your feed dealer if he likes the help you're going to give him."

"He could join us," said Frazier.

"But maybe he doesn't *want* to join you. Maybe he just wants to run a successful little feed store which served the farms you have gobbled up and collectivized."

"In such a case we'll simply have to do the best we can—for our conscience' sake as well as to avoid bad public relations," said Frazier. "The man has tied himself up with a moribund competitive society. All we can do is make his personal demise as painless as possible, unless he's intelligent enough to adjust to the new order."

"New order!" cried Castle. "That's another familiar name for the 'improvement' of people who get in your way."

Castle was bouncing in his chair. He seemed to feel that he had found Frazier's weak point at last, and he could scarcely contain himself. Frazier was taking his jibes with growing resentment.

"And I'll bet you have designs on the political machinery too," Castle continued. "You wouldn't always be satisfied with voting the Walden Ticket. You'd want to get the offices yourself, and you'd be strong enough to do it."

"Yes, I must admit you're right. But what's wrong with that? As soon as we're in the majority in any locality, we shall exercise our rights under a democratic form of government and take control."

"But you have several times suggested that you have little faith in democracy," Castle said.

"I will do more than suggest, if you like," said Frazier hotly. "But I am speaking of practical affairs, such as the recovery of taxes in the form of useful services. We have every intention of stepping into democratic politics for purposes of that sort as soon as possible. By reorganizing the local township and county governments we could reduce taxes, recover our own taxes in salaries by putting our own people in office, and at the same time raise the county to our own standards. The school system would naturally fall into our hands, and we might be able to adapt some of the schools to our own use and hence avoid the double taxation of private education. Who could object to that?"

"Almost anyone," said Castle, with unabating excitement. "And the fact that they'd object in vain proves how vicious the system is."

"It's the will of the majority, though," said Frazier. "And while I recognize that that's a form of despotism, we must use it temporarily to achieve a better government for all."

"Before you know it you'll have the Ethiopians wearing shoes!" cried Castle. "O brave new world, indeed!"

Frazier scowled.

"I've been called a Fascist before," he said quietly.

"I'll *bet* you have!" Castle growled.

"It's a convenient way to dispose of any attempt to improve upon a *laissez-faire* democracy," Frazier continued in the same quiet voice.

"And it's a convenient way to describe a form of government, too, I should say," said Castle, with less excitement. He was obviously annoyed that Frazier was unwilling to shout. "What's your answer?"

"I can see no similarity whatsoever between Walden Two and the gangsterdom of a Mussolini or Hitler," said Frazier.

"But you've admitted that it's antidemocratic," Castle insisted. "The people have no voice—"

"The people have all the voice they have any need for. They can accept or protest—and much more effectively than in a democracy, let me add. And we all share equally in the common wealth, which is the intention but not the achievement of the democratic program. Anyone born into Walden Two has a right to any place among us for which he can demonstrate the necessary talent or ability. There are no hereditary preferments of any sort. What you are complaining about is our undemocratic procedure outside the community, and I agree with you that it's despicable. I wish it were possible to act toward the world as we act toward each other. But the world insists that things be done in a different way."

"What about your élite? Isn't that a fascist device?" said Castle. "Isn't it true that your Planners and Managers exercise a sort of control which is denied to the common member?"

"But only because that control is necessary for the proper functioning of the community. Certainly our élite do not command a disproportionate share of the wealth of the community; on the contrary, they work rather harder, I should say, for what they get. 'A Manager's lot is not a happy one.' And in the end the Planner or Manager is demoted to simple citizenship. Temporarily, they have power, in the sense that they run things—but it's limited. They can't compel anyone to obey, for example. A Manager must make a job desirable. He has no slave labor at his command, for our members choose their own work. His power is scarcely worthy of the name. What he has, instead, is a job to be done. Scarcely a privileged class, to my way of thinking."

"There's another point of similarity, though," said Castle. "The successful communities of the past—and I still think comparisons are relevant—have usually had a strong figure at the head. Frequently the community has survived only as long as that leader. No matter what the constitutional structure of your society may be, it's quite possible that you are operating efficiently only because your government is in effect a dictatorship. Your members may be conforming out of submission to a dominating figure, or loyalty to a hero, or simple mesmerism, for that matter. And that's characteristic of Fascism, perhaps more than anything else."

"But who's the dictator here?" said Frazier with what seemed like unbelievable naïveté.

"Why, you, of course," said Castle.

"I?"

"Yes, you were the *primum mobile*, weren't you?"

Frazier smiled.

"I was? Well, I suppose you could say I gave the first push, but I'm not pushing now. There *is* no pushing, that's the point of the whole thing. Set it up right, and it will run by itself."

"Mr. Castle has decided that you are the Midget in the Machine," I said, "and that all the levers and gears we've been looking at during the past few days are so much window dressing."

"And I run it all by personal magnetism?"

"I wasn't entirely serious," said Castle. He was annoyed, but I could not decide whether he resented my reference or felt that his advantage was slipping.

"Have you seen anyone 'Heil Frazier' hereabouts?" said Frazier. "Have you seen any monogrammed F's on our walls or furniture or silver? Have you seen a new *Mein Kampf* in our library? In fact, have you heard anyone even so much as mention me? After all, you don't believe in telepathy, do you? Even Hitler had to come into contact with his people somehow, directly and through symbolic devices and customs. Where's the machinery of my dictatorship?"

"As a matter of fact," I said, "I ran into a woman this afternoon who had some difficulty in placing you when I mentioned your name."

Frazier smiled broadly, and I wondered again whether Mrs. Olson had been planted in my path.

"This is a world without heroes," he said quietly but with great finality. "We have got beyond all that."

"Then you've really created something new under the sun," I said, and Frazier nodded quietly. "Can you think of a single period of history which wasn't dominated by a great figure?" I turned to Castle, who was probably the most capable historian among us, but he merely shook his head absently. "I know there's a modern theory that history can be written without emphasizing personal exploits —the history of ideas, of political philosophies, of movements, and so on. But look how strongly the principle of personal leadership has survived in our own time. This is the century of Lenin, Hitler, Mussolini, Churchill, Roosevelt, Stalin. How can you possibly hope to dispense with so ubiquitous a feature of successful government?"

"A dominant figure in Walden Two is quite unthinkable," said Frazier. "The culture which has emerged from our experiments doesn't require strong personal leadership. On the contrary, it contains several checks and guarantees against it. As I explained before, no one in Walden Two ever acts for the benefit of anyone else except as the agent of the community. Personal favoritism, like personal gratitude, has been destroyed by our cultural engineers. No one is ever in debt to any figure, or any group short of the whole community. That's almost inevitable in a society in which economic preferment is lacking. It's impossible elsewhere.

"We deliberately conceal the planning and managerial machinery to further the same end. I doubt whether there are half a dozen members, aside from the Managers, who can correctly name all six Planners. The Managers are known to the members because they have a more direct responsibility, but they're more likely to be looked upon as servants than masters, although we strive for a neutral attitude.

"For the same reason," Frazier continued, "we discourage any sense of history. The founding of Walden Two is never recalled publicly by anyone who took part in it. No distinction of seniority is recognized. It's very bad taste to refer to oneself as an 'early member.' Give Steve and Mary a week to learn the ropes and you won't be able to tell them from the old-timers. And all personal contributions are either suppressed altogether or made anonymous. A simple historical log of the community is kept by the Legal Manager, but it's not consulted by anyone except Planners and Managers who need information."

"But why go to all that trouble?" said Castle. "Not all the great figures of history have been malevolent dictators. To allow an outstanding figure to emerge isn't necessarily to create a despot. Is there anything wrong with a personal figure?"

"You're slipping, Mr. Castle," said Frazier. "A moment ago it was I who was the Fascist. Yes, there's a great deal wrong with personal figures of any sort. After all, what's the function of the leader—of the hero? Have you ever thought that through? Isn't it to piece out an inadequate science of government? In a pre-scientific society the best the common man can do is pin his faith on a leader and give him his support, trusting in his benevolence against the misuse of the delegated power and in his wisdom to govern justly and to make war successfully. It's the only possible course when government remains an art.

"In the world at large we seldom vote for a principle or a given state of affairs. We vote for a man who pretends to believe in that principle or promises to achieve that state. We don't want a man, we want a condition of peace and plenty—or, it may be, war and want—but we must vote for a man. The leader or hero supplements a faulty science. That's his first function—to use his head and heart where science fails. We have no need for him here. Our Planners act perfectly well in practically complete anonymity.

"But the hero has another function—" Frazier continued. "To rally support, to accumulate power. It is the peculiar and extraordinary function of the hero-despot. The military, economic, and religious powers in the state are pledged to him through loyalty or submissiveness. A Napoleon could retain a substantial power of this sort even after being thoroughly despoiled by his enemies.

" 'The state is power, and the hero is the state!' What a faulty political design! It's true that many states wouldn't have come into existence except through the efforts of a leader. The structure is in that sense natural—but always in early forms of government. Here we have advanced beyond the need for personal figures either as specialists or as devices for holding power.

"No, Mr. Castle. A society which functions for the good of all cannot tolerate the emergence of individual figures. The leader principle has always failed in the long run. On the other hand, a society without heroes has an almost fabulous strength. It's high time that somebody gave it a try."

"Isn't the hero useful in inspiring emulation?" I said. "I can see why you don't want a child to imitate any one adult, but can you really carry through without heroes? What about nonpolitical leaders? Great athletes, for example?"

"We value skill and strength. But we don't value, and we certainly don't emphasize, personal triumph. That's not only unnecessary in a cooperative culture, it's dangerous. Our leaders aren't the men who can defeat the rest of us in battle, and we don't encourage that pattern elsewhere. We have no boxing or wrestling, and no games between teams, except chessmen! Our heroes, if you can call them that, are those who dive with exceeding grace, or polevault at a high setting of the bar. Their achievements are triumphs over nature or over themselves, and they're exactly on a par with our artists and musicians, our dressmakers, our cattle breeders. We don't keep them anonymous because we couldn't, and of course our youngsters imitate them and choose their temporary heroes. But we discourage hero *worship* as much as possible. It's a bad motive because it usually means an unwise choice of goals."

Frazier went to the door again as several people passed by. He called to someone.

"Will you tell Mr. and Mrs. Winton that I'd like to see them when they can spare a moment?" he said. He returned to us with an uncertain step.

"I should think a hero-less Walden Two would suffer by comparison when your young people learn about the great heroes of history," I said.

"We don't teach history," said Frazier. "We don't keep our young people ignorant of it, any more than we keep them ignorant of mycology, or any other subject. They may read all the history they like. But we don't regard it as essential in their education. We don't turn them in that direction and not many take it!"

"But history!" Castle protested. "The history of our country—of the civilization of which we are all a part. How can you neglect anything so important?"

"You're begging the question," said Frazier. "Important for what?"

"Why for the proper education of—a man of culture."

"You're still begging the question."

"Well—" said Castle, who seemed to be unprepared for this turn of affairs, "for perspective, for a detached view."

"Does history give perspective? You might advise a man to go down by the river to see Walden Two in perspective, but he wouldn't see it at all from there. How do we know that distant events are seen more clearly?"

"That's pretty strong," I said. "It's generally admitted that time brings a balanced judgment, a better sense of proportion."

"By falsifying the facts! Any single historical event is too complex to be adequately *known* by anyone. It transcends all the intellectual capacities of men. Our practice is to wait until a sufficient number of details have been forgotten. Of course things seem simpler then! Our memories work that way; we retain the facts which are easiest to think about.

"And that, by the way," Frazier continued, "is another count against the hero-leader—he misrepresents history. The hero, my dear Mr. Castle, is a device which the historian has taken over from the layman. He uses it because he has no scientific vocabulary or technique for dealing with the real facts of history—the opinions, emotions, attitudes; the wishes, plans, schemes; the habits of men. He can't talk about *them*, and so he talks about heroes. But how misleading that is! How inevitable that personal characteristics and private affairs be mixed with the hero type!" Frazier hitched himself up in his chair in a gross gesture of getting control of himself. "But we're getting away from the point," he went on. "I don't care how well historical facts can be known from afar. Is it important to know them at all? I submit that history never even comes close to repeating itself. Even if we had reliable information about the past, we couldn't find a case similar enough to justify inferences about the present or immediate future. We can make no *real* use of history as a current guide. We make a false use of it—an emotive use of it—often enough. No one denies that."

"I can't believe you're serious," said Castle. "Are you saying that you gain no perspective—I mean, no detached opinion—from a sense of history?"

"I mean that and more. Nothing confuses our evaluation of the present more than a sense of history—unless it's a sense of destiny. Your Hitlers are the men who use history to real advantage. It's exactly what they need. It obfuscates every attempt to get a clear appreciation of the present.

"Race, family, ancestor worship—these are the handmaidens of history, and we should have learned to beware of them by now. What we give our young people in Walden Two is a grasp of the *current* forces which a culture must deal with. None of your myths, none of your heroes—no history, no destiny—simply the *Now!* The present is the thing. It's the only thing we can deal with, anyway, in a scientific way. But we've got a long way from the dictator. Have I satisfied you that I have no personal ambitions, Mr. Castle?"

It was rather too rapid a switch, and Castle remained silent.

"What more can I do to convince you?" said Frazier. "What else would you like to know? You're free to study us at your pleasure. Stay as long as you like. You're paying your way, and we don't insist that our guests agree with us. On the contrary, we value an opponent worthy of our steel. If you can smoke out any vestige or threat of Fascism, we shall act at once. And we shall be eternally indebted."

"An anonymous indebtedness, I presume," I said dryly, "with no reference to the future implied in the word 'eternal.'"

"Anonymous, yes," said Frazier, apparently missing my point. "And let Mr. Castle tell us whether that fact alters his present motivation in any essential way. He's not, I'm sure, seeking a personal triumph any more than I." This was ambiguous, but I gave him the benefit of the doubt.

"The whole thing runs counter to a lot of modern psychology," I said. "Personal domination is a powerful motive."

"In a competitive world," said Frazier.

"But of great men, at least, in other respects. The geniuses—"

"Only the geniuses who have been great in the field of personal domination. The rest of us—" Frazier caught himself, but it was too late and he let it stand. Castle indulged in a prodigious smile. "The rest of us—have other motives, equally powerful and better adapted to a successful social structure. The last step in the long evolution of government is to employ unselfish motives where personal domination has always seemed ideally suited, even if always fatal."

Frazier scowled suddenly. I could not decide whether he was recalling his slip or whether he had realized what an extraordinary use of history and destiny he had just made.

"When I die," he went on hastily but in a dramatic manner, "I shall cease to exist—in every sense of the word. A few memories will soon follow me into the crematorium, and there will be no other record left. As a personal figure, I shall be as unidentifiable as my ashes. That's absolutely essential to the success of all the Waldens. No one has ever realized it before."

"But your contribution—the very plan of Walden Two itself—" I said.

"Ah, *that!*" Frazier explained, and there was an unholy gleam in his eye. "That's another story."

He stood up and walked briskly to the door. Castle and I overtook him in the Walk, and we made arrangements for the following day. We reached the passageway which led to Frazier's room and were saying good night when a young man came along the Walk. Frazier stopped him.

"By the way," he said, "whatever happened to the Wintons?"

"I heard they were all going swimming," said the young man.

Frazier looked at us with an embarrassed smile. He shrugged his shoulders and walked off without a word.

28

WELL, is he a Fascist?" I said to Castle as we were dressing on Sunday morning.

"I don't know. And I don't really care. After all, I'm a philosopher. I grant you our friend is extraordinarily skillful in handling practical matters. Not that I agree with much of what he has said—though I'm surprised that I agree with so much. But as a philosopher, I look for the fundamental verities on a different plane. There are some important general questions to be answered before I, for one, will sign on the dotted line. What about the dignity and integrity of the individual? Where does that come in? What about democracy? Frazier has hedged on that several times. And what about personal freedom? And responsibility?"

So far as I was concerned, questions of that sort were valuable mainly because they kept the metaphysicians out of more important fields. But I had respect for Castle's toughness, and I thought it quite possible that in his hands they would lead to profitable discussion.

"Why don't you go after him?" I said.

"Haven't had a chance. We always end up discussing specific processes. Conditioned reflexes, or something like that. The man shies away from a general issue like a colt from a piece of paper in the wind."

"I'd keep that simile to myself," I said. "Frazier might argue that a general issue was indeed no more substantial than a piece of paper in the wind. Or he might take the line of the positivists and contend that it was simply the wind on a piece of paper."

I was pleased with this, but Castle was either not listening or not amused. We finished dressing in silence and a little later made our way to the dining rooms.

Frazier was waiting for us. Rodge and Steve were with him, and the girls turned up shortly. Rodge helped them through the serving room, and it was perhaps this touch of chivalry which prompted Frazier to seat Barbara beside himself with a show of unpracticed manners. Barbara responded by springing into action.

"Thank you," she sang, giving him her number one smile.

Frazier was wearing a crisply pressed linen suit and a colorful bow tie. Barbara fingered the tie familiarly. "What an interesting design!" she said.

"Do you like it?" Frazier said. He turned to the rest of us. "It's from our own looms. We expect to develop quite a little industry along that line."

"You're always so technical," said Barbara, with a pout.

"I'm so sorry!" Frazier said, putting on his manners again. "I'm afraid you've found me rather a bore."

"Oh, no, I've loved every minute of it," said Barbara. "Only—don't you ever find time to just live?"

"Just live? Of course, I live. What do you mean?"

"I mean—well, you have such very scientific thoughts about people." Barbara was looking Frazier straight in the eye and staring him down from time to time.

"Does that make any difference?"

"But what do people seem like to you? Are they really *people?*"

"Why, nothing else, certainly."

"But your personal relations—are you always so— *scientific?*"

"Oh, I see what you mean. No, so far as I know I have experienced all the tender passions, at least as fully as most people."

"But I should be so afraid you were studying me. Or working on me with your theories."

"It's an interesting possibility."

Barbara pouted and then smiled, and Frazier dropped his eyes.

"But I'm afraid I must disappoint you," he said, with a businesslike marshaling of forces. "I have no more interest in you as material for a scientific investigation than if I were, let's say, a medical man, an anatomist." This obviously suggested more to Barbara than Frazier had intended, and he hastened to avoid further misunderstanding. "Do you think the anatomist is always imagining what you would look like when quick-frozen and sliced into nice thin sections, all properly stained?"

Even Frazier saw that this was not good table conversation, especially since most of us were eating some large sections of ham at the time, but he seemed unable to extricate himself. I let him suffer. "I mean to say," he went on rapidly, "that of course the anatomist doesn't—and neither do I—think of you as more than a charming young lady, whom it has been a delight to have as our guest."

This was such a ridiculous piece of behavioral engineering that I laughed aloud. Frazier, his embarrassment rising rapidly, pressed forward.

"Do you see my point?" he said. "It's always possible to behave as a scientist upon occasion, without letting it destroy the pleasure one takes in nature the rest of the time. The botanist can enjoy a flower garden—perhaps that's a better example. Take the botanist. Does his scientific knowledge necessarily interfere . . ."

He struggled on. Barbara was completely at sea and unable to help him. Rodge had turned sullenly to his breakfast. Castle was chuckling into his coffee cup, and Steve and Mary were rubbing ankles under the table. Frazier was in my hands, and I refused to help him.

He made his point half a dozen times under different guises, and eventually his harangue died a natural death. He had thrown in enough flattery to reassure Barbara, and when he turned to her with a final "Do you see?" she exclaimed rather indefinitely, "I'm so terribly glad!"

Frazier apparently had no immediate plans, except the suggestion that we might attend one of the Sunday services. These were already in progress by the time we had finished breakfast. We found that a new service would begin in about twenty minutes and therefore began to wander aimlessly about the Walk and lounges. I called Castle's attention to some of the sculpture which had particularly impressed me, and our group broke up.

A few minutes later, in looking for a portrait head which I especially wanted Castle to see, we entered one of the lounges just in time to hear Barbara saying, "But then why are you still a bachelor?"

She had managed to drift apart with Frazier in tow and was still quizzing him about his personal affairs. I would have admitted to a considerable curiosity along the same line, but of course no such approach was open to me. We retreated too rapidly to catch Frazier's reply, much as I should like to be able to record it here.

We reassembled in time for the service and started toward the theater, but Frazier dropped alongside me and said in a low voice, "Do you really want to hear this?" I shook my head. "Let's drop out then," he said and, taking my arm, turned me about.

"I'd almost forgotten what young ladies are like in a competitive culture," he said with a toss of his head in Barbara's direction. "Most amazing! What's her relation to Rogers? Is that an engagement ring?"

"I'm afraid it is."

"What does Rogers think about Walden Two?"

"He's been dreaming about it for two years, and it's all come true. But I'm afraid he's been dreaming about Barbara, too."

"But that's not such a hard choice, is it?"

"For Rogers it is. It all goes a long way back. They were engaged before Rodge went into the service."

"She's pretty in a physical way, but what does he see in her? I mean, besides sex?"

"I don't know. They both come from good families. They used to be pretty much alike, I suppose."

"Heaven forbid!"

"But Rodge went through the war and Barbara didn't."

"Ah, yes. That makes a difference. But good God, we can't let her catch a man like that! He's a fine fellow."

"I'm afraid he's caught, and caught for good," I said.

"Have you talked with him? Have you pointed out what he's doing? Have you shown him what this will look like ten years from now?"

"I've only let him talk it out a bit," I said.

"Oh, well, then. I must have a word with him."

"It may not do you any good. After all, Barbara's brand of behavioral engineering has a long tradition. And she's pretty skillful, I should imagine. She has some powerful forces under her control that you can't touch."

"Still, I must have a talk with him. We have pretty girls here, too."

We had walked in the direction of the personal rooms. We stopped and Frazier opened a door and waved me in. The room was in confusion. The bed was not only unmade, it looked as if it had not been made for weeks. The top of the desk was littered with books and papers, opened and unopened letters, pencils, a screw driver, a slide rule, and two empty glasses with traces of colored liquid in the bottoms. Books were piled irregularly on the floor in front of a small fireplace, and one pile was topped with a bundle of soiled clothes. Half a dozen canvases on stretchers were stacked against one wall. On the floor near the window stood a large flowerpot in which an unidentifiable plant had long since died of thirst.

Frazier took a pair of soiled pajamas from a small straight chair and urged me to sit down.

"In Walden Two," he said, as he dropped into an ancient swivel chair at his desk, "a man's room is his castle."

I surveyed the ruins in silence.

"I'm a curious study in opposites," Frazier went on. "The precision and order in my thinking is equaled only by the fantastic disorder of my personal habits. And since one's room is inviolate in Walden Two, behold the result! Elsewhere a certain neatness is mandatory. We hope that our children will naturally live in good order. But it's too much for some of us to achieve at this age. I can't put a book back when I'm through using it, and I've stopped trying—unless I'm working in one of the libraries, of course!"

I pulled out the remains of my pack of cigarettes and offered one to Frazier.

"Go ahead!" he said, passing me one of the glasses, which was apparently to serve as ash tray. "I don't smoke."

I straightened out a battered cigarette, tapped it firm, and lighted it.

"Well, what do you think of Walden Two?" Frazier said at last. I had felt the question coming, but it jarred me unpleasantly even so.

"I don't know," I said. "What should I think?"

"Well, is it working?"

"Admirably, I should say."

"Good. I thought you wouldn't be stupid enough to doubt that. Of course it's working. And what do you think of the life of the average member? Is it satisfying?"

"So far as I can see, you are all perfectly happy. I must confess that I made a little survey yesterday—"

"I heard about it," said Frazier impatiently. "But what about yourself? Have you any personal goal that wouldn't be more easily within reach here than at the University?"

"I don't know, Frazier. I really don't. I won't say I'm very happy about my academic life, but I'm not sure that all my motives are on the surface. How can I be sure that a very different kind of life will satisfy me at all?"

"There are some things we can't offer you, I'll admit," Frazier said. "But they aren't important. Is there really any choice in the matter?"

"I can only say," I said, resenting this shameless prose-lytizing, "that at the moment I'm not sold. There's a certain resistance—I can only be honest and tell you so. I don't know why. I'm not going to cook up reasons."

"Castle will be doing that," Frazier said. "You can borrow reasons from him. He'll have plenty. It's merely an emotional attitude, then?"

"I suppose so."

Frazier had been toying with some yellow tiles, about the size and shape of bread sticks, which lay in a small clearing in the middle of his desk. He saw that I was curious and explained that they were samples of a local clay, fired in different ways which were identified by numbers scratched on the surface. He tossed one of the tiles lightly in the air.

"How much of your attitude toward Walden Two," he said, "is really your attitude toward me?"

The question surprised me and I had no answer. Frazier rapped the tile with his knuckles and listened to its dull ring.

"It's better to get these things out into the open," he went on.

I could say nothing.

"Quite frankly, Burris, why do you dislike me?"

"Oh, I don't," I said, without being able to put much force into my words. "I think you've done a remarkable job."

"Job, yes. But you dislike me just the same. Isn't that true?"

I said nothing.

"You think I'm conceited, aggressive, tactless, selfish. You're convinced that I'm completely insensitive to my effect upon others, except when the effect is calculated. You can't see in me any of the personal warmth or the straightforward natural strength which are responsible for the success of Walden Two. My motives are ulterior and devious, my emotions warped. In a word—of all the people you've seen in the past four days, you're sure that I'm *one*, at least, who couldn't possibly be a genuine member of any community."

I still found nothing to say. It was as if Frazier were snatching the words away as I reached for them. He accepted my silence as assent.

"Well, you're perfectly right," he said quietly. Then he stood up, drew back his arm, and sent the tile shattering into the fireplace.

"But God *damn* it, Burris!" he cried, timing the "damn" to coincide with the crash of the tile. "Can't you see? *I'm—not—a—product—of—Walden—Two!*" He sat down. He looked at his empty hand, and picked up a second tile quickly, as if to conceal the evidence of his display of feeling.

"How much can you ask of a man?" he continued, looking at me earnestly. "Give me credit for what I've done or not, as you please, but don't look for perfection. Isn't it enough that I've made other men likable and happy and productive? Why expect me to resemble them? Must I possess the virtues which I've proved to be best suited to a well-ordered society? Must I exhibit the interests and skills and untrammeled spirit which I've learned how to engender in others? Must I wear them all like a damned manikin? After all, emulation isn't the only principle in education—all the saints to the contrary. Must the doctor share the health of his patient? Must the icthyologist swim like a fish? Must the maker of firecrackers pop?"

"We expect the physician to heal himself, I suppose," I said.

"I know of no remedy, and I'd be in no position to administer it if I did. I can keep myself acceptable to the community, as all who stay with us must. I ask no leniency in return for my part as founder. But there's never a complete rebirth. There's never total conversion. The final social structure we're working toward must wait for those who have had a full Walden Two heritage. They will come, never fear, and the rest of us will pass on to a well-deserved oblivion—the pots that were marred in making."

He picked up a piece of the tile which had caromed back from the fireplace and began to finger it idly. Suddenly he laughed.

"Shall we say that as a person I'm a complete failure, and have done with it? All right. Then what of Walden Two? Is it any the less real, any the less successful? Are its principles in any way challenged?"

He had begun to scrutinize the fragment in his hand more closely, running his finger along a sharp edge.

"No, Burris," he said. "You can safely leave me out. Forget me, and turn your face on heaven."

He stepped quickly to the fireplace and poked about among the fragments of tile. He seemed to be unable to locate something and returned to his desk to look at the identifying numbers on the remaining tiles.

"It must have been number seven," he said quietly. He held the fragment up to the light. "A remarkably sharp fracture," he said. "I must make a note of that."

29

C ASTLE got his chance to take up "general issues" that afternoon. A walk to the summit of Stone Hill had been planned for a large party, which included Mr. and Mrs. Meyerson and three or four children. It seemed unlikely that any serious discussion would be possible. But a storm had been threatening all morning, and at lunch we heard it break. The afternoon was again open. I detected a certain activity in the dining room as plans were changed. As we were finishing dinner, two young people approached our table and spoke to Rodge, Steve, and the girls.

"Do you play? Cornet, sax, trombone? We're getting up a concert. We even have a lonely tuba."

"You play, Steve," said Mary.

"Steve was the best little old trombone in the Philippines," said Rodge.

"Good! Anybody else? It's strictly amateur."

It appeared that Barbara could play popular tunes on the piano, mostly by ear, and it was thought that something might be arranged. They departed for the theater to look over the common stock of instruments, and Frazier, Castle, and I were left alone.

Castle immediately began to warm up his motors. He picked up an empty cigarette package which Barbara had left on the table, tore it in two, placed the halves together, and tore them again. Various husky noises issued from his throat. It was obvious that something was about to happen, and Frazier and I waited in silence.

"Mr. Frazier," Castle said at last, in a sudden roar, "I accuse you of one of the most diabolical machinations in the history of mankind!" He looked as steadily as possible at Frazier, but he was trembling, and his eyes were popping.

"Shall we go to my room?" Frazier said quietly.

It was a trick of Frazier's to adopt a contrasting tone of voice, and in this instance it was devastating. Castle came down to earth with a humiliating bump. He had prepared himself for a verbal battle of heroic dimensions, but he found himself humbly carrying his tray to the service window and trailing Frazier along the Walk.

I was not sure of the line Castle was going to take. Apparently he had done some thinking since morning, probably during the service, but I could not guess the result. Frazier's manner was also puzzling. His suggestion that we go to his room had sounded a little as if he were inviting a truculent companion to "step outside and say that again!" He had apparently expected the attack from Castle and had prepared the defenses to his satisfaction.

When we had settled ourselves in Frazier's room, with Frazier full-length on the bed, over which he had hastily pulled a cover, Castle began again in an unsuccessful attempt to duplicate the surprise and force of his first assault.

"A modern, mechanized, managerial Machiavelli—that is my final estimate of you, Mr. Frazier," he said, with the same challenging stare.

"It must be gratifying to know that one has reached a 'final estimate,'" said Frazier.

"An artist in power," Castle continued, "whose greatest art is to conceal art. The silent despot."

"Since we are dealing in 'M's,' why not sum it all up and say 'Mephistophelian'?" said Frazier, curiously reviving my fears of the preceding afternoon.

"I'm willing to do that!" said Castle. "And unless God is very sure of himself, I suspect He's by no means easy about this latest turn in the war of the angels. So far as I can see, you've blocked every path through which man was to struggle upward toward salvation. Intelligence, initiative—you have filled their places with a sort of degraded instinct, engineered compulsion. Walden Two is a marvel of efficient coordination—as efficient as an ant-hill!"

"Replacing intelligence with instinct—" muttered Frazier. "I had never thought of that. It's an interesting possibility. How's it done?" It was a crude maneuver. The question was a digression, intended to spoil Castle's timing and to direct our attention to practical affairs in which Frazier was more at home.

"The behavior of your members is carefully shaped in advance by a Plan," said Castle, not to be taken in, "and it's shaped to perpetuate that Plan. Intellectually Walden Two is quite as incapable of a spontaneous change of course as the life within a beehive."

"I see what you mean," said Frazier distantly. But he returned to his strategy. "And have you discovered the machinery of my power?"

"I have, indeed. We were looking in the wrong place. There's no *current* contact between you and the members of Walden Two. You threw us off the track very skillfully on that point last night. But you were behaving as a despot when you first laid your plans—when you designed the social structure and drew up the contract between community and member, when you worked out your educational practices and your guarantees against despotism—What a joke! Don't tell me you weren't in control *then!* Burris saw the point. What about your career as organizer? *There* was leadership! And the most damnable leadership in history, because you were setting the stage for the withdrawal of yourself as a personal force, knowing full well that everything that happened would still be your doing. Hundreds—you predicted millions—of unsuspecting souls were to fall within the scope of your ambitious scheme."

Castle was driving his argument home with great excitement, but Frazier was lying in exaggerated relaxation, staring at the ceiling, his hands cupped behind his head.

"Very good, Mr. Castle," he said softly. "I gave you the clue, of course, when we parted last night."

"You did, indeed. And I've wondered why. Were you led into that fatal error by your conceit? Perhaps that's the ultimate answer to your form of despotism. No one could enjoy the power you have seized without wishing to display it from time to time."

"I've admitted neither power nor despotism. But you're

quite right in saying that I've exerted an influence and in one sense will continue to exert it forever. I believe you called me a *primum mobile*—not quite correctly, as I found upon looking the term up last night. But I did plan Walden Two—not as an architect plans a building, but as a scientist plans a long-term experiment, uncertain of the conditions he will meet but knowing how he will deal with them when they arise. In a sense, Walden Two is predetermined, but not as the behavior of a beehive is determined. Intelligence, no matter how much it may be shaped and extended by our educational system, will still function as intelligence. It will be used to puzzle out solutions to problems to which a beehive would quickly succumb. What the plan does is to keep intelligence on the right track, for the good of society rather than of the intelligent individual—or for the eventual rather than the immediate good of the individual. It does this by making sure that the individual will not forget his personal stake in the welfare of society."

"But you are forestalling many possibly useful acts of intelligence which aren't encompassed by your plan. You have ruled out points of view which may be more productive. You are implying that T. E. Frazier, looking at the world from the middle of the twentieth century, understands the best course for mankind forever."

"Yes, I suppose I do."

"But that's absurd!"

"Not at all. I don't say I foresee the course man will take a hundred years hence, let alone forever, but I know which he should take now."

"How can you be sure of it? It's certainly not a question you have answered experimentally."

"I think we're in the course of answering it," said Frazier. "But that's beside the point. There's no alternative. We must take that course."

"But that's fantastic. You who are taking it are in a small minority."

Frazier sat up.

"And the majority are in a big quandary," he said.

"They're not on the road at all, or they're scrambling back toward their starting point, or sidling from one side of the road to the other like so many crabs. What do you think two world wars have been about? Something as simple as boundaries or trade? Nonsense. The world is trying to adjust to a new conception of man in relation to men."

"Perhaps it's merely trying to adjust to despots whose ideas are incompatible with the real nature of man."

"Mr. Castle," said Frazier very earnestly, "let me ask you a question. I warn you, it will be the most terrifying question of your life. *What would you do if you found yourself in possession of an effective science of behavior?* Suppose you suddenly found it possible to control the behavior of men as you wished. What would you do?"

"That's an assumption?"

"Take it as one if you like. *I* take it as a fact. And apparently you accept it as a fact too. I can hardly be as despotic as you claim unless I hold the key to an extensive practical control."

"What would I do?" said Castle thoughtfully. "I think I would dump your science of behavior in the ocean."

"And deny men all the help you could otherwise give them?"

"And give them the freedom they would otherwise lose forever!"

"How could you give them freedom?"

"By refusing to control them!"

"But you would only be leaving the control in other hands."

"Whose?"

"The charlatan, the demagogue, the salesman, the ward heeler, the bully, the cheat, the educator, the priest —all who are now in possession of the techniques of behavioral engineering."

"A pretty good share of the control would remain in the hands of the individual himself."

"That's an assumption, too, and it's your only hope. It's your only possible chance to avoid the implications of a science of behavior. If man is free, then a technology of behavior is impossible. But I'm asking you to consider the other case."

"Then my answer is that your assumption is contrary to fact and any further consideration idle."

"And your accusations—?"

"—were in terms of intention, not of possible achievement."

Frazier sighed dramatically.

"It's a little late to be proving that a behavioral technology is well advanced. How can you deny it? Many of its methods and techniques are really as old as the hills. Look at their frightful misuse in the hands of the Nazis! And what about the techniques of the psychological clinic? What about education? Or religion? Or practical politics? Or advertising and salesmanship? Bring them all together and you have a sort of rule-of-thumb technology of vast power. No, Mr. Castle, the science is there for the asking. But its techniques and methods are in the wrong hands—they are used for personal aggrandizement in a competitive world or, in the case of the psychologist and educator, for futilely corrective purposes. My question is, have you the courage to take up and wield the science of behavior for the good of mankind? You answer that you would dump it in the ocean!"

"I'd want to take it out of the hands of the politicians and advertisers and salesmen, too."

"And the psychologists and educators? You see, Mr. Castle, you can't have that kind of cake. The fact is, we not only *can* control human behavior, we *must*. But who's to do it, and what's to be done?"

"So long as a trace of personal freedom survives, I'll stick to my position," said Castle, very much out of countenance.

"Isn't it time we talked about freedom?" I said. "We parted a day or so ago on an agreement to let the question of freedom ring. It's time to answer, don't you think?"

"My answer is simple enough," said Frazier. "I deny that freedom exists at all. I must deny it—or my program would be absurd. You can't have a science about a subject matter which hops capriciously about. Perhaps we can never *prove* that man isn't free; it's an assumption. But the increasing success of a science of behavior makes it more and more plausible."

"On the contrary, a simple personal experience makes it untenable," said Castle. "The experience of freedom. I *know* that I'm free."

"It must be quite consoling," said Frazier.

"And what's more—you do, too," said Castle hotly. "When you deny your own freedom for the sake of playing with a science of behavior, you're acting in plain bad faith. That's the only way I can explain it." He tried to recover himself and shrugged his shoulders. "At least you'll grant that you *feel* free."

"The 'feeling of freedom' should deceive no one," said Frazier. "Give me a concrete case."

"Well, right now," Castle said. He picked up a book of matches. "I'm free to hold or drop these matches."

"You will, of course, do one or the other," said Frazier. "Linguistically or logically there seem to be two possibilities, but I submit that there's only one in fact. The determining forces may be subtle but they are inexorable. I suggest that as an orderly person you will probably hold —ah! you drop them! Well, you see, that's all part of your behavior with respect to me. You couldn't resist the temptation to prove me wrong. It was all lawful. You had no choice. The deciding factor entered rather late, and naturally you couldn't foresee the result when you first held them up. There was no strong likelihood that you would act in either direction, and so you said you were free."

"That's entirely too glib," said Castle. "It's easy to argue lawfulness after the fact. But let's see you predict what I will do in advance. Then I'll agree there's law."

"I didn't say that behavior is always predictable, any more than the weather is always predictable. There are often too many factors to be taken into account. We can't measure them all accurately, and we couldn't perform the mathematical operations needed to make a prediction if we had the measurements. The legality is usually an assumption—but none the less important in judging the issue at hand."

"Take a case where there's no choice, then," said Castle. "Certainly a man in jail isn't free in the sense in which I am free now."

"Good! That's an excellent start. Let us classify the kinds of determiners of human behavior. One class, as you suggest, is physical restraint—handcuffs, iron bars, forcible coercion. These are ways in which we shape human behavior according to our wishes. They're crude, and they sacrifice the affection of the controllee, but they often work. Now, what other ways are there of limiting freedom?"

Frazier had adopted a professorial tone and Castle refused to answer.

"The threat of force would be one," I said.

"Right. And here again we shan't encourage any loyalty on the part of the controllee. He has perhaps a shade more of the feeling of freedom, since he can always 'choose to act and accept the consequences,' but he doesn't feel exactly free. He knows his behavior is being coerced. Now what else?"

I had no answer.

"Force or the threat of force—I see no other possibility," said Castle after a moment.

"Precisely," said Frazier.

"But certainly a large part of my behavior has no connection with force at all. There's my freedom!" said Castle.

"I wasn't agreeing that there was no other possibility —merely that *you* could see no other. Not being a good behaviorist—or a good Christian, for that matter—you have no feeling for a tremendous power of a different sort."

"What's that?"

"I shall have to be technical," said Frazier. "But only for a moment. It's what the science of behavior calls 'reinforcement theory.' The things that can happen to us fall into three classes. To some things we are indifferent. Other things we like—we want them to happen, and we take steps to make them happen again. Still other things we don't like—we don't want them to happen and we take steps to get rid of them or keep them from happening again.

"*Now,*" Frazier continued earnestly, "if it's in our power to create any of the situations which a person likes or to remove any situation he doesn't like, we can control his behavior. When he behaves as we want him to behave, we simply create a situation he likes, or remove one he doesn't like. As a result, the probability that he will behave that way again goes up, which is what we want. Technically it's called 'positive reinforcement.'

"The old school made the amazing mistake of supposing that the reverse was true, that by removing a situation a person likes or setting up one he doesn't like—in other words by punishing him—it was possible to *reduce* the probability that he would behave in a given way again. That simply doesn't hold. It has been established beyond question. What is emerging at this critical stage in the evolution of society is a behavioral and cultural technology based on positive reinforcement alone. We are gradually discovering—at an untold cost in human suffering —that in the long run punishment doesn't reduce the probability that an act will occur. We have been so preoccupied with the contrary that we always take 'force' to mean punishment. We don't say we're using force when we send shiploads of food into a starving country, though we're displaying quite as much *power* as if we were sending troops and guns."

"I'm certainly not an advocate of force," said Castle. "But I can't agree that it's not effective."

"It's *temporarily* effective, that's the worst of it. That explains several thousand years of bloodshed. Even nature has been fooled. We 'instinctively' punish a person who doesn't behave as we like—we spank him if he's a child or strike him if he's a man. A nice distinction! The immediate effect of the blow teaches us to strike again. Retribution and revenge are the most natural things on earth. But in the long run the man we strike is no less likely to repeat his act."

"But he won't repeat it if we hit him hard enough," said Castle.

"He'll still *tend* to repeat it. He'll *want* to repeat it. We haven't really altered his potential behavior at all. That's the pity of it. If he doesn't repeat it in our presence, he will in the presence of someone else. Or it will be repeated in the disguise of a neurotic symptom. If we hit hard enough, we clear a little place for ourselves in the wilderness of civilization, but we make the rest of the wilderness still more terrible.

"Now, early forms of government are naturally based on punishment. It's the obvious technique when the physically strong control the weak. But we're in the throes of a great change to positive reinforcement—from a competitive society in which one man's reward is another man's punishment, to a cooperative society in which no one gains at the expense of anyone else.

"The change is slow and painful because the immediate, temporary effect of punishment overshadows the eventual advantage of positive reinforcement. We've all seen countless instances of the temporary effect of force, but clear evidence of the effect of not using force is rare. That's why I insist that Jesus, who was apparently the first to discover the power of refusing to punish, must have hit upon the principle by accident. He certainly had none of the experimental evidence which is available to us today, and I can't conceive that it was possible, no matter what the man's genius, to have discovered the principle from casual observation."

"A touch of revelation, perhaps?" said Castle.

"No, accident. Jesus discovered one principle because it had immediate consequences, and he got another thrown in for good measure."

I began to see light.

"You mean the principle of 'love your enemies'?" I said.

"Exactly! To 'do good to those who despitefully use you' has two unrelated consequences. You gain the peace of mind we talked about the other day. Let the stronger man push you around—at least you avoid the torture of your own rage. *That's* the immediate consequence. What an astonishing discovery it must have been to find that in the long run you could *control the stronger man* in the same way!"

"It's generous of you to give so much credit to your early colleague," said Castle, "but why are we still in the throes of so much misery? Twenty centuries should have been enough for one piece of behavioral engineering."

"The conditions which made the principle difficult to discover made it difficult to teach. The history of the Christian Church doesn't reveal many cases of doing good to one's enemies. To inoffensive heathens, perhaps, but not enemies. One must look outside the field of organized religion to find the principle in practice at all. Church governments are devotees of *power*, both temporal and bogus."

"But what has all this got to do with freedom?" I said hastily.

Frazier took time to reorganize his behavior. He looked steadily toward the window, against which the rain was beating heavily.

"Now that we *know* how positive reinforcement works and why negative doesn't," he said at last, "we can be more deliberate, and hence more successful, in our cultural design. We can achieve a sort of control under which the controlled, though they are following a code much more scrupulously than was ever the case under the old system, nevertheless *feel free*. They are doing what they want to do, not what they are forced to do. That's the source of the tremendous power of positive reinforcement—there's no restraint and no revolt. By a careful cultural design, we control not the final behavior, but the *inclination* to behave—the motives, the desires, the wishes.

"The curious thing is that in that case the *question of freedom never arises.* Mr. Castle was free to drop the matchbook in the sense that nothing was preventing him. If it had been securely bound to his hand he wouldn't have been free. Nor would he have been quite free if I'd covered him with a gun and threatened to shoot him if he let it fall. The question of freedom arises when there is restraint—either physical or psychological.

"But restraint is only one sort of control, and absence of restraint isn't freedom. It's not control that's lacking when one feels 'free,' but the objectionable control of force. Mr. Castle felt free to hold or drop the matches in the sense that he felt no restraint—no threat of punishment in taking either course of action. He neglected to examine his positive reasons for holding or letting go, in spite of the fact that these were more compelling in this instance than any threat of force.

"We have no vocabulary of freedom in dealing with what we want to do," Frazier went on. "The question never arises. When men strike for freedom, they strike against jails and the police, or the threat of them—against oppression. They never strike against forces which make them want to act the way they do. Yet, it seems to be understood that governments will operate only through force or the threat of force, and that all other principles of control will be left to education, religion, and commerce. If this continues to be the case, we may as well give up. A government can never create a free people with the techniques now allotted to it.

"The question is: Can men live in freedom and peace? And the answer is: Yes, if we can build a social structure which will satisfy the needs of everyone and in which everyone will want to observe the supporting code. But so far this has been achieved only in Walden Two. Your ruthless accusations to the contrary, Mr. Castle, this is the freest place on earth. And it is free precisely because we make no use of force or the threat of force. Every bit of our research, from the nursery through the psychological management of our adult membership, is directed toward that end—to exploit every alternative to forcible control. By skillful planning, by a wise choice of techniques we *increase* the feeling of freedom.

"It's not planning which infringes upon freedom, but planning which uses force. A sense of freedom was practically unknown in the planned society of Nazi Germany, because the planners made a fantastic use of force and the threat of force.

"No, Mr. Castle, when a science of behavior has once been achieved, there's no alternative to a planned society. We can't leave mankind to an accidental or biased control. But by using the principle of positive reinforcement—carefully avoiding force or the threat of force—we can preserve a personal sense of freedom."

Frazier threw himself back upon the bed and stared at the ceiling.

"But you haven't denied that you are in complete control," said Castle. "You are still the long-range dictator."

"As you will," said Frazier, waving his hands loosely in the air and then cupping them behind his head. "In fact, I'm inclined to agree. When you have once grasped the principle of positive reinforcement, you can enjoy a sense of unlimited power. It's enough to satisfy the thirstiest tyrant."

"There you are, then," said Castle. "That's my case."

"But it's a limited sort of despotism," Frazier went on. "And I don't think anyone should worry about it. The despot must wield his power for the good of others. If he takes any step which reduces the sum total of human happiness, his power is reduced by a like amount. What better check against a malevolent despotism could you ask for?"

"The check I ask for," said Castle, "is nothing less than democracy. Let the people rule and power will not be misused. I can't see that the nature of the power matters. As a matter of fact, couldn't this principle of 'positive reinforcement,' as you call it, be used by a democratic government just as well as by your dictatorship?"

"No principle is consistently used by a democratic government. What do you mean by democracy, anyway?"

"Government by the people or according to the will of the people, naturally," said Castle.

"As exemplified by current practices in the United States?"

"I suppose so. Yes, I'll take my stand on that. It's not a perfect democracy, but it's the best there is at the moment."

"Then I say that democracy is a pious fraud," said Frazier. "In what sense is it 'government by the people'?"

"In an obvious sense, I should say."

"It isn't obvious at all. How is the people's will ascertained? In an election. But what a travesty! In a small committee meeting, or even a town hall, I can see some point in voting, especially on a yes-or-no question. But fifty million voters choosing a president—that's quite another thing."

"I can't see that the number of voters changes the principle," said Castle.

"The chance that one man's vote will decide the issue in a national election," said Frazier, speaking very deliberately, "is less than the chance that he will be killed on his way to the polls. We pay no attention whatsoever to chances of that magnitude in our daily affairs. We should call a man a fool who bought a sweepstakes ticket with similar odds against him."

"It must mean something or people wouldn't vote," said Castle.

"How many of them would go on voting if they were free of a lot of extraneous pressures? Do you think a man goes to the polls because of any effect which casting a vote has ever had? By no means. He goes to avoid being talked about by his neighbors, or to 'knife' a candidate whom he dislikes, marking his X as he might defile a campaign poster—and with the same irrational spite. No, a man has no logical reason to vote whatsoever. The chances of affecting the issue are too small to alter his behavior in any appreciable way."

"I believe the mathematicians have a name for that fallacy," said Castle. "It's true that your chances of deciding the issue get smaller as the number of voters increases, but the stakes get larger at the same rate."

"But do they? Is a national election really an important issue? Does it really matter very much who wins? The platforms of the two parties are carefully made as much alike as possible, and when the election is over we're all advised to accept the result like good sports. Only a few voters go on caring very much after a week or two. The rest know there's no real threat. Things will go on pretty much the same. Elections are sometimes turned by a few million voters who can't make up their minds until election day. It can't be much of an issue if that's the case."

"Even so, it's important that the people *feel* they've chosen the government they want," said Castle.

"On the contrary, that's the worst of it. Voting is a device for blaming conditions on the people. The people aren't rulers, they're scapegoats. And they file to the polls every so often to renew their right to the title."

"I daresay there are defects in the machinery of democracy," said Castle. "No one wholly approves of the average presidential campaign. The will of the people is likely to be unduly influenced, and perhaps incorrectly determined. But that's a matter of technique. I think we will eventually work out a better system for ascertaining what the people want done. Democracy isn't a method of polling opinion, it's the assignment of power to that opinion. Let's assume that the will of the people can be ascertained. What then?"

"I should ask you that. What then, indeed? Are the people skilled governors? No. And they become less and less skilled, relatively speaking, as the science of government advances. It's the same point I raised in our discussion of the group nursery: when we've once acquired a behavioral technology, we can't leave the control of behavior to the unskilled. Your answer is to deny that the technology exists—a very feeble answer, it seems to me.

"The one thing the people know," Frazier continued, "and the one thing about which they should be heard is how they like the existing state of affairs, and perhaps how they would like some other state of affairs. What they conspicuously don't know is how to get what they want. That's a matter for specialists."

"But the people have solved some pretty important problems," I said.

"Have they, in fact? The actual practice in a democracy is to vote, not for a given state of affairs, but for a man who claims to be able to achieve that state. I'm not a historian"—Frazier laughed explosively—"quite the contrary—but I suspect that that's always what is meant by the rule of the people—rule by a man chosen by the people."

"Isn't that a possible way out, though?" said Castle. "Suppose we need experts. Why not elect them?"

"For a very simple reason. The people are in no position to evaluate experts. And elected experts are never able to act as they think best. They can't experiment. The amateur doesn't appreciate the need for experimentation. He wants his expert to *know*. And he's utterly incapable of sustaining the period of doubt during which an experiment works itself out. The experts must either disguise their experiments and pretend to know the outcome in advance or stop experimenting altogether and struggle to maintain the *status quo*."

"'With all her faults, I love her still,'" said Castle. "I'll take democracy. We may have to muddle through. We may seem laughable to your streamlined Planners. But we have one thing on our side—freedom."

"I thought we had settled that," said Frazier.

"We had. But apparently not as you thought," said Castle. "I don't like despotism."

Frazier got up and went to the window. The rain had stopped, and the distant hills beyond the river had become visible. He stood with his back to us for perhaps a minute, which seemed very long against the energetic tempo of our conversation. Finally he turned.

"Can't I make you understand?" he said, holding out his hands in a gesture of appeal. "*I don't like despotism either!* I don't like the despotism of ignorance. I don't like the despotism of neglect, of irresponsibility, the despotism of accident, even. And I don't like the despotism of democracy!"

He turned back to the window.

"I don't think I follow you," said Castle, somewhat softened by Frazier's evident emotion.

"Democracy is the spawn of despotism," Frazier said, continuing to look out the window. "And like father, like son. Democracy is power and rule. It's not the will of the people, remember; it's the will of the majority." He turned and, in a husky voice which broke in flight like a tumbler pigeon on the word "out," he added, "My heart goes out to the everlasting minority." He seemed ready to cry, but I could not tell whether it was in sympathy for the oppressed or in rage at his failure to convince Castle.

"In a democracy," he went on, "there is *no* check against despotism, because the principle of democracy is supposed to be itself a check. But it guarantees only that the *majority* will not be despotically ruled."

"I don't agree that the minority has no say," said Castle. "But in any case it's better that at least half the people get what they want, instead of a small élite."

"There you are!" said Frazier, jumping up again just as he had started to sit down. "The majority are an élite. And they're despots. I want none of them! Let's have government for the benefit of all."

"But that isn't always possible," said Castle.

"It's possible much oftener than under a democracy. There are seldom any issues which have to be decided in an all-or-none fashion. A careful planner could work out a compromise which would be reasonably satisfying to everyone. But in a democracy, the majority solve the problem to their satisfaction, and the minority can be damned.

"The government of Walden Two," he continued, "has the virtues of democracy, but none of the defects. It's much closer to the theory or intent of democracy than the actual practice in America today. The will of the people is carefully ascertained. We have no election campaigns to falsify issues or obscure them with emotional appeals, but a careful study of the satisfaction of the membership is made. Every member has a direct channel through which he may protest to the Managers or even the Planners. And these protests are taken as seriously as the pilot of an airplane takes a sputtering engine. We don't need laws and a police force to compel a pilot to pay attention to a defective engine. Nor do we need laws to compel our Dairy Manager to pay attention to an epidemic among his cows. Similarly, our Behavioral and Cultural Managers need not be compelled to consider grievances. A grievance is a wheel to be oiled, or a broken pipe line to be repaired.

"Most of the people in Walden Two take no active part in running the government. And they don't want an active part. The urge to have a say in how the country should be run is a recent thing. It was not part of early democracy. The original victory over tyranny was a constitutional guarantee of personal rights, including the right to protest if conditions were not satisfactory. But the business of ruling was left to somebody else. Nowadays, everybody fancies himself an expert in government and wants to have a say. Let's hope it's a temporary cultural pattern. I can remember when everyone could talk about the mechanical principle according to which his automobile ran or failed to run. Everyone was an automotive specialist and knew how to file the points of a magneto and take the shimmy out of front wheels. To suggest that these matters might be left to experts would have been called Fascism, if the term had been invented. But today no one knows how his car operates and I can't see that he's any the less happy.

"In Walden Two no one worries about the government except the few to whom that worry has been assigned. To suggest that everyone should take an interest would seem as fantastic as to suggest that everyone should become familiar with our Diesel engines. Even the constitutional rights of the members are seldom thought about, I'm sure. The only thing that matters is one's day-to-day happiness and a secure future. Any infringement there would undoubtedly 'arouse the electorate.'"

"I assume that your constitution at least can't be changed without a vote of the members," I said.

"Wrong again. It can be changed by a unanimous vote of the Planners and a two-thirds vote of the Managers. You're still thinking about government by the people. Get that out of your head. The people are in no better position to change the constitution than to decide upon current practices."

"Then what's to prevent your Planners from becoming despots?" I said. "Wouldn't it really be possible?"

"How?" said Frazier.

"Oh, in many ways, I imagine."

"Such as?"

"Well, if I were a Planner with a yen for despotism, I would begin by insinuating into the culture the notion that Planners were exceptional people. I would argue that they should be personally known to the members, and should therefore wear an identifying badge or uniform. This could be done under the guise of facilitating service to the members, but eventually the Planners would be set off as a separate caste. Then they'd be relieved from menial work on the ground that they were too busy with the affairs of the community. Then special quarters, perhaps quite luxurious, would be built for them. I'd bring the Managers around to this change in the constitution by giving them better quarters also. It would all be carefully propagandized, of course. Eventually more and more of the wealth of the community would be diverted to this élite, and I would come out with a true despotism. Isn't that possible?"

"If you mean, 'Isn't despotism possible?' the answer is yes," said Frazier. "Cultures which work for the advantage of a few last a long time. Look at India, where the oppressed aren't even aware that they are sick and miserable. But are the people strong, productive, progressive? If not, then the culture will eventually be replaced by competing cultures which work more efficiently. Our Planners know this. They know that any usurpation of power would weaken the community as a whole and eventually destroy the whole venture."

"A group of despotic Planners might be willing to sacrifice the community," I said. "They wouldn't necessarily suffer if it failed. They could simply abscond with the funds."

"That would be a catastrophe. Like an earthquake, or a new and frightful epidemic, or a raid from another world. All we can do is take reasonable precautions. Your hypothetical case strikes me as implausible, that's all I can say."

"But isn't that just the weakness of your antidemocratic attitude?" Castle said. "Haven't you lost your guarantee against the usurpation of power?"

"There's no power to usurp," said Frazier. "There's no police, no military, no guns or bombs—tear-gas or atomic —to give strength to the few. In point of physical force the members are always clearly in power. Revolt is not only easy, it's inevitable if real dissatisfaction arises.

"And there's little real wealth to tempt anyone. It isn't true that the Planners could abscond with the funds. Our wealth is our happiness. The physical plant of the community would be practically worthless without the members.

"And then remember that the Planners are part of a noncompetitive culture in which a thirst for power is a curiosity. They have no reason to usurp. Their tradition is against it. Any gesture of personal domination would

255

stand out as conspicuously as the theft of the bulletin board."

"But it's human to dominate," said Castle, "in any culture."

"That's an experimental question, Mr. Castle. You can't answer it from your armchair. But let's see what a usurpation of power would amount to. Insofar as the Planners rule at all, they do so through positive reinforcement. They don't use or threaten to use force. They have no machinery for that. In order to extend their power they would have to provide more and more satisfying conditions. A curious sort of despotism, Mr. Castle."

"But they might change to a different sort of power."

"That would require a unanimous vote. But the Planners are eventually demoted to simple citizenship. Their terms of office are staggered, and some of them are always so close to retirement that they wouldn't share in the selfish consequences. Why should they vote for the change?

"Usurpation of power is a threat only in a competitive culture," Frazier continued. "In Walden Two power is either destroyed or so diffused that usurpation is practically impossible. Personal ambition isn't essential in a good governor. As governmental technology advances, less and less is left to the decisions of governors, anyway. Eventually we shall have no use for Planners at all. The Managers will suffice."

Frazier turned to me in an open gesture of appeasement.

"Democracy is not a guarantee against despotism, Burris. Its virtues are of another sort. It has proved itself clearly superior to the despotic rule of a small élite. We have seen it survive in conflict with the despotic pattern in World War II. The democratic peoples proved themselves superior just because of their democracy. They could enlist the support of other peoples, who had less to fear from them than from an aggressive élite. They could marshal greater manpower in the long run because everyone had a stake in victory and few were suffering from the strain of forcible coercion. The despots couldn't convert the people they conquered while pretending to be a superior race. Every principle which seemed to strengthen the governmental structure of Fascism when the war began proved to be an eventual weakness.

"But the triumph of democracy doesn't mean it's the best government. It was merely the better in a contest with a conspicuously bad one. Let's not stop with democracy. It isn't, and can't be, the best form of government, because it's based on a scientifically invalid conception of man. It fails to take account of the fact that in the long run *man is determined by the state*. A *laissez-faire* philosophy which trusts to the inherent goodness and wisdom of the common man is incompatible with the observed fact that men are made good or bad and wise or foolish by the environment in which they grow."

"But which comes first," I asked, "the hen or the egg? Men build society and society builds men. Where do we start?"

"It isn't a question of starting. The start has been made. It's a question of what's to be done from now on."

"Then it's to be revolution, is that it?" said Castle. "If democracy can't change itself into something better—"

"Revolution? You're not a very rewarding pupil, Mr. Castle. The change won't come about through power politics at all. It will take place at another level altogether."

"What level?"

Frazier waved his hand toward the window, through which we could see the drenched landscape of Walden Two.

"Well," said Castle, "you'd better hurry up. It's not a job to be done on four hours a day."

"Four hours a day is exactly what it needs," said Frazier with a smile. He lay back upon the bed, looking rather tired.

"I can think of a conspicuous case in which the change you're advocating is coming about at the level of power politics," I said.

Frazier sat up quickly, with obvious effort. He looked at me suspiciously.

"Russia," I said.

"Ah, Russia," he said with relief. He showed no inclination to go on.

"What about Russia, though?"

"What about it, indeed?"

"Isn't there a considerable resemblance between Russian communism and your own philosophy?"

"Russia, Russia," Frazier murmured evasively. "Our visitors always ask that. Russia is our rival. It's very flattering—if you consider the resources and the numbers of people involved."

"But you're dodging my question. Hasn't Russia done what you're trying to do, but at the level of power politics? I can imagine what a Communist would say of your program at Walden Two. Wouldn't he simply tell you to drop the experiment and go to work for the Party?"

"He would and he does."

"And what's your answer?"

"I can see only four things wrong with Russia," Frazier said, clearly enjoying the condescension. "As originally conceived, it was a good try. It sprang from humanitarian impulses which are a commonplace in Walden Two. But it quickly developed certain weaknesses. There are four of them, and they were inevitable. They were inevitable just because the attempt was made at the level of power politics." He waited for me to ask him what the weaknesses were.

"The first," he said, as soon as I had done so, "is a decline in the experimental spirit. Many promising experiments have simply been dropped. The group care of children, the altered structure of the family, the abandonment of religion, new kinds of personal incentives—all these problems were 'solved' by dropping back to practices which have prevailed in capitalistic societies for centuries. It was the old difficulty. A government in power can't experiment. It must know the answers or at least pretend to know them. Today the Russians contend that an optimal cultural pattern has been achieved, if not yet fully implemented. They dare not admit to any serious need for improvement. Revolutionary experimentation is dead.

"In the second place, Russia has overpropagandized, both to its own people and to the outside world. Their propaganda is much more extensive than any which ever enslaved a working class. That's a serious defect, for it has made it impossible to evaluate their success. We don't know how much of the current vigor of Russian communism is due to a strong, satisfying way of life, and how much to indoctrination. You may call it a temporary expedient, to counteract the propaganda embedded in an older culture. But that need has long since passed, yet the propaganda continues. So long as it goes on, no valid data on the effectiveness of Russian communism can be obtained. For all we know, the whole culture would fall apart if the supporting attitudes were taken away. And what is worse, it's hard to see how they can ever be taken away. Propaganda makes it impossible to progress toward a form of society in which it is unnecessary.

"The third weakness of the Russian government is its use of heroes. The first function of the hero, in Russia as elsewhere, is to piece out a defective governmental structure. Important decisions aren't made by appeal to a set of principles; they are personal acts. The process of governing is an art, not a science, and the government is only as good or as long-lasting as the artist. As to the second function of the hero—how long would communism last if all the pictures of Lenin and Stalin were torn down? It's a question worth asking.

"But most important of all, the Russian experiment was based on power. You may argue that the seizure of power was also a temporary expedient, since the people who held it were intolerant and oppressive. But you can hardly defend the continued use of power in that way. The Russians are still a long way from a culture in which people behave as they *want* to behave, for their mutual good. In order to get its people to act as the communist pattern demands, the Russian government has had to use the techniques of capitalism. On the one hand it resorts to extravagant and uneven rewards. But an unequal distribution of wealth destroys more incentives than it creates. It obviously can't operate for the *common* good. On the other hand, the government also uses punishment or the threat of it. What kind of behavioral engineering do you call that?"

Frazier spat into the flowerpot in a gesture of disgust. Then he held out his hands with an exaggerated shrug and drew himself slowly to his feet. He had evidently had enough of Castle's "general issues."

A^{ND} SO had I. I could not see that our discussion, energetic as it had been, had added anything to our understanding of Walden Two except an occasional glimpse of some new behavioral technique.

Castle was quite right in saying that Frazier shied away from generalities. Walden Two was not founded on them, but on specific behavioral and cultural laws and techniques. I could easily believe that the question of freedom might never arise, and I suspected that Castle's "threat of despotism" could be reduced to a practical problem in defining the functions of Managers. In some strange way Frazier had undercut all the standard issues in political science, and they seemed scarcely worth debating.

He proceeded to drive his point home with a concrete demonstration. With no word of explanation he opened the door and waved us into the hall. Then, setting an awkwardly slow pace, he led us toward the common rooms.

The community had sprung into life now that the rain had stopped, and small groups were emerging from the personal rooms on their way out-of-doors. We followed the general movement to a common locker room, where all heavy outdoor clothing was kept. Two or three members were putting on rubbers or heavy shoes, and one was trying on a battered fisherman's hat. A band of young people in yellow slickers, who had been for a long walk during the storm, were cleaning their shoes or rubbers in the "dirt trap" at the entrance.

We reached the common rooms and moved idly along the Walk. Frazier maintained a strict silence, but he looked from side to side earnestly, as if everything we passed were of the utmost importance. Castle and I were taken in, and we gave the place a thorough examination. The music rooms emitted various pleasant noises through their closed doors, and the studios were dotted with animated talkers. The reading rooms and lounges were all occupied, in spite of the clearing weather. Through their windows the Walden Two landscape appeared even fresher and more beautiful, thanks in part to our industrious and painstaking window-washing.

We swung about in the direction of the Ladder. The children were coming up for Sunday night supper, and Frazier contrived that we should be swept into the serving room with them. They broke up into groups, roughly according to age, filled their trays skillfully and graciously, and chose places without quarreling. The few adults with them were mostly young parents, perhaps not more than five years older than the oldest child. Some of them were apparently not on duty but merely taking a meal with the children for the fun of it.

We withdrew from the serving room and approached the top of the Ladder. Frazier allowed us to catch a glimpse of it and then drew us back along the Walk. We entered one of the lounges and went to the windows to look out over the landscape, which was dotted here and there with groups of people enjoying the fresh green countryside.

Frazier allowed perhaps a minute to pass. Then he turned to Castle.

"What were you saying about despotism, Mr. Castle?"

Castle was taken by surprise, and he stared at Frazier as a deep flush crept over his face. He tried to say something. His lips parted but no words came. Frazier broke into a loud, nervous laugh, which startled the other occupants of the room, and he gave Castle a hesitant slap on the back which did not seem to fit the mood of the piece or the role he was playing.

Suddenly he looked toward the Walk, raised a finger, and nodded, as if he were signaling to someone with whom he had an appointment. Several people were visible through the door, but none of them seemed to respond to Frazier's signal. I suspected that he was faking. He had felt the need for a quick exit and could think of no better way to achieve it.

He backed away from us awkwardly, nodding rapidly, his mouth agape, as if he had forgotten the word for "Good-bye."

"Supper at seven?" he called from the door.

He turned without waiting for an answer and disappeared along the Walk.

31

As we left the dining rooms after a simple Sunday-night supper, Frazier turned to Rodge.

"Want to show you something," he said and drew him away from us.

Steve and Mary were joined by several young people, and Barbara opened up on one of the more interesting males. Castle had brought a couple of cigars, and he suggested that we stroll outside for a smoke. I accepted, but I hoped I was not to spend the whole evening alone with him. He had been in jubilant spirits during supper, and I suspected that he had settled the problem of Walden Two to his satisfaction. Frazier, I was sure, had been assigned to some thoroughly ignominious pigeonhole.

My suspicion was correct. Castle considered himself the conquering hero of the afternoon, and he was not at all disturbed by my suggestion that Frazier probably looked upon himself in the same light. The truth was, these warriors had never met on the same field or with the same weapons. Frazier had no use for general principles and could not see their relevance in evaluating the accomplished fact of Walden Two. On the other hand, Castle had seemed to miss the point of Frazier's practical epilogue. Frazier had left too much to histrionics and had failed to drive home the incompatibility of a theoretical despotism and an unmistakable freedom in fact.

The pigeonhole into which Frazier had been tossed was labeled, of course, "Fascist." I could not get Castle to define the term very clearly, but it involved an élite—that much was certain. The government of Walden Two was admittedly only a limited Fascism, since the proceeds of the community were not unfairly diverted. That would come in time, Castle thought, but he did not say how or why. Frazier and the other Planners, and some of the Managers, were currently an élite just because they ruled. There was a diversion of power, if not of material goods. When I pointed out that the techniques of ruling did not involve power, Castle replied with a skeptical snort. He would not admit that any kind of government could function without force.

His argument enabled me, in turn, to put him into a pigeonhole. He was the philosopher—too unfamiliar with the facts and methods of science to have any feeling for the potency of behavioral engineering. Frazier might have indulged in general principles if he had so desired. The governmental design and creation of a happy people, regardless of any issue of freedom, involved some beautiful general principles. But he had had no interest in doing so, and Castle could not do it for himself.

I was sick of the whole discussion. No matter how I might defend Frazier, Castle would be "of the same opinion still." I scarcely replied to his occasional questions, and as soon as we had finished our cigars—I was reminded of Hans Castorp again—I suggested that we rejoin our friends. But they were not to be found, and I seemed unable to escape. In desperation I consulted the bulletin board and learned that the afternoon concert of the Philharmonic had been recorded and was being rebroadcast on the Walden Network. My suggestion that we listen to it appealed to Castle because we could hear it in our room and he would have a chance to finish the batch of term papers which he had brought with him.

In each personal room, and each guest room as well, there was a loudspeaker through which several programs were piped from a control room. I turned the selector switch until I struck the symphony, which was playing an unfamiliar work, probably Mozart. I climbed straightway to my bunk and stretched out in pointed relaxation, making clear that I was not inclined toward further discussion. Castle responded by opening his brief case and taking out a stack of neatly bound papers. He dropped into a chair and went to work with a deep sigh, which I suspected was unconscious and habitual.

Though I had disposed of Castle, I could not escape from myself. My mind was a chaotic jumble. The music mocked me with its distressing order and simplicity and added to my confusion. I could not listen to more than a few bars at a time, nor stick to any one line of thought for more than a moment. I would reflect that I was scheduled to leave Walden Two within sixteen or eighteen hours, but that I was as far as ever from knowing whether I wanted to leave. Then I would realize that I had never had any thought of signing up, and I damned Frazier for maneuvering me into a position in which I had to make a decision. I thought of Steve and Mary and how simple their choice had been. I had no doubt whatsoever that they were right. Then I thought of Rodge and the extraneous tie which was preventing him from following his better judgment. I knew what Frazier would say: my own judgment was similarly distorted. I could not shake off the sheer habit of academic life. It seemed as inevitable as it was unsatisfying.

I rolled about on the bunk trying to suppress my thoughts by adopting various postures of relaxation, but without success. Finally I climbed down, grabbed my toothbrush, and went to the washroom. I returned, got into my pajamas, and climbed back into bed. I turned to the wall and pulled the sheet over my face to shield myself from Castle's light. In an effort to forget the intellectual bombardment going on around me, I set out resolutely to recall all the poetry I could remember. The first lines which came were:

> "But at my back I always hear
> Time's wingèd chariot hurrying near."

32

ALTHOUGH Castle finished his batch of papers before turning in, he was up bright and early the next morning and bouncing about the room in the best of spirits. He packed his bag with fastidious care and placed it with his brief case beside the door. Then he slapped his hands together and stood rocking slightly on his heels while I finished packing. He was whistling a monotonous tune through his teeth.

We set off toward the dining rooms with Castle half a step ahead of me.

"That was a good set of papers," he said suddenly, almost smacking his lips. "Some quite interesting ideas. I sense a gradual improvement in the quality of our students as the years go by. They come closer and closer to my expectations. Have you noticed it?"

"All I know is, I've come to expect less and less."

"Now, now, Burris. Don't let Frazier get you down. That anti-academic bias of his—it's pure emotion. What was Frazier's history, by the way—academically, I mean?"

"I don't know."

"I suspect he never had a chance to teach. Was never recommended to a good job, probably. Lone wolf—unstable—some such thing as that. This prejudice of his is sour grapes."

My long practice in taking that sort of thing from Castle saved me from blowing up. I recognized the stage he had reached and knew that nothing could be done about it. Castle was by no means a second-rater. His learning was considerable and he was known as a skillful debater, although Frazier had found him an easy mark. As long as his mind remained open, I valued him as a stimulating companion. The fact that he worked best in the heat of battle appealed to me. His conversation was better than his rather sickly publications, and I regarded this as a virtue.

But Castle occasionally indulged in an extreme act

of self-deception which would not have been out of place in the clinical picture of a psychotic. In the early stages of a discussion he would entertain all points of view with tolerance and candor. He was willing to endure uncertainty and tension and intellectual disorder. For a long time his mind would stay open. Then it would snap shut like a clam.

He had made an honest effort to understand Frazier during the first three days of our visit, and to reconcile what he saw and heard with his established opinions. Much of the time it was evident that he was a tortured soul. Then the strain had become too great, and he had seized upon the hypothesis of Fascism as a way out. I had seen the solution coming—he had tried a preliminary skirmish or two—but the full force with which it took possession of him was nevertheless surprising. There was a complete eclipse of all possible doubt, and the energy which had previously gone into reconciling or sorting out various ideas now went into bolstering his hypothesis. He was like a child who thinks he sees the outline of an animal in the pebbles on a beach and immediately rearranges them here and there until there can be no possible question.

We found Steve and Mary already at breakfast, and my first impulse was to shield them from Castle's skepticism, but this proved to be unnecessary. Castle treated their evident happiness with good-natured tolerance—they were foolish to be so happy, but at least they were not hurting anyone. Walden Two might go on forever, and Steve and Mary live out their lives in storybook bliss; Castle would remain unshaken. Quite consistently he took no special joy in the fact, which was soon apparent when Rodge and Barbara joined us, that Rodge was not going to sign up.

When we had finished a lingering breakfast, we reported at the Work Desk, but no jobs that could be handled in the remaining time were available, and we were asked to consider our account closed. Steve and Mary, who were already on a four-credit basis, had elected to work during the supper period that evening in order to be with us as long as possible.

We went out to the lawn and presently discovered Frazier walking rapidly toward us from the pond. I did not want to see him. He had failed to convert Rodge, and I was afraid he would be in a bad mood. I had wasted his time with a visitor irrevocably committed to the outside world. Walden Two had exceeded all his fondest dreams; what more could Rodge ask? But I should have learned to expect the unexpected from Frazier. He was glowing with good spirits, and greeted us in a very friendly manner. When he saw that Rodge was embarrassed and avoided a direct greeting, he went out of his way to lay a hand on his shoulder and address a few pleasant remarks to him and Barbara.

I was wrong, too, in my fear that he would reopen his attack on me. His gambit on Sunday morning had led to a very different sort of game when he digressed to justify himself. The morning which lay before us was his only chance, and I was sure he would not miss it. But I had reached no decision, and I desperately wanted to avoid discussion. My knees actually buckled when Frazier took my arm and said, "Burris, would you like to come along while I do my stint for the day?"

It was obviously a move to get me alone. He could easily have put in his single hour of physical labor at some other time. But I could scarcely decline the invitation, and we walked silently down the road toward the shops. I waited uneasily for his opening move, but he broke the silence only once or twice and then merely to make some trivial comment upon the progress of the season.

We entered the machine shop, which was again deserted. Frazier drew a stool close to one of the workbenches and indicated that it was for me. Then he set to work to clean up the littered bench. It took me a minute or two to realize that this was his work for the day, for I recalled the utter confusion of his personal room.

"I'm probably the most untidy person in history," he said, as if he knew that the point would occur to me, "but I take a strange delight in getting order out of chaos. I like to salvage tangled wire and string and sort out a scrap heap of nails and screws. The Freudians have a word for it." He glanced at me with a restrained smile and dropped a small wrench into place in a rack. "I leave a standing request for jobs of this sort," he added. He swept together a little pile of dust and bits of wood and metal, from which he began to rescue all serviceable pieces. "It's not an hour well spent, for we could buy most of what I salvage for a few cents. But once in a while I find something of value—a drill or small tool— that would otherwise be thrown away. Even so, I'm afraid the Work Desk indulges me. It helps on the foreign exchange, however, and the place needs to be swept anyway."

This sort of chatter went on for some time, and I began to feel more at ease. Evidently he had no intention of pressing me, and I finally ventured to bring the conversation around to Walden Two myself.

"There's just one thing I want to say, Frazier," I said, after a long pause. "Never mind my opinion of you as a person. I won't deny that your little essay in telepathy yesterday morning was pretty successful. But I want you to know I admire the job you've done. It's a magnificent piece of work. The simple fact is, I envy you."

"You needn't, you know," he said, a little too quickly.

"I don't mean I envy your life at Walden Two— though it seems ideal." I drew back from this line as fast as possible. "I mean I envy you an ambitious experiment, successfully carried through. It must be a source of tremendous satisfaction."

"It is."

"And if I must say it, Frazier—I concede the point: you're a genius."

"Nonsense, Burris! Don't be a fool!" I had expected a mild disclaimer, but his manner was almost violent. "I'm no more distinguished as an intellect than I am a person. You can see that for yourself. I have no exceptional ability whatsoever. I'm not a facile mathematician, or a particularly clear thinker. I'm not well read. When I open a book, a thousand arguments beset me and I have to put it away. I'm certainly not a scholar. Once in a while I get a flash of insight, but only after an industrious sorting of material which is no more inspired than what I'm doing with this dust pile right now. You can hear my mind creak in the pompous cadences of my prose. Don't think I don't know it."

"But what about Walden Two?"

"That's an achievement, Burris, say what you will. It's the crowning achievement in the history of the human intellect to date, and make what you will of that! The splitting of the atom pales into insignificance beside it."

"Then what about yourself? I'm afraid we're talking at cross-purposes."

"But Walden Two didn't require genius! I have only one important characteristic, Burris: I'm stubborn. I've had only one idea in my life—a true *idée fixe.*"

"What idea is that?"

"To put it as bluntly as possible—the idea of having my own way. 'Control' expresses it, I think. The control of human behavior, Burris. In my early experimental days it was a frenzied, selfish desire to dominate. I remember the rage I used to feel when a prediction went awry. I could have shouted at the subjects of my experiments, 'Behave, damn you! Behave as you ought!' Eventually I realized that the subjects were always right. They always behaved as they should have behaved. It was I who was wrong. I had made a bad prediction."

Frazier laughed suddenly and at length.

"And what a strange discovery for a would-be tyrant," he exclaimed at last, "that the only effective technique of control is unselfish!"

He continued to laugh softly.

"But you can scarcely complain," I said. "You've gained your control, I'm beginning to see that."

He looked at me suspiciously for a moment, but then seemed to agree. He nodded slowly.

"And you've had the fun of being a pioneer," I went on. "You've skimmed the cream. It's going to be all too easy and dull for those who follow."

"That's nonsense, too, Burris," said Frazier, resuming some of his former violence. "Can you cite a single instance in the history of science to bear you out? When has a scientific discovery ever made things easy? It may clarify some *former* obscurity or simplify a *former* difficulty, but it always opens up problems which are more obscure and more difficult—and more interesting! Use your imagination, man! Look at what remains to be done!"

Frazier finished cleaning the surface of the bench with a small hand brush and moved to a fresh job on the other side of me.

"I'm sorry to be stupid," I said, swinging around on my stool, "but what does remain to be done? It seems to me that the whole venture is running very smoothly. I suppose you mean the development of other Waldens —your program of expansion."

"I mean nothing of the sort. That will be interesting to watch, but I'll take no active part in it. I expect to remain at Walden Two."

"But what's left to be done at Walden Two? So far as I can see, your job is practically finished. The community is self-sufficient, and it provides an interesting and satisfying life for everyone."

Frazier flared angrily.

"Do you think I'd be satisfied with *that?*" he shouted. "Do you think I'd be content with a set of cultural conditions in which mankind was in *equilibrium?* A successful culture in that sense is only the beginning—the very minimal achievement of a behavioral technology."

"But surely no mean achievement when you consider the condition of the world today."

"The world's a poor standard. Any society which is free of hunger and violence looks bright against that background. But live in Walden Two a month or so and you will get a fresh point of view. You will shake off the pessimism which fills the abysmal depths to which we've sunk, and you will begin to see the potentialities of man. You will begin to expect great things of men, and see the chance of getting them, too.

"Could you really be happy in a static world, no matter how satisfying it might be in other respects?" Frazier went on. "By no means! Nor would you wish to engineer general happiness for everyone under static conditions. We must never be free of that feverish urge to push forward which is the saving grace of mankind."

"That feverish urge has got us into a pretty sorry mess," I said.

"It has indeed. And that's another reason why we can't be satisfied with a static culture. There's work to be done, if we're to survive. To stand still would be to perish. The discrepancy between man's technical power and the wisdom with which he uses it has grown conspicuously wider year by year. We become aware of it when an atomic bomb blasts an open gulf, but the separation has gone on steadily for a long time. It's no solution to put the brakes on science until man's wisdom and responsibility catch up. As frightening as it may seem—as mad as it may seem to the contemplative soul—science must go on. We can't put our rockets and our atomic piles in museums—like the locomotives in Erewhon. But we must build men up to the same level. We can't retreat, but we must straighten our lines. We must reinforce the weak sectors—the behavioral and cultural sciences. We need a powerful science of behavior.

"Any sensible man must know why science is misused, Burris. Look at modern education and its niggling support! Look at the culture of the average American community! Look at the machinery of government! Where among them can you expect to find the inculcators of wisdom? But wait until we've developed a science of behavior as powerful as the science of the atom, and you will see a difference."

"Yes, but you aren't going to get a powerful science of behavior just by wishing for it. It will take more than a spot of genius. You must have financial support. You must be able to attract and hold the enthusiasm and energy of talented men. You must have material for extensive research. Think of what is needed to get a really large-scale science of behavior under way!"

Frazier laughed heartily.

"My dear fellow!" he said at last. "Can't you see that your specifications are precisely those of Walden Two?"

I caught my breath and stared at him.

"I'll let you in on a secret," he continued, lowering his voice dramatically. "You have just described the *only* side of Walden Two that really interests me. To make men happy, yes. To make them productive in order to assure the continuation of that happiness, yes. But what else? Why, *to make possible a genuine science of human behavior!*

"These things aren't for the laboratory, Burris. They're not 'academic questions.' What an apt expression! They concern our very lives! We can study them only in a living culture, and yet a culture which is under experimental control. Nothing short of Walden Two will suffice. It must be a real world, this laboratory of ours, and no foundation can buy a slice of it."

Frazier dropped the brush he had been using and thrust his hands into his pockets. He held himself rigid, as if to divert all his energy into speech.

"What remains to be done?" he said, his eyes flashing. "Well, what do you say to the design of personalities? Would that interest you? The control of temperament? Give me the specifications, and I'll give you the man! What do you say to the control of motivation, building the interests which will make men most productive and most successful? Does that seem to you fantastic? Yet some of the techniques are available, and more can be worked out experimentally. Think of the possibilities! A society in which there is no failure, no boredom, no duplication of effort!

"And what about the cultivation of special abilities? Do we know anything about the circumstances in the life of the child which give him a mathematical mind? Or make him musical? Almost nothing at all! These things are left to accident or blamed on heredity. I take a more optimistic view: we can analyze effective behavior and design experiments to discover how to generate it in our youth. Oh, our efforts will seem pretty crude a hundred years hence. They may seem crude now, to the expansive soul. But we've got to make a start. There's no virtue in accident. Let us control the lives of our children and see what we can make of them."

Frazier began to pace back and forth, his hands still thrust in his pockets.

"My hunch is—and when I feel this way about a hunch, it's never wrong—that we shall eventually find out, not only what makes a child mathematical, but how to make better mathematicians! If we can't solve a problem, we can create men who can! And better artists! And better craftsmen!" He laughed and added quietly, "And better behaviorists, I suppose!

"And all the while we shall be improving upon our social and cultural design. We know almost nothing about the special capacities of the *group*. We all recognize that there are problems which can't be solved by an individual—not only because of limitations of time and energy but because the individual, no matter how extraordinary, can't master all the aspects, can't think thoughts big enough. Communal science is already a reality, but who knows how far it can go? Communal authorship, communal art, communal music—these are already exploited for commercial purposes, but who knows what might happen under freer conditions?

"The problem of efficient group structure alone is enough to absorb anyone's interest. An organization of a committee of scientists or a panel of script writers is far from what it could be. But we lack control in the world at large to investigate more efficient structures. Here, on the contrary—here we can begin to understand and build the Superorganism. We can construct groups of artists and scientists who will act as smoothly and efficiently as champion football teams.

"And all the while, Burris, we shall be increasing the net power of the community by leaps and bounds. Does it seem to you unreasonable to estimate that the present efficiency of society is of the order of a fraction of one per cent? *A fraction of one per cent!* And you ask what remains to be done!"

He stood still for a moment, then glanced at his watch and started for the door.

"Let's get out of here!" he said, pushing the door wide open with his foot.

33

I HAD some difficulty in keeping up with Frazier as he strode through the pines toward the main buildings. It became clear that he was not going to rejoin our group, for he turned off to the left in the direction of Stone Hill. I followed him to a well-worn path which led into the woods, and after a sharp climb we struck off through low bushes to the right. In a few minutes we came to a strong welded fence with a barbed wire strung above it. Frazier grasped the fence on one side of a post and gave a sharp tug upward. It came loose and coiled away from the post. We passed through beneath the barbed wire, replaced the fence, and walked on as rapidly as the heavy underbrush permitted.

The upper rim of the stone quarry appeared suddenly at our feet, and I drew back in alarm at the precipitous drop which confronted us. Frazier walked casually along the rim to a mossy bank, where he threw himself full-length upon the ground. I followed more cautiously and sat down several feet from the edge, breathing heavily from the rapid climb. Presently Frazier sat up. He drew a small telescope from his pocket and adjusted it carefully.

"We call this ledge the 'Throne,'" he said, as he put the glass to his eye. "Practically all of Walden Two can be seen from it. I come up occasionally to keep in touch with things. Right now, I'm looking at the foundation of the new shop just north of the garage. They seem to be pouring the last of the concrete this morning. And there's Morrison at the piggery again. More inoculations, I presume. And over here—a load of early kale going into the poultry house. . . . The cattle are far up in the pasture today. I wonder why? . . . And there's the mailman nudging his old Ford over the hill. Our boy ought to— Yes, there he is—emptying the box into the basket on his bike. . . . The corn looks good. I wish we could irrigate over that way. It would save a lot of— Something seems to be wrong with the cultivator. Stopping and starting. No, there it goes. No, it's stopping again. Someone getting a lesson, I guess. . . . There's old Mrs. Ackerman out for a walk again. And that must be Esther with her."

This had begun as an account for my benefit, but it fell away into the merest mumble. Frazier had apparently forgotten me. He finally took the glass from his eye, collapsed it, and restored it to his pocket. I shifted my position to attract his attention, and I thought I saw him start. He laughed nervously.

"Not a sparrow falleth," he said, patting the glass in his pocket. He laughed again.

We were silent as he lay back on the ground.

"It must be a great satisfaction," I said finally. "A world of your own making."

"Yes," he said. "I look upon my work and, behold, it is good."

He was lying flat on his back, his arms stretched out at full length. His legs were straight but his ankles were lightly crossed. He allowed his head to fall limply to one side, and I reflected that his beard made him look a little like Christ. Then, with a shock, I saw that he had assumed the position of crucifixion.

I was extraordinarily ill at ease. My heart was still pounding from my rapid climb, and from my fright as we reached the ledge. And, for all I knew, the man beside me might be going mad.

"Just so you don't think you're God," I said hesitantly, hoping to bring matters out into the open.

He spoke from the rather awkward position into which his head had fallen.

"There's a curious similarity," he said.

I suffered a moment of panic.

"Rather considerably less control in your case, I should imagine," I said, attempting to adopt a casual tone.

"Not at all," he said, looking up. "At least, if we can believe the theologians. On the contrary, it's the other way round. You may remember that God's children are always disappointing Him."

"While you are in complete command. Well, I congratulate you."

"I don't say I'm never disappointed, but I imagine I'm rather less frequently so than God. After all, look at the world *He* made."

"A joke's a joke," I said.

"But I'm not joking."

"You mean you think you're God?" I said, deciding to get it over with.

Frazier snorted in disgust.

"I said there was a curious similarity," he said.

"Don't be absurd."

"No, really. The parallel is quite fascinating. Our friend Castle is worried about the conflict between long-range dictatorship and freedom. Doesn't he know he's merely raising the old question of predestination and free will? All that happens is contained in an original plan, yet at every stage the individual seems to be making choices and determining the outcome. The same is true of Walden Two. Our members are practically always doing what they want to do—what they 'choose' to do—but we see to it that they will want to do precisely the things which are best for themselves and the community. Their behavior is determined, yet they're free.

"Dictatorship and freedom—predestination and free will," Frazier continued. "What are these but pseudo-questions of linguistic origin? When we ask what Man can make of Man, we don't mean the same thing by 'Man' in both instances. We mean to ask what a few men can make of mankind. And that's the all-absorbing question of the twentieth century. What kind of world can we build—those of us who understand the science of behavior?"

"Then Castle was right. You're a dictator, after all."

"No more than God. Or rather less so. Generally, I've let things alone. I've never stepped in to wipe out the evil works of men with a great flood. Nor have I sent a personal emissary to reveal my plan and to put my people back on the track. The original design took deviations into account and provided automatic corrections. It's rather an improvement upon Genesis."

"Blasphemy doesn't become you, Frazier. It's not your style."

"Then let's drop the theology. I have no wish to be blasphemous. But I'm not talking nonsense, either. The competitive talents which have made man pre-eminent —right up to the invention of the atomic bomb—aren't enough for the step he must take next. Being competitive, they are incompatible with the good of all mankind. Man's superior endowment has emerged from a struggle for survival and that fact has left its beastly mark. Those who survive have destroyed, and they have not survived unscathed. We justify our genius for warfare by arguing that we should otherwise have been destroyed, but that's only another way of saying that we want our own way. And our success encourages us to be more and more aggressive. By its very nature the struggle to survive cannot give birth to a noncompetitive intelligence."

"But you acquired and developed the behavioral technology responsible for Walden Two in a competitive culture. You were operating under the principle of the survival of the fittest."

"Of course! No one is more competitive—more aggressive—than I," said Frazier. He caught himself and added, "Except when I'm following the Walden Two Code, of course."

"Then the old life must have had within it the seeds of the new," I said. "There was only one plan, and it wasn't yours. Instead, you were merely a part of it. An instrument, if you will. I felt the same inconsistency in our discussion of human nature. You said you had no faith in the innate goodness of man, and needed none in the design of Walden Two. Yet you are, after all, a man. You argued that a government which left men alone, trusting to their goodness, could not muddle through to a satisfactory culture. Yet you yourself muddled through. You are the fruit of the system which you condemn as unfruitful."

"The science of behavior is full of special twists like that," said Frazier. "It's the science of science—a special discipline concerned with talking about talking and knowing about knowing. Well, there's a motivational twist, too. Science in general emerged from a competitive culture. Most scientists are still inspired by competition or at least supported by those who are. But when you come to apply the methods of science to the special study of human behavior, the competitive spirit commits suicide. It discovers the extraordinary fact that in order to survive, we must in the last analysis *not* compete."

"That's a little too glib, Frazier. It's still true that the old order worked something out. You can't get around that by stepping out of the main current and claiming the position of co-creator."

"Perhaps I must yield to God in point of seniority," Frazier said, with a smile. He stopped unexpectedly, as if the consequences did not please him. "Though I might claim," he continued with some warmth, "that I made a more explicit statement of my plan. I could claim a more *deliberate* control. The evolution of human intelligence may not have been deliberately planned. The final state of affairs may not have been foreseen. Perhaps we are merely reading a plan into the world after the fact. But there's no doubt whatever that Walden Two was planned in advance pretty much as it turned out to be. In many ways the actual creation of Walden Two was closer to the spirit of Christian cosmogony than the evolution of the world according to modern science."

"We're back with the theologians again," I said, with a laugh, "and for good reason. Like them, you're not indifferent to power. To use a term which I professionally dislike, you have a sizable God complex."

"Of course I'm not indifferent to power!" Frazier said hotly. "And I like to play God! Who wouldn't, under the circumstances? After all, man, even Jesus Christ thought he was God!"

He stared at me in silence, as if to see whether I had caught the full significance of his remark. He was not challenging me, and there was no hint of blasphemy. His tone had been almost devout. He spoke as if Jesus were an honored colleague whose technical discoveries he held in the highest esteem. There was an implication, too, which I did not wish to question, that his own achievement had given him an insight into the personal problems of a great reformer, a sympathy for weaknesses which were beyond my ken. I judged him only with great diffidence.

He drew out his telescope again and began to examine various details of his handiwork. We heard a slight disturbance in the direction of the lawn, and he swung his glass about, but the view was cut off by the main building. He continued to peer through the glass for several minutes.

"There's another point of similarity," he said at last when he saw that I was not going to speak. "I don't know whether you'll understand this, Burris. I expect you'll laugh. But try to forget your professional cynicism."

He dropped the telescope and hesitated for a moment. Then he flung his hand loosely in a sweeping gesture which embraced all of Walden Two.

"These are my children, Burris," he said, almost in a whisper. "I love them."

He got to his feet and started back along the ledge. I followed carefully. He turned into the underbrush and waited for me to catch up. He was embarrassed and rather confused.

"What is love," he said, with a shrug, "except another name for the use of positive reinforcement?"

"Or vice versa," I said.

34

T HE DISTURBANCE on the lawn grew noisier as we
came down the hill from the Throne. The sheep
were baaing, the Bishop was barking savagely, and from
time to time someone shouted. As we came round the
end of the main building, we saw that one of the sheep
had escaped from the portable fold. The Bishop was
using encircling tactics to drive it back, but the cloth-
marked string was apparently equally formidable from
either side, and whenever the sheep approached the fold,
it veered off on a new path of escape. In the excitement,
the rest of the flock had pressed into the far corner and
other sheep were being forced through the string. Several
men and women had formed a ring to keep them together. Everyone seemed to be waiting for a figure who
was calmly approaching from the pasture across the
brook. I found myself drawn into the emergency, but
Frazier grasped my arm and we stopped at some distance.

"It doesn't work, even with sheep, you see," he said.

"What doesn't?"

"Punishment. Negative reinforcement. The threat of
pain. It's a primitive principle of control. So long as
we keep the fence electrified, we have no trouble—provided the needs of the sheep are satisfied. But if we re-
lent, trouble is bound to arise sooner or later."

I was jolted by this detachment. Frazier was obviously
much more concerned about the principle involved than
about the escaped sheep.

"Society isn't likely to convert to positive reinforcement
in the control of its sheep," I said impatiently.

"It couldn't," he replied seriously. "It couldn't convert
because it's not raising sheep for the good of the sheep.
It has no net positive reinforcement to offer. Nothing
short of an insurmountable fence or frequent punishment will control the exploited."

"The string works pretty well. There must be something to be said for punishment."

"It would scarcely work at all except for the Bishop. And the Bishop is *not* controlled by punishment. A sheep dog has a strong inclination to herd sheep—by definition. The Bishop *wants* to keep our sheep in their fold—it's his life. And we feed and shelter him and arrange for the propagation of his kind because he wants to do what we want done. It's like the cat in the grocery store—both the cat and the grocer want mice killed. It's a very satisfying sort of symbiosis."

The man had arrived from the pasture and was restoring order. The Bishop was called off, a section of the string was taken down, and the escaped sheep was herded back into the fold.

"The cooperation of man and dog is very different from the slavery of man and beast," said Frazier. "When will the society of man and man be classed with the former instead of the latter?"

We heard someone laughing and turned to discover that Castle had been watching the affair from one of the benches along the wall of the building. He laughed again in a rather forced manner when he saw that we had spotted him.

"The revolt of the angels!" he shouted as he arose and came toward us, nursing his fading merriment. I glanced at Frazier and saw that he was annoyed. Castle achieved a final guffaw as he joined us.

"Your behavioral engineering, Mr. Frazier," he said, swallowing hard as if he had almost choked, "may be all very well up to a point. But I can't say it's perfect—not yet, at any rate." He laughed again, with some effort.

Frazier looked at me, as if to make sure that I understood, and then shrugged his shoulders and walked off without a word.

Castle was startled. He turned surprisingly red as he watched Frazier's retreat.

"I thought he was tougher than that," he said. "Can't

he take a joke? I don't understand. I don't understand at all."

"I'm surprised to hear you admit it," I said quietly and with great satisfaction.

35

WE LEARNED from Steve, as we assembled for lunch, that a community truck would take us on the first leg of our journey home. The time to leave was not far off, and we began to eat lunch without Frazier, who had not appeared. Castle seemed to think he was sulking in his tent. He recounted the episode of the sheep in great glee and drew a parallel with Walden Two as a whole. It was skillful enough, but fundamentally dishonest. I followed Frazier's example and said nothing.

We returned to our rooms for our luggage and then waited on the lawn. A truck came up the road from the barns, and Steve ran to meet it and leaped aboard. When it had stopped, he let down the tailboard with an amusing air of proprietorship and began to load the bags. The truck contained half a dozen bales of straw, which were to be delivered along the way. A large piece of canvas had been thrown over them to protect our clothes.

We stood about uneasily, waiting for Frazier. Steve ran to look for him around the end of the building, and dashed down to the flower gardens to survey the windows of the common rooms. He then decided to try the dining rooms but ran into Frazier at the door. Frazier put a hand on his shoulder, and they came up to us together.

I started to express our thanks, but Frazier reminded me of our labor-credits and of the Walden Two Code. He shook hands with Rodge and Barbara and helped them aboard. Then he turned to Castle and held out his hand pleasantly.

"Mr. Castle," he said, "you have given us furiously to think."

Castle seemed almost ashamed. He responded to Frazier's friendly manner in kind and shook hands for an unnecessarily long time. He climbed awkwardly aboard with a heavy grunt.

Frazier turned to me. He was relaxed and casual, and held out his hand with a smile. He tossed his head slightly in Castle's direction, as if there were a secret understanding between us.

"Come back," he said quietly, as we shook hands. I nodded in a meaningless way and climbed aboard.

Steve and Mary got in, Steve drew up the tailboard and signaled to the driver, and the truck began to move down the road.

Frazier stood for a long time, waving both arms loosely in the air.

We found places, comfortable in a primitive sort of way, among the bales of straw. It was an open truck, but a tarpaulin had been drawn over uprights to make a roof. As the truck crept slowly down the slope toward the pines, rolling gently from side to side, I saw myself for a moment in a covered wagon crossing a trackless plain. We were all moved by our leave-taking and remained silent until we reached the highway. Then, as the truck picked up speed and the tarpaulin began to flap noisily, our spirits revived and we fell into a holiday mood.

Half an hour later we entered a small town and drew to a stop at a dirty restaurant which served as bus station. We had scarcely alighted when the bus came into sight. Steve hailed it, and while our bags were being stored, we said good-bye to him and Mary. It was done hurriedly, and perhaps fortunately so. Rodge promised to come back to be Steve's best man, and Barbara expressed her desolation at being unable to come, too. Steve grasped my hand gratefully and with unbelievable force. Castle entered the bus, then thoughtfully backed out to allow Barbara to enter ahead of him. In the confusion the driver found it difficult to sell us tickets and make change with the right persons, and he did not conceal his impatience.

The bus was nearly full. I squeezed along the aisle and found a single seat at the back, from which I could wave good-bye to Steve and Mary through a miniature window. I pressed my face close to the glass to be sure they would identify my fluttering hand.

I enjoyed being alone. Far up toward the front of the bus, Castle occasionally bent across the aisle to speak to Rodge, and I was glad I could not hear. I wanted solitude and time. Since morning I had successfully kept myself from thinking of my relation to Walden Two, but this could not go on forever. And for some reason I felt pressed. My anxiety was mounting steadily. The bus which lifted and fell and curved so gracefully along the road might have been Time's wingèd chariot itself, no longer at my back but whisking me off into the future as Walden Two receded into history.

We reached the city surprisingly quickly, and Castle and I carried our bags a block or two to the railroad station. I was to be alone with him again, for Barbara had telephoned friends, and she and Rodge were staying over until an evening train.

In the waiting room Castle resumed an intermittent harangue. In a way he was more completely absorbed in Walden Two than I, for the most trivial details suggested comparisons. His audible remarks were frequently incoherent, and I could make sense of them only by guessing at the energetic silent discourse which was taking place behind them. He was not yet free of Frazier's magic, but he had reached and was holding to a decision. From every point of view—logical, psychological, factual—Walden Two appeared to him obviously impossible. The discrepancies would vanish in time.

"For one thing," he said, "you can be sure someone will 'get' Frazier before things have gone much farther. It may be the government, it may be rival religious or economic forces, or perhaps just some envious individual inside or outside the community. But someone will get him, you may be sure of that. Joseph Smith was murdered by an angry mob, Eric Janson was shot by a jealous rival, John Humphrey Noyes fled to Canada. Look at history, man!"

I knew what Frazier would say to that. These early communities had almost nothing in common with Walden Two, in fact or in theory. How could one draw any inferences? Frazier had seen the danger of aggression against Walden Two, and had provided for it well enough.

The possibility of working out a satisfying life of one's own, making the least possible contact with the government, was the brightest spot in Frazier's argument. I thought of the millions of young people who were at that moment choosing places in a social and economic structure in which they had no faith. What a discrepancy between ideal and actuality—between their good will toward men and the competitive struggle in which they must somehow find a place! Why should they not work out a world of their own?

That was the Thoreauvian side of Frazier, and I liked it. Why fight the government? Why try to change it? Why not let it alone? Unlike Thoreau, Frazier would pay his taxes and compromise wherever necessary. But he had found a way to build a world to his taste without trying to change the world of others, and I was sure he could carry on in peace unless the government took some monstrously despotic turn.

Nor was I ready to laugh off Frazier's plans for expansion. On several points he was dead right. The important lasting conquests in the history of mankind—Frazier himself had made this appeal to history—had come about, not through force, but through education, persuasion, example. Frazier's program was essentially a religious movement freed of any dallying with the supernatural and inspired by a determination to build heaven on earth. What could stop him?

Castle's voice broke into my meditations.

". . . behavioral engineering," he was saying. "If you really had a technology which could manipulate human behavior, you could raise some puzzling questions. But isn't that wishful thinking?"

The evidence, I thought, seemed clear enough. Frazier had claimed some innovations in behavioral techniques which I wanted to know more about, but I could imagine a potent technology composed of the principles already used by politicians, educators, priests, advertisers, and psychologists. The techniques of controlling human behavior were obvious enough. The trouble was, they were in the hands of the wrong people—or of feeble repairmen. Frazier had not only correctly evaluated this situation but had done something about it. I was not ready to accept his educational practices as unquestionably the best. Frazier himself still regarded them as experimental. But they were at least well along toward a crucial test, which was more than could be said for their counterparts in the world at large. Their potency had already been too clearly demonstrated elsewhere in their misuse. Frazier had all the technology he could possibly need.

". . . regimentation," Castle was saying. "Pretty cleverly concealed, but regimentation just the same. A curious sort of voluntary goose-step. Why should all those people subscribe to a code or submit to the subtle coercions of a Behavioral Manager? 'Don't gossip!' 'Carry your dishes to the kitchen!' It reminds me of a well-organized girls' camp. I'll grant you it's efficient. But I want to be free. No codes, no psychological suasions. I'm not taking any, thank you."

The enormity of Castle's intellectual sin! Could he really believe that he was free of codes and psychological suasions? Could he look upon his life as a succession of deliberate acts? Why, he parted his very hair by a code!

"The man's unread," Castle was saying. "You would think he was the first social thinker in history. These things take on a different light when one has read Plato, Rousseau, John Stuart Mill. Frazier needs a good course in the humanities."

Was Castle by any chance baiting me? A good course

in the humanities! He must have known my reaction to that! Nothing aroused me quicker than the suggestion that we abandon science in dealing with the problems of society. I could not comfortably defend nine-tenths of what passed for social science—but it was better to see that a thing was clearly nonsense than to wander around in the all-embracing fog of social philosophy. I could understand the satisfaction which men like Castle might find in turning from current problems to ancient treatises. An old book is a welcome relief from the uncertainty and disappointment which are inevitable in the scientific study of a new field. Historical research can take the place of scientific inquiry and give one time out for an honorable snooze, while pretending to carry on. Fortunately, my sense of personal failure had not yet forced me to such extremes.

". . . in the face of nature," Castle was saying. "Blood is thicker than water. And blood will tell. Can you deny that? Where does your behavioral engineering come in there? The family has a *biological* basis."

I suppose it had. And so had "race." I thought of all the violence that had been committed in the name of "blood relationship." Yet aside from the role of physical resemblance, I could not see that hereditary connections could have any real bearing upon relations between men. A "sense of family" was clearly dependent upon culture, for it varied in all degrees among cultures. The important thing was not that two people were related, but that they had been told they were related. Better not to bring the matter up at all. The family was only a little race, and it had better go. It was no longer an efficient economic or social unit or transmitter of culture—its current failure was increasingly evident. A unit of another magnitude would have to dispense with "blood ties," as Frazier clearly saw.

". . . not a man you could warm up to," Castle was saying. "He lacks the human touch. I've never seen such colossal conceit. The man has set himself up as a little tin god."

Tin or otherwise, I had been through all that, and was sure Castle had nothing to offer. Frazier had, I thought, appraised himself correctly. His evaluation was accurate, if not always tactful. I had learned to allow for his mannerisms in this respect and they no longer bothered me. In fact, I had begun to like him, in a way. He was not bad company. It is true, my ego suffered an inevitable wound now and then, but I had kept my self-respect and most of my opinions. I could even look forward to seeing him again.

Castle excused himself and walked to the middle of the waiting room. He made a survey of the doors and booths which lined the walls and, spotting what he was looking for, trotted off.

The tempo and tenor of my thinking immediately changed. Some sort of order came into my thoughts. Castle had induced me to defend Frazier and Walden Two, and now that he was gone I realized that my thinking had acquired direction. I had prevented stalemate. With a little more time I might win through to some positive decision.

Suddenly I found myself dashing across the waiting room and tossing my bag upon a counter marked "Parcels Checked." I caught the attention of a boy back among the shelves, placed a dime beside the bag, and called to him to keep the ticket. In the street I made for the nearest corner and was soon out of sight of the station.

I dropped into a slower pace and passed through several blocks of shadowy warehouses. I emerged into a blighted area in which rows of decaying stores had been converted into squalid living quarters. Dirty children played in dirty streets, tired and unkempt women leaned on window sills, hopeless men stood about in sullen groups. But I drew no comparison with Walden Two. The contrast was too massive to fit into the delicate play of forces in my mind. Walden Two had nothing in common with the human devastation about me now. It was absurd to ask which life one would choose, if these were the alternatives.

I came to a boulevard and followed it to a pleasanter part of the city. It led to a small park, and I dropped upon a bench to rest. Before long I found myself absently reading a page of newspaper which lay on the bench beside me. A headline brought me to my senses:

DIGNITY OF MAN
BACCALAUREATE
ADDRESS THEME

I picked up the paper. The president of my university had been in the city, making his most recent version of a standard speech. The article was rewritten from a press release and badly handled, but it would have been difficult to do serious damage to so distinguished an assemblage of clichés. The theme was the "Task of Education in the Postwar World," and phrases like "encouraging individual initiative," "ministering to the whole man," "stimulating a spirit of inquiry," "fostering an open mind," and "restoring the dignity of the human soul," were packed tightly together. As usual, I was not sure what any of these utterances meant, though I experienced a nebulous sense of agreement. Insofar as they had meaning at all, they seemed to refer to worth-while goals. But on one point my reaction was definite: it was obvious that no one, least of all the speaker, had any notion of how to set to work to attain them.

As a teacher I had given little thought to the "philosophy of education." Teaching was a job to be done without benefit of perspective or program. I knew, as all teachers know, that education was inadequately supported. That was perhaps not its own fault, but its outmoded techniques certainly were. Furthermore, education was completely bewildered as to its place in the world of the future. It could inspire no sense of belonging to a movement, no *esprit de corps*. I could get no satisfaction from atavistic or nostalgic attempts to reconstruct a happier era, and so I contented myself with doing the day's work.

Now, fresh from my experience at Walden Two, I saw that this could not go on. But I also saw that educators themselves could not save the situation. The causes were too deep, too remote. They involved the whole structure of society. What was needed was a new conception of man, compatible with our scientific knowledge, which would lead to a philosophy of education bearing some relation to educational practices. But to achieve this, education would have to abandon the technical limitations which it had imposed upon itself and step forth into a broader sphere of human engineering. Nothing short of the complete revision of a culture would suffice.

As I let the paper fall to the ground I relinquished my hold on my unrewarding past. It was all too clear that nothing could be made of it. I would go back to Walden Two. I do not remember actually reaching a decision. I simply knew at last that only one course of action lay before me. The matter had probably been determined for days—from the beginning of time, Frazier would have said—but suddenly I was aware of it. I knew what I was going to do.

I sat motionless for a long time, strangely exhausted. I became interested in a shabby figure sprawling on the bench opposite me, and gazed in fascination at his shoes, through the worn soles of which I could see plugs of newspaper. Gradually the practical necessity of getting back to Walden Two forced itself upon me, and I conceived the fantastic notion of walking back. I am not sure that I did not consider crawling back on all fours. Certainly I had in mind some sort of religious pilgrimage— some act of expiation. But the main point was that I wanted to make my return as physically evident as possible, beyond any possibility of doubt. A long, exhausting forced march seemed the only course.

I remembered the bag in the parcel room and began to walk back toward the station. I wondered how Castle had reacted to my disappearance. Probably he had not been alarmed, or even puzzled. I was fairly sure he would not wait for me, for he was anxious to get back to the University. I entered the station cautiously and made a hasty survey of the waiting room. He was gone. With growing reassurance I retrieved my bag and carried it to the express office. I took out my only clean shirt, a pair of socks, my razor, my toothbrushes, and a few other items. I rolled them into a bundle and fashioned it into a sort of knapsack with some cord supplied by the expressman. I dispatched the bag to Canton, to be held until I called for it from Walden Two.

There was something about the small bundle on my back, compared with the heavy bag which I had just got rid of, which filled me with an exhilarating sense of freedom. I was "traveling light," and this seemed to mean a certain lightheadedness. I had sense enough to return to the station to get a refund on my unused ticket, but that was to be my last responsible act for a long time.

As I left the ticket window, occupied with placing the refund in my billfold, I stumbled against a large rack of books. I steadied the rack and started to move on. But something had caught my eye and I turned and took a copy of *Walden* from the rack. It was a cheap paper-covered edition, which slipped comfortably into my pocket. I paid the clerk at the newsstand a quarter, reflecting that Thoreau would have been delighted at the price, and walked on with frank satisfaction in the good omen.

On my way out of the station, I passed a telegraph counter. For a fleeting moment I remembered the University. Should I at least serve notice of my defection? I stepped up to the counter, feeling as I sometimes felt after seeing a particularly debonair hero in the movies. I picked up a pencil and began to swing it by its chain, as I considered how to phrase my message. A pretty young clerk pushed a pad of blanks along the counter in my direction, and stood watching me. She seemed to sense my extraordinary self-confidence.

I set to work and entered the name and address of the president in expansive block letters. Then, unmindful of standard telegraphic style and struggling to control my euphoric abandon, I printed slowly and with great care:

MY DEAR PRESIDENT MITTELBACH
STOP YOU MAY TAKE YOUR STUPID
UNIVERSITY . . .

The pretty clerk behind the counter was reading the message upside down with professional skill. She seemed, indeed, to be a few words ahead of me, for in a pleasant but occupationally standardized tone she sang out, "I'm sorry, sir, but I'm afraid we can't accept that type of message."

The weather was not particularly appropriate for my pilgrimage back to Walden Two. It would have fitted my mood if it had been starting to rain or at least if night were coming on. I wanted to battle an element. But it was an ordinary, unheroic, rather warm afternoon. More-over, it took me more than an hour to get outside the city, and it is difficult to capture the atmosphere of an important mission while walking on sidewalks.

Eventually I struck the countryside and began to feel duly conspicuous as a solitary figure. I kept to the gravel on the left side of the road and held to a rhythmic stride which I tried to avoid breaking at all cost. A few cars slowed down to offer me a lift, but I waved them all on and shook my head in an exaggerated manner which would be clearly understood from a distance.

I felt warm blood coursing through my veins. This was what I had really wanted. I was on my own at last, and ahead of me lay a future of my own making.

On a sudden impulse I pulled out the copy of *Walden* and turned to the last page. I had always thought of the last paragraph as a blemish. Its apparent mysticism and its obscurity were unlike the rest of the book and quite un-Thoreauvian. But now I knew that I would un-derstand every word of it, and as I walked on I read it with feverish excitement:

I do not say that John or Jonathan will realize all this; but such is the character of that morrow which mere lapse of time can never make to dawn. The light which puts out our eyes is darkness to us. Only that day dawns to which we are awake. There is more day to dawn. The sun is but a morning-star.

36

I wanted to end my story there.

"Perhaps it's rather indefinite," I said to Frazier, "but I like the idea of trailing off that way. The reader will be more inclined to go on thinking about it. Let him take me back to Walden Two in his imagination."

We were going over the manuscript in Frazier's room before turning it over to the Office of Information, at whose request I had written it.

"I think you'd better give the reader the whole story," Frazier said. "After all, you must realize that some fool professor is going to assign your book as outside reading in a course in political science. 'The Critics of Democracy'—something like that. You'd better be explicit."

"But isn't it obvious how the story ends?"

"Not obvious at all. I can think of half a dozen different ent endings, equally plausible.'

I suspected he was bluffing.

"Tell me one," I said.

"Well, let's see. You set out on the long voyage home —back to Walden Two. But it starts to rain. Cold rain for June, and by morning you're drenched and exhausted. You're stumbling along at a snail's pace. You're sneezing, and you have a fever. Passing through a small town you attract the attention of the law. But the constable sees you're not drunk and takes you to a doctor. It's too late. You have pneumonia. You're done for. You 'never get to Carcassonne.' The pity of it. The spiritual waste."

"Another," I insisted.

"Well, let's say you start your long walk of penance, completely humbling yourself before a superior mind." Frazier said this without a smile. He will never learn. "But your feet begin to hurt. Then they blister, and you start to worry about infection. Penance is one thing, but a 'strep' heel is another. A truck pulls off the road and stops to give you a lift. This time you *don't* wave it on.

No, there's no point in being a damn fool. You're not a religious man anyway, and this sort of thing doesn't come natural. You will *ride* to Walden Two—who'll know the difference?

"The driver's a talkative fellow, who has picked you up because he was bored. You find him interesting. He's picturesque. You begin to wonder whether there will ever be any really picturesque people in Walden Two. You've always liked big cities, because of the chance to meet so many different types. Maybe that's what you really want after all—the festering beggars, the drunks, the down-and-outers at the mission, the street musicians, the painted whores—everything that makes life fascinating. The Real People in the Saroyan House Saloon.

"The driver starts talking politics—world politics these days, of course—and what he says seems pretty sensible. Just for a moment you get a flash of that old cherished belief in the innate good sense of the common man. Being an academic person you've damned well got to believe in innate good sense, because it can't be left up to the professors.

"Well, the upshot is, you ride on past the ravine, taking a quick look back in the mirror without letting the driver see what you're doing, and you stop for gas in the next town, and you buy the driver a drink, and he buys you one, and all the while he seems like a nicer and *nicer* guy." Frazier did a poor imitation of a drunk. "After all, that's Life."

"That makes two," I said, "and I suppose you could give me six if I insisted. But does that prove anything? What about a little ambiguity? As a matter of technique."

"The fact of the matter is," Frazier said, "the end of your personal history doesn't mean a damn, one way or the other. What the reader wants to know is: What was Walden Two really like? He sees it through your eyes, that's true—I don't mean to leave you out of the story entirely. But as soon as the picture of Walden Two is complete, the book's finished. You might as well leave out that stuff in the railroad station and park. But if you're going to work the personal angle in, go all the way. Finish it up."

As a matter of fact there is very little more to tell. I did come back to Walden Two, and I walked back, all the way. But I took it at a sensible rate. As Frazier had surmised, I am not given to castigation of either the flesh or the spirit. That became clear during the first five or six miles. I walked because I wanted time to think. Not to reconsider my decision but to untangle my motives, to evaluate half a dozen personal objectives.

There were practical matters to be attended to. My affairs at the University would have to be wound up. I had dropped my plan to telegraph my resignation, but the connection would certainly be severed when I failed to appear to give my final examination. I would have to ask the Faculty Club to pack and send my personal effects. And there were some bills. But I was resolved not to go back to take care of these things personally. I had wasted enough of my life taking care of things. I preferred to spend the time instead in a little walking tour, every step of which would bring me closer to Walden Two.

What would remain of the halfhearted hopes and dreams of the past decade? My professional plans, for example? I had never really liked teaching as it had to be done in a university. Now I might be able to attract a few people who cared about my field of interest and to whom I could unburden myself. It would be a pleasure not to worry about being too obscure for the dull, too obvious for the bright, or unfair to those who were taking the course for practical purposes. Some of my research I thought I could carry on, too. Perhaps I could get a little space in one of the workshops. Or I could build my own laboratory! Of mud!

And I would have time for a little diversion. Perhaps I would have another try at the "Well-Tempered Clavichord." I could dispense with the sentimentally fortified music which I had turned to for relief from long days in the classroom. And I could give up detective stories! There were still some novels of Trollope I hadn't read, and one of Jane Austen, too. And I had been amazed at the clairvoyance with which the Walden Two librarians had collected most of the books I had always wanted to read.

And I would have time to write! Time to think would be nearer the truth. Time to evaluate. Time to plan.

But first—and who knows for how long—I would have time to rest.

It was noon when I turned in at the ravine and climbed to the top of the bank and saw Walden Two again. I had been gone three days and had walked about sixty miles. I felt fine. The stiffness and soreness that had beset me on the second day had been walked off, and my legs were growing strong. My step was light, and I could feel the ball of each foot pushing the earth down from me as I walked.

I crossed the little bridge, turned past the workshops, and went on through the pine grove. Suddenly I heard footsteps. Someone was running to overtake me.

"Professor Burris!"

It was Steve. We shook hands warmly, and I must confess that there were tears in my eyes.

"I've come back, Steve," I said. "I've come back to stay."

"I've been watching for you," said Steve. "Mr. Frazier told me you were coming back."

Mr. Frazier!

I glanced fearfully upward toward the Throne. There was no one there. But I saw the familiar features of Walden Two stretched before me, just as I had recalled them, again and again, on my journey back, and I drew a deep breath of satisfaction.

Frazier was not in his heaven. All was right with the world.